T0371727

Advising Upwards

For Patrick, with thanks

Advising Upwards

A Framework for Understanding and Engaging Senior Management Stakeholders

Edited by
LYNDA BOURNE

Routledge
Taylor & Francis Group

LONDON AND NEW YORK

First published in paperback 2024

First published 2011 by Gower Publishing

Published 2016 by Routledge
4 Park Square, Milton Park, Abingdon, Oxon OX14 4RN

and by Routledge
605 Third Avenue, New York, NY 10158

Routledge is an imprint of the Taylor & Francis Group, an informa business

© 2011, 2016, 2024 selection and editorial matter, Lynda Bourne; individual chapters, the contributors

The right of Lynda Bourne to be identified as the author of the editorial material, and of the authors for their individual chapters, has been asserted in accordance with sections 77 and 78 of the Copyright, Designs and Patents Act 1988.

All rights reserved. No part of this book may be reprinted or reproduced or utilised in any form or by any electronic, mechanical, or other means, now known or hereafter invented, including photocopying and recording, or in any information storage or retrieval system, without permission in writing from the publishers.

Trademark notice: Product or corporate names may be trademarks or registered trademarks and are used only for identification and explanation without intent to infringe.

Publisher's Note
The publisher has gone to great lengths to ensure the quality of this reprint but points out that some imperfections in the original copies may be apparent.

British Library Cataloguing in Publication Data
Advising upwards : a framework for understanding and engaging senior management stakeholders.
    1. Communication in management. 2. Teams in the workplace – Management.
3. Managing your boss.
    I. Bourne, Lynda.
    658.4'5–dc22

Library of Congress Cataloging-in-Publication Data
Bourne, Lynda.
    Advising upwards : a framework for understanding and engaging senior management stakeholders / Lynda Bourne.
        p. cm.
    Includes bibliographical references and index.
    ISBN 978-0-566-09249-7 (hbk. : alk. paper) 1. Management. 2. Organizational behavior.
3. Organizational effectiveness. 4. Corporate governance. I. Title.

    HD31.B6337 2011
    658.4'095–dc22

                                                                            2011015705

Cover design with thanks to Flux Creative, Melbourne, Australia.

ISBN: 978-0-566-09249-7 (hbk)
ISBN: 978-1-03-283844-1 (pbk)
ISBN: 978-1-315-56579-8 (ebk)

DOI: 10.4324/9781315565798

Contents

List of Figures

List of Tables

About the Editor

Dr Lynda Bourne PMP®, FAIM, is an international authority on stakeholder engagement using the *Stakeholder Circle*®: www.stakeholder-management.com. She works with organisations globally to manage change through managing the relationships essential for successful delivery of organisational outcomes.

She has presented these ideas at conferences and seminars in Europe, Russia, Asia, North and South America, and Australia to audiences from the IT, construction, defence and mining industries. Her book *Stakeholder Relationship Management* was published in 2009. She has contributed to books on stakeholder engagement, and has published papers in many academic and professional journals, including a chapter in 2010 on stakeholder engagement in Project Management Offices (PMO) for the Project Management Institute's (PMI) publication – *PMOSIG Program Management Office Handbook*.

She was 2010 President of the PMI's Melbourne Chapter and has contributed a quarterly column for PMI's *PM Network* since 2008. She can be contacted at lyndab@stakeholder-management.com.

About the Contributors

Alfonso Bucero, MSc, PMP®, is an independent project management consultant and speaker. He is founder, partner and director of BUCERO PM Consulting in Spain. Bucero has a MSc in computer science engineering, and he is a frequent contributor to international project management conferences and workshops. Alfonso is active in the Project Management Institute (PMI) taking on many volunteer leadership roles: this year he was elected as Component Mentor for the South of Europe. He is involved in managing projects worldwide: project management is his passion. He is the author of *Project Management – a New Vision*, co-author of *Project Sponsorship* and author of *Today is a Good Day* (published 2010). Alfonso received a PMI Distinguished Contribution Award in 2010. His motto is 'Passion, Persistence and Patience'. He can be contacted at alfonso.bucero@bucero.com .

Randall L. Englund, MBA, BSEE, NPDP, CBM, is an author, speaker, trainer, university instructor, professional facilitator and executive consultant for the Englund Project Management Consultancy (www.englundpmc.com, englundr@pacbell.net). He draws upon experiences as a former Senior Project Manager with Hewlett-Packard Company (HP) for 22 years and as an installation supervisor for GE Medical Systems. He is co-author of three books in the business and management field – *Creating an Environment for Successful Projects*, *Creating the Project Office* and *Project Sponsorship* – and has contributed to blogs, articles, as well as chapters in other management books. Randy is both a long time member of and frequent seminar presenter for the Project Management Institute (PMI).

Robert N. Higgins V, PMP® is a fenestrator, an entrepreneur and a digital coach. Robert lives in Tokyo, Japan and manages high-profile architectural global projects. He holds a Bachelor of Arts in Cultural Anthropology from Fort Lewis College in Durango, Colorado. He has extensive global project management experience including in China and specialises in multicultural project teams. Robert Higgins believes that understanding culture is invaluable to creating harmony and building high performance teams. He can be contacted at RobertHigginsV@gmail.com

Dr David Hillson is The Risk Doctor (www.risk-doctor.com). He is a leading thinker and expert practitioner in risk management who writes and speaks widely on the topic. He specialises in both strategic and tactical risk, with a particular interest in risk psychology.

David is active in the Project Management Institute where his risk work has been recognised with both the PMI Fellow award and the PMI Distinguished Contribution Award.

He is also an Honorary Fellow of the Association for Project Management (APM), and a Fellow of the Institute of Risk Management (IRM). David is a Chartered Manager and was elected a Fellow of the RSA to contribute to its Risk Commission.

Soon Kheng Khor (SK) is a founder of Asia ICT Project Management (www.asiaictpm.com). He has 22 years of working and management experiences in Europe, the USA and Asia. He managed to deliver mission and life-critical integrated system for five airports, three of them in China. He is a certified Professional Management Professional (PMP®) and successfully trained 500 PMPs® since 2005. He is a Registered Charted Engineer with Engineer Ireland and obtained his degree in computer science from University of Dublin, Trinity College, Ireland. He can be contacted at skhor@asiaictpm.com.

Bob McGannon PMP®, GWCPM is Director of Mindavation, a United States and Australia-based organisation focusing on increasing business capabilities in the portfolio management, programme and project management space by providing programme delivery consultants basic through to advanced training workshops and coaching. Bob has worked with beginning to advanced programme and project personnel from over 15 countries, with a wide variety of industry backgrounds. He is the author of the Intelligent Disobedience blog, which can be accessed at http://mindavation.com/IDBlog. Bob can be reached via email at rmcgannon@mindavation.com.

Ruth Murray-Webster is an organisational change consultant, Managing Partner of Lucidus Consulting Ltd, www.lucidusconsulting.com, and a Visiting Fellow at Cranfield School of Management. Her professional interests and experience centre on the competences required for individuals to manage change and the culture of organisations as they seek to improve and advance. Ruth's work has been published previously in project and programme management-related journals and conference proceedings and in the books *Understanding and Managing Risk Attitude* and *Managing Group Risk Attitude*, both published by Gower.

She holds a Master of Business Administration degree from Henley Management College where she carried out research into the effect of cultural differences on business success within international joint ventures. She is currently studying for a Doctorate at Cranfield School of Management. She can be contacted at ruth@lucidusconsulting.com.

Jürgen Oschadleus MBA, MAIPM, PMP® is an experienced international speaker, educator and consultant on project leadership, influence and effective communication. He combines a background in history and education with a fascination for sport and psychology to challenge people's thinking and help them create new mental connections, apply knowledge and achieve the outcomes they seek. Jürgen, director of Act Knowledge and managing partner of Valense, welcomes your views on effective stakeholder engagement; contact him at advisingupwards@actknowledge.com.

Arthur Shelley is the founder of Intelligent Answers, a behavioural and capability development consultancy business. He is the author of two books, *The Organizational Zoo* (2007) and *Being a Successful Knowledge Leader* (2009). Formerly the Global Knowledge Director for Cadbury Schweppes he managed projects in Asia, Europe, America and Australia. He teaches knowledge management and applied research in RMIT's MBA programme and facilitates professional networking forums: Melbourne Knowledge Management Leadership Forum and the Organizational Zoo Ambassadors Network. See www.organizationalzoo.com.

S. Jonathan Whitty, more familiarly Jon Whitty, is an engineer at heart who originally hails from Wales in the United Kingdom. He is currently Senior Lecturer in Project Management at the School of Management and Marketing at the University of Southern Queensland, Brisbane, Australia.

He is probably best known for his opinions on the concept of complex project management and for his evolutionary approach to project management research. His email is whitty@usq.edu.au, his website www.usq.edu.au/users/whitty.

Preface

Over the last ten years of consulting, writing and training in all aspects of stakeholder engagement in organisations in different countries and different industries, it has become clear that the issues of the 'impossible manager', the unhelpful sponsor exist everywhere. This is fuelled by the *command and control* culture and results in a huge gap in understanding between those who are responsible for leading and managing the organisation – the CEO and leadership team – and those who work further down the line in delivering tactical and operational outcomes. It is one thing to provide organisations and their people with tools and training to better understand who the *right* stakeholders are and techniques to communicate effectively and measure that effectiveness. It is an entirely other thing to provide the team with the knowledge, support or the maturity to understand how to *manage upwards*: how to gain credibility, provide the most appropriate information, and express that information in the best possible way.

There are a few basic precepts that I recommend to people when wanting to begin building credibility with managers:

1. Understand their expectations and provide information in the context of those (possibly fluid) expectations.

2. Make them (your managers) look good – ensure they are always prepared to deal with bad news, or for meetings. Shield them from potential embarrassment – their embarrassment can be also yours. It will build your credibility if your boss sees you as an ally and not a threat. Understand that they also have to advise upwards and

may be having the same difficulties as you are in being heard or getting the support they need.

3.   Always speak in business language – this not only reduces confusion but also gives the perception that you are allied and not one of another group (who speak technical jargon).

There is no doubt that these tips are useful, but of course there is much more to successfully managing upwards or advising upwards. There are so many factors to be considered: and there does not appear be much help or guidance available.

So I asked my colleagues to help!

The contributors to this book are all experts in their field, and have developed new ways of approaching the issues that need to be addressed. They come from all fields ranging from academics to experienced practitioners. But they all have one thing in common – interesting ideas to contribute.

I hope that the ideas expressed in this book are useful to all those who need to manage the expectations of their senior stakeholders.

Dr Lynda Bourne, PMP, FAIM
CEO, Stakeholder Management, Pty Ltd
Melbourne Australia

Introduction

Lynda Bourne

The work that an organisation does to deliver its business strategy usually involves change: to manage change successfully it is also essential to manage relationships and to manage uncertainty. While the relationships with stakeholders involve all types of groups and individuals, relationships with senior stakeholders seem most difficult. With this group of stakeholders the stakes are high, they have most to lose if things go wrong and often see things differently from those who are below them in the organisation's hierarchy.

Anyone – everyone – who has ever worked in an organisation (of any type) will have encountered at least one 'difficult' senior stakeholder. They may set aggressive deadlines or impossible tasks, have unrealistic expectations of the outcomes but are not prepared to discuss or modify these expectations, are 'too busy' to discuss details or issues, or are not interested in progress reports but angry when things go wrong. The purpose of this book is to provide new approaches to understanding the expectations of these senior stakeholders, and tools and techniques to enhance effectiveness and to build trust and confidence in their minds.

Succeeding in today's corporate environment requires a different management paradigm from the traditional view promoted by Western business schools and sustained by a universal corporate culture of 'command and control'. The stress and anxiety experienced in coping with change is borne by everyone in an organisation, not just the managers, but also all members of the organisation and stakeholder community. However, it is probably fair to say that this stress and anxiety is felt in different ways.

There is a highly complex and dynamic 'organism' in the space between an organisation's strategic vision and the (tactical) work being done to deliver that vision. Around this 'zone', theoretically, management's vision has clear direction and clear outcomes, and through clear transmission of strategic (organisational) visions into tactical objectives, outcomes will be delivered to the required time, cost and quality. In reality the outcomes are unpredictable. This is the landscape of uncertainty and ambiguity that must be navigated to manage the expectations of senior stakeholders.

Inevitably, rogue stakeholders (supporting one of the conflicting parties, or seeking to establish ascendancy over other stakeholders, regain control or with other hidden agendas) will incite conflict or cause trouble. This trouble can come in the form of seeking to cancel the work or change its scope or technical direction, reduce the funding, or perhaps requiring additional or different reporting. It may come as a result of the turbulence caused by another management attempt to resume control within the organisation. Or it might just be the product of lack of trust in the team and its management.

The actions of these stakeholders and the consequences of the actions can be averted or at least minimised through sustained effective communication: communication whose purpose is clear, whose format and content is appropriate to the requirements of each important stakeholder and whose effectiveness is monitored and modified as necessary to meet the needs of the activity and the expectations of the stakeholder. The most successful communication will come from teams who have established credibility through a sustained campaign to develop a reputation for delivery of results and fearless good advice.[1]

A paradigm shift in management thinking is needed to succeed in managing the successful delivery of outcomes within the turbulent environment of a modern organisation. To succeed, vigilance and flexibility are necessary. Management of relationships and engagement of important stakeholders are keys to success in the dynamic environment of these organisations. It is time to question the command and control ethos and look at more useful and appropriate ways to influence senior management[2] – *advise upwards*. Such strategies can only be effective if implemented with a clear understanding of the culture of the organisation and the culture of the stakeholders who have been identified as important to the success of the work.

---

1   See Chapters 1, 2, 3 and 10 this volume.
2   Chapter 4 offers insights on how the culture can move from 'command and control' to a 'sponsor' culture.

Organisational Culture

The dynamics of the global economy and the ensuing increased complexity have consequences for organisations and their people. Traditional management theory and practice has been firmly in the grip of Taylor's scientific management theory which defines management as *organising, planning and controlling*, based on 'rational analysis of task requirements and human motivations to perform them' (Streatfield 2001, p. 8). The emphasis has been on ensuring that the manager is 'in control'. This is the culture of management that is sustained through management education and through the selection of managers with that education to continue to 'control' aspects of the organisation and thus sustaining existing organisational culture.[3]

Schein (1985) defines *culture* in terms of systems of symbols, ideas, beliefs, values and of distinctive forms of behaviour. Trompenaars and Hampden-Turner (1997, p. 13) define it as 'a shared system of meanings (that) dictates what we pay attention to, how we act and what we value'. Simply put, *culture* is: 'how we do things around here' and *cultural norms* are the unwritten rules of behaviour. How we do things around here varies with each group and/or organisation, therefore there can be no universal law of organisational management or a universal management toolkit.

Three factors are especially important in determining corporate culture:

1.　System of authority between superiors and subordinates.[4]

2.　Relationships between employees and their organisation.[5]

3.　Employees' views about the organisation and his/her place in it. (Trompenaars 1993, p. 157).

3　These ideas are covered in detail through alternative perspectives on the culture of management in modern Western organisation in Chapter 8.
4　This will be a product of many factors: national, professional, industrial, even the dominance of specific generations – see Chapters 6, 7 and 8.
5　Chapter 1 defines a structured process for developing an understanding of the relationships within the stakeholder community and mapping this community to ensure awareness of its networks and complexities. Chapter 3 discusses the most appropriate ways to craft communication to engage those stakeholders.

Hierarchy and Authority

Talbot (2003) proposed that the development and creation of industrial and post-industrial organisational forms derives from military models, traced back to military organisational innovations of Napoleon in the early nineteenth century. Infrastructure projects such as the Western Railroad of the US were the catalyst for the hierarchical and bureaucratic line and staff management structure. Adopted by other railroads, it became the dominant management structure – the traditional functional structure. The language and culture of management as we practice it today has direct links to this military connection (Talbot 2003, p. 331). Mintzberg (1979, p. 27) refers to the 'chain of command' of organisation structure. The military culture is echoed in the metaphor of business as war, whose reference manual is Sun Tzu, *the Art of War* and whose language includes such terminology as 'indefensible claims', targets, 'arguments shot down in flames' (Lakoff and Johnson 1981, p. 4).[6]

The structure, culture and language of the military has been the predominating one in the world of organisations, and still drives the dominant paradigm by which senior management is 'in command' and therefore 'in control'. The implication of the traditional, military-based organisational culture is that it is management who generate ideas, make decisions and provide leadership, and it is staff's role to work to deliver management vision. This formal authority, with its control over rewards and punishment, does not automatically provide the means to influence people to do or not do something. Such influence is achieved through the exercise of *personal power* in the form of expertise, loyalty or charisma, or through *political power*. In situations where goodwill, flexibility or self-motivation and responsibility are required, the command and control approaches of coercive power simply do not work (Yukl 1998, Chapter 8).

The Manager's Dilemma

To understand what it means to be an executive in a large organisation, it is important to explore the nature and culture of organisational leadership: what it takes to reach an executive position, and the demands of decision-making in today's competitive environment. There is extensive literature on leadership and what makes a good leader. Despite that, newly appointed executives

---

6   Chapter 9 discusses the concepts of metaphors in more detail and its application in organisations for advising upwards.

struggle to make the transition to the ranks of the senior leadership team, often having to change the management 'habits' that actually got them to their current position and become more strategic, think more holistically and learn to delegate. This personal reinvention must occur at the same time that the new executive is grappling with the pressures and urgent requirements of the new role.

Management theories of leadership have emphasised (or developed) the concept of the *CEO as hero*. Jim Collins describes a different way of thinking about leadership (Collins 2001). From his research into the leadership of long-term sustainable organisations – 'what makes an organisation *great*?' – he developed a hierarchy of leadership qualities and characteristics culminating in 'level 5' leadership which he has defined as a blend of 'humility and will' that moves a company to sustainable greatness. The CEO as hero equates to Collins' 'level 4' leadership. This is the paradox of leadership – the qualities that Collins identified for most effective leadership do not necessarily result in the CEO or other executives being the 'front man' of the organisation or the one that must lead the troops into battle. The level 5 leader is a strategist, recognising the path that an organisation must take for success, but also empowering the management team to meet the challenges. The expectations of executives in modern Western organisations is at level 4: the advising upwards approaches outlined in this book should be directed to assisting the CEO and executive team to take on level 5 characteristics.[7]

The qualities of leadership that have been described in this section match the requirements of the executives from Watkins' (2003) study and provide a starting point for identification of the characteristics that managers of an organisation's funded and approved activities require from a *sponsor*. It also provides an alternative perspective for those who will have to develop communication strategies to enlist the support of senior stakeholders and engage and assist them in the work that has to be done to deliver successful outcomes.

The Importance of an Effective Sponsor

The role of the sponsor is seen to be vital to success even though the roles and responsibilities are not clearly defined or agreed. The Office of Government

---

7   Chapter 5 discusses aspects of decision-making and Chapter 10 looks at how teams and their managers can assist the organisation's leadership in making this transition.

Commerce (OGC) defines the sponsor role as 'the interface between project ownership and delivery'. Characteristics of this role are (Office of Government Commerce UK 2008):

- Adequate knowledge and information about the business and the work of the activity or its outcomes to be able to make informed decisions; and

- Ability to network effectively, negotiate well and influence people and build and maintain robust relationships with stakeholders within and outside the activity.

The roles and responsibilities of the sponsor may be perceived as onerous or time-consuming if the individual:

- Does not understand the objectives of the activity, the processes and practices used to implement the deliverables; or

- Does not clearly understand the role; or

- Is not interested in doing so.

The command and control management style will not easily adapt to this role. The nature of the work within an organisation often causes change and with that change uncertainty and anxiety, affecting not only the team but also the leadership.[8]

Change, Uncertainty and Anxiety

Being 'not in control' is often viewed as management incompetence. Traditional expectation is that management should be able to anticipate important potential changes and put in place controls to ensure that only the intended outcomes were realised. But managers only work with part of the picture. When *unknown unknowns* cause unplanned outcomes, the reaction of senior management is often to perceive that the activity is out of control. The solution of choice is usually to introduce more or more rigorous and/or aggressive control mechanisms such as more detailed or frequent reporting, or in extreme situations, change team personnel, or impose an additional layer of management.

---

8   Chapter 4 provides direction on how to build the sponsorship culture within an organisation.

Uncertainty and ambiguity affect everyone in the organisation, through all levels. Managers respond by applying solutions that promise to be effective. The situation is exacerbated by the inability of each group to see the point of view of the other. The nature of these asymmetric relationships (power) means that those at the top cannot understand the impact of the change and controls they impose, and those at the bottom cannot understand the reasons for management requiring these changes. The most powerful stakeholders will most likely believe that they must control all outcomes, moving to impose more controls when results do not meet expectations.

Other forms of organisational structure are evolving. One form worthy of note is 'patterns of relationships between people' (Stacey 2001, p. 140) where structure, power relations and forms of organising are not fixed, but vary in unpredictable ways according to events and relationships that occur within and outside of the group. An example of this form is the circular form developed by Hesselbein (1996) for the Scouting Association in the US. Because there is no hierarchal structure apparent in the depiction of this (circular) organisational form, authority and decision-making have to be redefined: conversation and collaboration develops communication and interaction. Conversation forms the group, organisation or community (Fonseca 2002, p. 7) and facilitates action, knowledge transfer and resolution of issues. It is in 'conversation' – in organisational terms, communication – that the key to successfully managing the expectations of senior stakeholders and advising upwards lies.

Everyone who has been involved in delivering organisational outcomes has a horror story about working with difficult stakeholders. These usually involve:[9]

- The difficulty and frustration of working in the command and control management culture, and 'being heard' by senior management.

- How lack of experience can cause the manager and team to try desperate measures or just give up and provide the senior stakeholder with whatever they want, even if it is not in the best interests of the organisation or the current work.

---

9   Chapter 1 uses the case study of Heathrow Terminal 5. For another more personal case study see Bourne (2011) 'Advising upwards: managing the perceptions and expectations of senior management stakeholders' *Management Decision*.

- How focus on one stakeholder can lead to neglect of other equally important but less vocal stakeholders and subsequent perception of failure of the activity.

- How everyone reacts (not necessarily logically) to uncertainty.

The stress and anxiety experienced in coping with change is borne by everyone in an organisation, not just the managers, but also all members of the organisation's community.

To reduce the stress and manage the anxiety it is essential to:

- Identify stakeholders for each phase of the work. At each phase there may be a different mix of stakeholders, and those identified as most important.

- Be clear on what a successful outcome means for each of the important stakeholders. Knowing these expectations means that the manager can target messages to gain the support and influence of each stakeholder, within the framework of what was considered 'successful' (Bourne 2009).

- Understand that inevitably there will be conflicting expectations within the group of senior stakeholders who have been assessed as important. Awareness of these conflicts and the influence of other stakeholders and targeted communication assists in the achievement of the best outcome.

- Know that with experience of operating in the power structures of the organisation, and learning from mistakes, advising upwards and the ability and willingness to operate becomes a better understood and unconscious mode of managing difficult stakeholders.

- Build credibility within the organisation through a reputation in the industry, and utilise the influence networks developed and sustained over time.

- Recognise that it takes time and continuous effort to analyse and review the stakeholder community, understand the expectations of the important stakeholders, develop targeted communication strategies and negotiate with those stakeholders who had conflicting expectations.

Understanding how to work within the power structures of the organisation is an important skill worth acquiring because access to resources (financial, human, material and informational) must be negotiated. The team is often without organisational authority or status and so must rely on other attributes to achieve the organisation's outcomes. These attributes are summarised as the ability to:

- Build credibility through the reputation for successful management and leadership;

- Develop and maintain networks as a source of influence and access to power;

- Be willing to operate within the power structures of the organisation;

- Understand the expectations of stakeholders and to communicate in the language that matches their own roles and experience;

- Recognise that the groundwork must be laid *before* a crisis occurs through targeted communication of progress, including fearless but fully analysed reporting of issues or risks; and

- Help the sponsor assist the manager and team deliver success to the organisation.

Managing a senior manager's optimistic expectations needs a strong relationship between the team and its stakeholders. Consistency, perseverance and determination are important in building respect. The development of stakeholders' perceptions of the individual's personal credibility, wider personal and professional relationships, contacts and networks are all essential elements that go towards building the respect needed to change senior stakeholders' perceptions. These wider relationships must be built not just for the project, but maintained long-term.

The techniques for managing the expectations of senior stakeholder and managing the behaviours of difficult colleagues (who are also stakeholders) used successfully appear to be instinctive. In reality successful approaches are partly instinctive and partly developed from experiences from a variety of sources, both business and personal. A framework is offered to assist individuals in an organisation to build relationships with senior stakeholders through building credibility so that when support is needed it is readily given. Data from surveys seeking to understand how managers make the transition from middle management to the ranks of the senior leadership team, or how CEOs emerge from the senior leadership team to lead organisations, recognises that each transition requires a major change in behaviour and that the same guidelines apply each time. These guidelines recognise the need to learn from others, to understand and manage the expectations of their stakeholders, and to build and maintain relationships within and around the individual's sphere of influence.

The Structure of the Book

Part I, 'Advancing the Fundamentals', looks at some of the most important and fundamental aspects of management and leadership within organisations. It seeks to advance traditional thinking into the realm of what needs to occur for advising upward. The chapters in this section look at engaging senior management within organisations through understanding their expectations and through effective communication to engage them in support of the work; managing risk throughout the different layers of the organisation and in particular what happens in the often overlooked middle layers of the enterprise; understanding the processes of influence and developing credibility to better engage senior stakeholders; and finally helping senior stakeholders to grow into the role of sponsor through insights into how an organisation can develop the culture of sponsorship to increase success.

Chapter 1, 'Why is stakeholder relationship management so difficult?', uses the construction and opening for operation of the Heathrow Terminal 5 (T5) as a case study. It explores the concept of the importance of knowing who the 'right' stakeholders are at any time in the life cycle of the work that an organisation does to deliver its business strategies. The disastrous opening week of T5 caused the reputation of British Airways to be negatively affected. Subsequent investigation identified inadequate training of staff and poor preparation for changes connected to a new terminal with infrastructure and new processes as major causes. In addition, the 'urgency' created by the senior stakeholder – BA's CEO – resulted in important preparations to be overlooked. Finally the chapter proposes a new approach to investing in stakeholder relationship management in the form of the concept of 'zero cost of stakeholder management' based on the 'zero cost of quality'. The logic is as follows: the more time and planning invested early in better understanding of the stakeholder community of T5, the less rework in the form of customer satisfaction and reputational damage and therefore lower costs.

Chapter 2, 'Enterprise risk management: managing uncertainty and minimising surprise', looks at risk as it exists at the various levels of an organisation. It provides advice on communicating about risks between these levels to manage uncertainty and minimise surprises, with an emphasis on proactive management rather than reaction. Risk relates to the most fundamental purposes of any organisation through the links between risk and objectives. The focus is on Enterprise Risk Management (ERM), an integrated and hierarchical approach to risk management across the organisation. These are the two key aspects of ERM: how to manage risk across boundaries within an organisation and how to report risk upwards to the appropriate level for both attention and action. By looking at the four types of risk to the organisation – risk *to* the enterprise; risk *of* the enterprise; risk *within* the enterprise; risk *across* the enterprise – the chapter is able to provide guidance for those wishing to implement ERM in an effective way.

Chapter 3, 'Conversations that engage: the challenge of advising senior managers', first describes the nature of giving advice; how even solid well-intentioned advice is often ignored in favour of decisions based on emotion or instinct or even sometimes sheer wrong-headedness: this frequently results in poor decisions. A discussion of how the brain processes information is followed by a discussion of principles in how better to deliver advice that is 'heard' and acted on by others, particularly senior stakeholders. This is achieved through creating a platform of trust and credibility and developing a reputation as a 'trusted advisor'. Aristotle's three approaches based on *ethos* (personal character), *pathos* (emotional appeal and relationship) and *logos* (logic and reason) are discussed: influence is therefore about balancing the three dimensions and framing advice in terms that can be best appreciated and understood by others.

Chapter 4, 'From commander to sponsor: building executive support for project success', addresses both the role of sponsorship and how to advise upwards when a sponsorship culture is weak, ineffective, unfamiliar, good but not great, or missing. The chapter first describes the importance of (and need for) sponsors who are supportive and who also understand the sponsor's role.

It is based on the principle that moving from the traditional organisation's command and control culture to one that fosters a more collaborative approach is essential for the organisation's success. In command and control organisations it is common to encounter 'accidental sponsors' who often do not understand the role and even may not know that they are sponsors of a project! The authors provide some useful, practical advice on what the managers or the team members can do to engage their sponsors or other senior stakeholders, drawing on their own vast experience to apply the lessons they have learned to assist managers and leaders to become more effective. Executives need training, experience and practice to be effective sponsors. Excellence in sponsorship needs to be every manager's mantra for achieving more in the organisation.

Part II, 'The Effects of Culture', explores how different aspects of culture affect an organisation and its people. Ideas range from a discussion on how groups shape information and make decisions, an exploration of the phenomenon of 'groupthink' and other influences on decision making – the 'triple strand' of influences on perception of risk and risk attitude. This is followed by an exploration of the true differences between the ideas and cultures of Western-trained managers and Chinese-trained managers and how to succeed in Chinese organisations. An exploration of the 'Nintendo®' generation includes guidelines for this (younger) generation on how to apply the skills they have learned in gaming to success in organisational culture. Finally, a fresh look at the culture of management in Western organisations where the application of a Darwinian perspective provides insight into the issues around training and succession planning in today's organisations.

Chapter 5, 'How groups shape information and decisions', begins with the proposition that groups of people working in teams are central to organisational life: there are very few individuals who have the necessary influence to lead an organisation by themselves. The focus is on: what constitutes information that is suitable for *upwards* stakeholders in decision-making; and practical guidance on how to overcome communication and decision-making barriers to engage and influence stakeholders more effectively. The guidance includes an analysis of decision-making, a discussion of groupthink and how to avoid it, or at least reduce its impact, and finally a discussion about the triple strand of influence on perception of risk and risk attitude.

Chapter 6, 'East meets West: working with a Chinese boss', presents an insider's view of the differences between Western-trained management culture and Chinese management culture. Most managers understand the concept of 'saving face' and possibly even the '*Quanxi*' relationship (a network of contacts and influence). However there are subtleties in operating in the environment of Chinese management culture that can only be described and explored by someone who actually grew up in that culture. The author of this chapter has the added advantage of also being educated and having worked in Western organisational culture, and so is able to explain to us what these subtleties actually are. Three case studies describe common situations in organisational life, handled differently in each culture: ordering coffee, concepts of authority and responsibility, and conflict resolution. The next step is to understand how to survive in a Chinese organisation, and in particularly how to give advice: do you 'hint'? Do you allow the boss to think it is his idea? Do you remind him of essential things in meetings? If you do, what is the best way to do it?

Chapter 7, 'The new new Confucian communication game', provides essential information for those over 25 on the new generation of under-25s – the 'gamer' or 'Nintendo®' generation. Organisational issues on how to control reputation, coordinate projects and ensure that the organisation's knowledge assets are retained and enhanced may be achieved in the new environments of the twenty-first century. It will be through the combination of the ancient wisdoms of Confucian thinking and the sophisticated *always on communication* approach of the latest generation of employees – the gamers. The chapter provides advice to gamers on how to harness the skills and thinking processes honed through online games to organisational life. This will support advancement of their culture under the new paradigms of communication and leadership. For those of us seeking to understand how to communicate with and lead the new generation of knowledge workers there are explanations and translations of the seemingly foreign concepts and language of the gamer generation. Ultimately it seems the medium of communication has changed, but many of the Confucian principles still apply – good businesses have potent leaders, organisations with potent leaders don't need command and control, there is only limited opportunity for success for individuals who seek to operate alone. Only when part of a team and utilising the power of the team can true success be achieved. Be flexible, but recognise that true success often only comes after long efforts – 'grinding'.

Chapter 8, 'How to train your manager: a Darwinian perspective', provides an alternative view to the modern organisation where the behaviours that are rewarded are the ability to plan and organise: these behaviours allow a manager to survive in the corporate world, are taught in management schools and are considered to be the important characteristics of successful managers. In the same way that Darwin's theory of natural selection has been applied to explain the evolution and continuance of particular characteristics and species, this chapter explores the idea that behaviours, ideas and techniques are selected and passed on from person to person, from manager to manager, from manager to senior manager. Behaviours that provide survival advantages to managers will reinforce the views and expectations of senior stakeholders. Credibility and trust are built through always providing senior stakeholders with reports, information and behaviours that comfort them, and thus reducing their anxiety and uncertainty.

Part III, 'Being Extraordinary', looks at two unique approaches to advising upwards: the first through the use of metaphor to characterise management behaviours according to culturally accepted comparisons with animals. The second by the application of 'intelligent disobedience' – an approach that suggests that there are times when it is better to deliberately disobey a manager's directions or the organisation's rules for the benefit of the organisation.

Chapter 9, 'Creative metaphor as a tool for stakeholder influence', uses metaphor to identify specific types of behaviours exhibited by individuals within an organisation. Through application of a defined set of characteristics teams can be formed and relationships built based on an understanding of which behaviours work well together and which do not. These metaphors are intuitive and also applicable across all cultures. In this chapter there is a development of methods to use the knowledge gained about individual and group (stakeholder) behaviours to build and maintain the appropriate relationships with those who matter. The awareness of this metaphorical approach has been shown to assist in developing better communication to engage and influence stakeholders.

Chapter 10, 'Intelligent disobedience: the art of saying "no" to managers', provides a new approach to advising upwards through suggesting that experienced managers must use their own discretion at times in the best interests of the organisation. Decision-making requires information that is timely and of good quality, but both the decision-maker and advisors usually operate under constraints that restrict the time, effort and attention in such a way that the wrong or at least suboptimal decisions are made. Through intelligent disobedience managers and leaders will make courageous decisions in the best interests of the business but not necessarily according to the rules, processes or practices of the organisation or the instructions of their senior stakeholders. Using a case study to identify situations that may require intelligent disobedient actions, the chapter provides guidance and reassurance for those who recognise that they may sometimes need to take a courageous but maverick approach to the situation.

References

Bourne, L. 2009. *Stakeholder Relationship Management: a Maturity Model for Organisational Implementation*. Farnham: Gower.

Bourne, L. 2011. Advising upwards: managing the perceptions and expectations of senior management stakeholders. *Management Decision* June.

Collins, J. 2001. Level 5 leadership: The triumph of humility and fierce resolve. *Harvard Business Review* 79(1): 66–77.

Fonseca, J. 2002. *Complexity and Innovation in Organizations*. London: Routledge.

Hesselbein, F. 1996. *Managing in a World That is Round*. New York: Leader to Leader Institute, http://leadertoleader.org/about/index.html.

Lakoff, G. and M. Johnson 1981. *Metaphors We Live By*. Chicago, IL: The University of Chicago Press.

Mintzberg, H. 1979. *The Structure of Organisations*. Englewood Cliffs, NJ: Prentice-Hall.

Office of Government Commerce UK 2008. *Project Sponsor*. Retrieved 13 June 2008, from www.ogc.gov.uk.

Schein, E.H. 1985. *Organisational Culture and Leadership*. San Francisco, CA: Jossey Bass.

Stacey, R.D. 2001. *Complex Responsive Processes in Organizations; Learning and Knowledge Creation*. London: Routledge.

Streatfield, P. 2001. *The Paradox of Control in Organizations*. London: Routledge.

Talbot, P.A. 2003. Management organisational history – a military lesson? *Journal of European Industrial Training* 27(7): 330–340.

Trompenaars, F. 1993. *Riding the Waves of Culture: Understanding Cultural Diversity in Business*. London: Economics Books.

Trompenaars. F. and Hampden-Turner, C. 1997. Riding theWaves of Culture: Understanding Cultural Diversity in Business. London: Nicholas Brealey.

Watkins, M. 2003. *The First 90 Days*. Boston, MA: Harvard Business School Press.

Yukl, G. 1998. *Leadership in Organisations*. Sydney: Prentice-Hall.

PART I
Advancing the Fundamentals

1

Why is Stakeholder Relationship Management so Difficult?

Lynda Bourne

Whatever your role in an organisation your work will only be considered successful if key stakeholders perceive that deliverables or outcomes meet their needs. Perceptions of success or failure are heavily influenced by the effectiveness of client, project or other team's communications and relationships with its stakeholder community, particularly those in management or decision-making roles.

Studies have consistently shown that a critical factor in creating successful outcomes is the active support of senior management stakeholders, particularly the sponsor of a given project or activity. Successful managers understand this and are willing to do whatever is necessary to ensure that this group of stakeholders is prepared to support the work to its (successful) conclusion. This requires the manager, and the team, to be skilful at *advising upwards*, using effective stakeholder management techniques to engage the support of senior executives and to manage their expectations.

Crafting *advice* to senior management to achieve required outcomes from communication is as much an art as a science. Effective communication requires a clear understanding of the objective of the communication and the skills to create messages that are focused: on the *right* people, at the *right* time and with the *right* information in the *right* format.

Introduction

Much of the work that an organisation must do to deliver its business strategy generates change. The challenge for organisations to deliver successful outcomes to activities, projects or programmes in a climate of uncertainty is met by ensuring that all those groups and individuals affected by the change – stakeholders – are engaged in a way that encourages and, ideally, ensures their collaboration.

We are social animals: we don't thrive in isolation, in fact our behaviour is largely driven by reciprocity; you do or say something to me and that will condition a response. We need to build relationships in our personal and professional lives to be effective human beings. Building relationships requires us to understand two important factors: first, a sustainable relationship provides benefits to both parties; and secondly communication is the *only* tool to build and maintain robust relationships. This is indisputably the case in personal relationships, but the same factors apply to professional relationships. We all communicate: in many cases, with little thought or unconsciously, but we need to appreciate that the most effective communication, personal or professional, is planned – we know the purpose of the communication, we are certain that the relationship is important and we are clear about the level of effort we need to apply to the communication activity. Stakeholder engagement is complex and 'getting it right' can be time-consuming. By understanding which stakeholders are important and how best to provide the information that meets their needs, as well as the needs of the organisation, it is possible to reduce some of the difficulties inherent in communication and stakeholder engagement. Engaging stakeholders to ensure their continued collaboration involves constant vigilance in a changing landscape of relationships with diverse stakeholders whose support, interests and influence may fluctuate unpredictably.

This chapter applies the processes that support effective communication to the task of building and maintaining robust relationships with organisational stakeholders, through analysis of a case study – that of the construction and opening of Heathrow Terminal 5. They may be seen as two distinct projects: one considered very successful and the other considered to have marred the reputation of British Airways staff and management because of the first disastrous week of operation. The first section will analyse the factors, both positive and negative, that led to development of *perception* of the success of the first and failure of the second. The second section describes a structured methodology, the *Stakeholder Circle®*,[1] which provides guidance for teams to identify which of an organisation's stakeholders are the 'right' stakeholders for any particular time in the life of the activity and to define the best approach to communicating effectively for maximum collaboration. Finally, there is a discussion of the common problems that teams encounter, that of engaging senior management stakeholders – *advising upwards* – for the essential support that each project needs for survival.

THE CASE STUDY: HEATHROW TERMINAL 5

The focus of this discussion of Heathrow's Terminal 5 (T5) is on the following two stages:

1.   Construction of the terminal for British Airport Authority (BAA), supported by enlightened contractual arrangements.

2.   British Airways (BA) opens its facilities to the public and begins operation.

Construction

The £4.3bn Heathrow T5 project has been acknowledged as the 'most successful UK construction project' due to innovative project management practices which focused on collaboration (Potts 2006).[2] This collaboration was achieved through an emphasis on integrated teams, early risk management to anticipate, manage and reduce risks associated with the project, and an acceptance by BAA of total risk in all contracts, rather than the previous adversarial approach of contract negotiation.

Under the 'new' approach to construction project management resulting from the Egan Report (Egan 1998), T5 had been completed on time and within budget at the human cost of two fatalities, compared with a project of this size managed under traditional arrangements which would potentially have resulted in average time overruns of two years, 40 per cent budget overruns and six to eight fatalities. This change in BAA's culture was described as a

---

1   The *Stakeholder Circle®* is a registered trademark of Mosaic Project Services Pty Ltd, Australia.
2   The terminal was designed by Richard Rogers Partnership – now Rogers, Stirk, Harbour and Partners: see www.richardrogers.co.uk. The firm received a Royal Institute of British Architects (RIBA) London award in June 2008 for the building.

'watershed' (Potts 2006), creating an environment for early problem-solving, sharing of information and collaboration.

The Opening

T5 was designed exclusively for BA's use. Features of the new terminal included:

- Seamless check-in designed to eliminate queuing.

- Improvements in punctuality with all BA flights arriving and departing from one terminal.

- State-of-the-art baggage system using technology already in use at other airports to streamline the retrieval of passenger's baggage.

T5 was officially opened on 14 March 2008 by HM Queen Elizabeth and began operating in 27 March, 2008. From that first day flights had to be cancelled, passengers were stranded and over 30,000 pieces of baggage were lost. An enquiry conducted by the House of Commons Transport Committee in 2008 described a series of issues and blunders resulting from poor planning and inadequate preparation of BA staff (House of Commons Transport Committee 2008).

The Chief Executive Officer (CEO) of BA, Willie Walsh, stated in an interview[3] that he and his management took a 'calculated risk':

> *The company had known there were problems with the building from September when BA began to move in its staff and test systems. It was not 100% complete ... managers had reviewed their decision to open as planned on March 27 on a weekly basis and had decided that the problems caused by delaying the move to [October] ... would be greater than those caused by pressing ahead.*

Staff arriving for their morning shifts at T5 on that first day, encountered a number of issues:[4] a scarcity of staff car parking places, with staff overflow car

---

3   business.timesonline.co.uk 'Airline tie-ups loom as crunch hits'; 18 May 2008, Dominic O'Connell.
4   www.bbc.co.uk 'What went wrong at Heathrow's T5?'; 31 March 2008.

parks closed; delays in passing through security; no familiarity with the new terminal building and the new systems.

The House of Commons report (2008) provided additional information:

- Baggage handlers claimed that they had not been adequately trained and did not have any support or back-up even on the first day.

- BA asked for volunteers to make up additional numbers to provide this support, but due to low morale staff were not prepared to attend on their day off.

- Check-in staff continued to add bags to the system, causing the new baggage handling system to overload, because baggage handlers were not removing them quickly enough off the belts. *There was no override switch to stop the belts!*

AN ANALYSIS

The construction of the terminal was acknowledged as a success from a time, cost, scope and quality perspective, but also from the perspective of the *soft skills* of proactive management of risk and reduction of disputes and conflicts. There was a focus on collaboration: the project owner, BAA, recognised that reducing conflict and the use of integrated teams would increase productivity. The innovative focus on collaboration reflected the inclusive flavour of the development of the Egan report – inviting representation and input from other industries, and excluding representatives of the construction industry (Crane 2010).

Inadequate staff training for the opening of T5 was a clear indicator of BA's lack of understanding of the importance of training and preparation of staff for implementation. There was no contingency on that first day, no recognition that something might go wrong:

- Management did not ask staff to come in early to counteract the effect of any potential delays in entering a building they had not entered before.

- They did not offer overtime or offer to pay for additional staff, merely asking staff to come on their day off to help out.

- The baggage handlers appear to have not been trained at all – they did not know how to work within the new processes or technology.

- The baggage handling system appeared to have no back-up system to support the new complex system.

What does the experience of the T5 construction project and its implementation tell us about success and failure? BA's reputation was damaged from the events of T5's opening. Its failure was a failure to manage the *people* side – poor preparation of the people responsible for operation of the facility. If T5's success was to be judged just on the completion of the construction project it would continue to be known as a success, but the perception of the travelling public and many other stakeholders is that T5 'does not work'.[5]

LESSONS LEARNED

Whether the focus was on the successful construction of T5 or the 'unsuccessful' opening, the common element of both the success and the failure was in the areas of stakeholder engagement and effective communication. On the one hand, the focus of the construction project on collaboration, integrated teams, proactive risk management and long-term contracting relationships. On the other hand, the *absence of* recognition and engagement of all stakeholders, indicated by the failure to prepare the staff for the immense changes of working within the new building and its infrastructure, or involve staff through adequate training and include contingencies on the first couple of days of operation. Even more important was the inability of the implementation team to engage the CEO (the most important stakeholder). He did not understand the consequences of meeting the aggressive goals that he imposed upon the project to open the terminal before it was totally ready; and before the staff and the important stakeholders were prepared for the changes.

The examples of both T5 projects illustrate the importance of proactive risk management, development of long-term contractual relationship, and stakeholder engagement, in particular the recognition of the negative influence of the most senior stakeholder's unrelenting drive to meet that aggressive deadline.

We don't know who the project manager was for the opening: the public face of BA at the time was the CEO, Willie Walsh. He has been quoted in the

---

5   This is still the case at the time of writing (2011).

House of Commons report as knowing there were risks in opening before all the infrastructure was complete. Management *had decided* he said, that the problems caused by delaying the move would be greater than those caused by meeting whatever obligations dictated opening at the scheduled date.

The common theme for both projects is stakeholder engagement: when stakeholders are engaged and informed they are instrumental to success; when they are not engaged and not informed, success becomes elusive. The next section of this chapter will explore the concepts of stakeholder engagement and effective communication.

Stakeholder Relationship Management

Stakeholders are defined as 'Individuals or groups who will be impacted by, or can influence the success or failure of an organisation's activities' (Bourne 2009).

Stakeholders are groups or individuals who supply critical resources, or invest funds, career or time in pursuit of the organisation's business strategies or goals. Alternatively, stakeholders may be groups or individuals opposed to the organisation or some aspect of its activities. By definition, a stakeholder has a stake in the activity. This stake may be:

- An *interest* in the outcome, an individual or group affected by the work or the outcome, whether direct or indirect;

- *Rights* (legal or moral);

- *Ownership*, such as intellectual property rights, or real property rights; or

- *Contribution* in the form of knowledge (expertise or experience) or support (in the form of funds, human resources, or advocacy).

Only when the needs (expectations) of each stakeholder and the stake or stakes they may have in the outcome are known and understood is it really possible to begin to understand the drivers or business needs of a sponsor or other senior management stakeholders for what may in reality be unrealistic targets. With this realisation messages can be crafted and a communication campaign or programme begun to attempt to 'educate' the senior management stakeholder on what can be achieved in the context of what they need. The sponsor's needs cannot be assumed and may not even be related to the work itself, but this understanding of needs and expectations is crucial. It is a fundamental starting point for any campaign to reach agreement on alternative objectives and the management of the perception of the sponsor himself *but also* the perceptions of the stakeholders of the sponsor.

THE METHODOLOGY

The *Stakeholder Circle* methodology is based on the concept that success of an organisation's activities to achieve its business strategies and objectives (often projects) depends on the engagement and involvement of the stakeholder community. Figure 1.1 shows the relationships between the activity[6] and its stakeholders. All decisions or understanding of the relationships are made from the perspective of the manager of the activity. Surrounding the work itself is the team; often overlooked in many stakeholder engagement processes, just as it appeared to be by the management of British Airways during the opening of T5. Surrounding the team is the community of stakeholders that has been identified as being important to the success of the activity *at the current time – time 'now'* in the life of the activity. The outermost circle references potential stakeholders: those who may, or will, be important to the success of the work at a later stage.

By differentiating current stakeholders and potential stakeholders in this way, confusion about which stakeholders are important at any particular time and how best to manage the current relationships will be minimised, while ensuring that planning for future relationships is managed effectively. The stakeholders in the outer circle must also be considered in risk-management planning because they may cause the activity to be at risk of failure in the future. Alternatively, these stakeholders may need to be considered in an organisation's marketing plans, as potential customers.

---

6   The concepts defined in this chapter and the methodology applies to *all* activities that an organisation approves, resources and funds to achieve its strategies and goals. Many organisations now use the discipline of project management to deliver these goals and strategies. So when 'project' is referred to in this chapter it can be interpreted in the widest sense to mean any activity, temporary or ongoing, that an organisation performs.

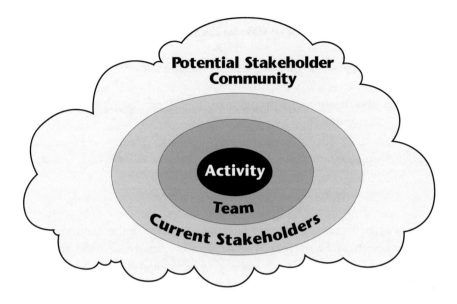

Figure 1.1 The *circle* of stakeholders

MANAGING STAKEHOLDER RELATIONSHIPS

The *Stakeholder Circle* is a five-step methodology that provides a flexible but structured approach to understanding and managing relationships within and around the activity. The methodology is based on the concept that any activity can only exist with the informed consent of its stakeholder community, and that managing the relationships between this community and the team will increase the chances of success. The stakeholder community consists of individuals and groups, each with a different potential to influence the activity's outcome positively or negatively. The team must develop knowledge about this community and appreciation of the right level of engagement. This information will help define the appropriate level and content of communication needed to influence stakeholder's perceptions, expectations and actions. Stakeholder relationship management is complex and cannot be reduced to a formula: each person is unique and the relationships between people reflect that uniqueness and complexity.

The *Stakeholder Circle* enables the team to accumulate information necessary for the engagement of its stakeholders. It consists of five *steps*:

Step 1: identification of all stakeholders;

Step 2: prioritisation to determine who is important;

Step 3: visualisation (mapping) to understand the overall stakeholder community;

Step 4: engagement through effective communications; and

Step 5: monitoring the effect of the engagement.

The next section of this chapter describes the *steps* of the methodology and how to apply them for increased understanding of the specific and unique community of the project or activity and to provide guidance on stakeholder relationship management practices.

STEP 1: IDENTIFY

Step 1: identify consists of three activities:

1.   Developing a list of stakeholders.

2.   Identifying *mutuality*:

   -   How each stakeholder is important to the work of the project; and
   -   What each stakeholder expects from success (or failure) of the project, or its outcomes.

3.   Categorise: document each stakeholder's:

   -   *Influence category*: these are *upwards, downwards, outwards* and *sideways*; and
   -   Relationship to the organisation – whether they are *internal* to the organisation or *external*.

The output of this step will be a list of *all* stakeholders that fit the definition of stakeholder.

HOW MANY STAKEHOLDERS? BEWARE OF 'STAKEHOLDER MYOPIA'!

Some organisational activities are large and complex, and may affect many stakeholders. For example, construction of public facilities or national infrastructure projects will affect private citizens, landowners and the natural and historical environment. For such projects, it is essential to recognise and accept that there will be large numbers of stakeholders. There is often an unconscious boundary on what a 'good number' of stakeholders can be – this is *stakeholder myopia*. It is important for the team and for their management to understand that while the initial number of stakeholders identified may appear unwieldy or overwhelming, *step 2: prioritise*, provides a structured and logical means to prioritise the key stakeholders for the current time.

MUTUALITY

The application of mutuality to stakeholder relationship management addresses the two-way nature of any relationship whether personal, family or work-related. Two additional questions must be asked to gauge and then document both characteristics of each stakeholder:

1.   *'How is this stakeholder important to us? What is their stake?'*

2.   *'What does this stakeholder require from the success or failure of the work's execution or its outcomes?'*

The answer to the first question establishes that this person or group actually is a stakeholder and what their potential contribution to the project's success (or failure) may be. Generally, a stakeholder is important to the project because they are an important source of funds, personnel or materials or can impact the success or failure of the project through either action or inaction.

The answer to the second question establishes the stakeholder's expectations or requirements of the success or failure of the project. Generally a stakeholder will have expectations of personal or organisational gain through either the success or failure of a particular organisational activity. An understanding of the two parts of the relationship with the stakeholder community is crucial to subsequent steps in the stakeholder mapping process and to developing targeted communication strategies.

The final task in *step 1* is to categorise the listed stakeholders according to the type of influence that they can have on the work or its outcomes, or that the work and outcomes can hold over the stakeholders. This is the start of the refinement of the raw list of stakeholders into more manageable information.

INFLUENCE CATEGORIES

There are two sets of *influence* to consider:

1. Is the *influence* of the stakeholder *upwards, downwards, outwards* or *sideways?* These categories are shown in Figure 1.2.

2. Is the stakeholder part of the organisation or outside it: *internal* to the organisation or *external* to the organisation?

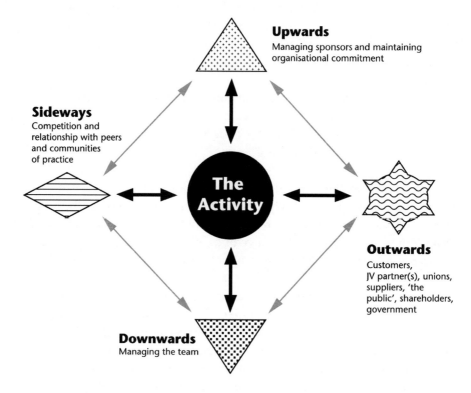

Figure 1.2   *Influence* categories

Upwards defines the influence that senior management, especially the sponsor, exert over the activity. *Downwards* denotes team members, whether full-time staff, consultants, contractors or specialists who work with the manager to achieve the objectives or outcomes of the activity. *Outwards* stakeholders are those outside the team and will include individuals and groups such as end users, government, regulators, the public, shareholders and lobby groups. Finally *sideways* stakeholders are peers of the manager, industry groups and managers within the organisation who are considered to be at the same level professionally. Categorisations for *internal* and *external* are primarily directed to the information necessary for planning communication.

STEP 2: PRIORITISE

Most stakeholder management methodologies rely on an individual's (or the team's) subjective assessment of who is important. The approach adopted in the *Stakeholder Circle* methodology attempts to provide consistency in decision-making about stakeholders. It does this through a structured decision-making process where team members agree on and rate the characteristics of stakeholders to assess their relative importance.

How to Understand who is Important

The results from *step 1: identify* are the starting point for *step 2: prioritise*. For complex high-profile activities, the unranked, unrefined list can be quite large.[7] *Step 2* provides a system for rating and therefore ranking stakeholders. The ratings are based on three aspects:

1.   *Power*: the power an individual or group may have to permanently change or stop the project or other work.

2.   *Proximity*: the degree of involvement that the individual or group has in the work of the team.

3.   *Urgency*: the importance of the work or its outcomes, whether positive or negative, to certain stakeholders (their stake), and how prepared they are to act to achieve these outcomes (stake).

---

7   In working with organisations using the *Stakeholder Circle* methodology and software for mapping and managing stakeholder relationships, the author has assisted in projects that have over 300 stakeholders (both individuals and groups) identified in the first step.

The team applies ratings to each stakeholder, for 1–4 for *power*, and *proximity*, (where 4 is the highest rating) and 1–5 for each of the two parts of *urgency – value* and *action* (where 5 is highest).

Why Choose these Prioritisation Attributes?

The three attributes of *power, proximity and urgency* are the essential elements for understanding which stakeholders are more important than others. The definition of *power* used in *step 2: prioritise* describes the relative power to 'kill' or 'save' the project or activity, or cause permanent change. It is not necessary to identify the type of power that a stakeholder wields, it is essential only to understand the extent to which the stakeholder has power over the continuation of the work itself, the extent to which they must be consulted, or at the lowest level, that they have no power at all.

Rating for *proximity* provides a second way of identifying how a stakeholder may influence the work or its outcomes. Its contribution is the acknowledgement of the importance of regular, close and often face-to-face relationships in influencing the outcomes of the work.[8] The immediacy of this relationship contributes to trust between members of the team, and more effective work relationships as the team members understand the strengths and weaknesses of those they work with on a regular basis (Granovetter 1973). An individual's ability to access independently all other members of the team (Rowley 1997), develops a stronger team culture, and enhances the team's ability to achieve group goals. Groups work best when they have met each other face-to-face at least once; and that they work even more effectively if co-located[9] (McGrath 1984).

Urgency is based on the concept described in Mitchell, Agle and Wood (1997) whose theory described two conditions that may contribute to the notion of urgency:

1.   Time sensitivity: work that must be completed in a fixed time, such as a facility for the Olympic Games.

---

8   *Proximity* simply defines how stakeholders are involved in the work of the project or activity.
9   This research, conducted in the 1980s, may soon be superseded by research into Generation Y's communication preferences for online forms and text messaging: see Chapter 7, 'The new new Confucian communication game'.

2.   Criticality: an individual or group feels strongly enough about an issue to act, such as environmental or heritage protection activists.

In the *Stakeholder Circle*, *urgency* is rated through analysis of two subcategories: the *value* that a stakeholder places on an outcome of the work, and the *action* that they are prepared to take as a consequence of this stake. The inclusion of *urgency* in the prioritisation ratings balances the potential distortion of an organisational culture that identifies stakeholders with a high level of hierarchical power as most important. If *power* and *proximity* are the only measures, stakeholders such as the 'lone powerless voice' who can cause significant damage to successful outcomes if ignored will not be acknowledged.

STEP 3: VISUALISE – MAPPING COMPLEX DATA

The objective of every stakeholder mapping process is to:

- Develop a useful list of *current* stakeholders;

- Assess some of their key characteristics;

- Present data to assist the team's planning for engaging these stakeholders;

- Reduce subjectivity;

- Make the assessment process transparent;

- Make the complex data collected about the stakeholders easy to understand; and

- Provide a sound basis for analysis and discussion.

Presenting complex data effectively will be directly useful to two important stakeholder groups: the organisation's management generally requires information in the form of lists, tables, pictures or graphics, whereas the project team responsible will need charts and graphics for analysis of the community to highlight potential issues. The mapping from the *Stakeholder Circle* fulfils all of these requirements.

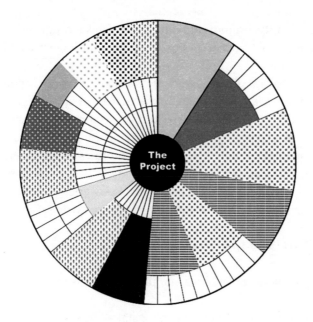

Figure 1.3   A map of a stakeholder community

THE STAKEHOLDER CIRCLE

The *Stakeholder Circle* (Figure 1.3) shows a multidimensional map of the activity's stakeholder community, produced from data gathered during *steps 1 and 2* of the *Stakeholder Circle* methodology.

Key elements of the *Stakeholder Circle* are:

- Concentric circles that indicate distance of stakeholders from the work of the activity or project;

- The size of the block represented by its relative length on the outer circumference, indicates the scale and scope of influence of the stakeholder; and

- The radial depth of the segment indicates the stakeholder's degree of power.

Figure 1.4 provides the key for reading the *Stakeholder Circle*.

The *Stakeholder Circle* represents the work of the activity surrounded by its stakeholder community.

The activity leader or project manager represents the work, and all dimensions of the stakeholder analysis are relative to this person; e.g. *downwards* represents the team members working for the leader.

Four concentric circles represent the *proximity* of the stakeholders to the work and their *power*. The closer a stakeholder is to the work, the nearer it will be drawn to the centre of the circle.

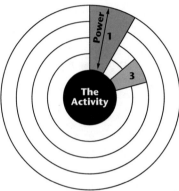

Stakeholders are represented by segments of the circle.

The *power* of the stakeholder is represented by the radial depth of the segment.

Stakeholder 1 has a *power* of 4 and can 'kill' the project; it 'cuts the circle'. This person is a key stakeholder.

Stakeholder 3 has a *power* rating of 2, a significant informal capacity to cause change. This stakeholder is also very close to the work, possibly a team member.

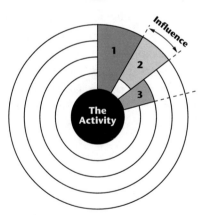

The importance of each stakeholder and their degree of influence is indicated by the relative size of each segment measured on the outer circumference of the circle. The larger the segment, the more influential the stakeholder.

The most important stakeholder (with the highest level of influence) is plotted at position 1, starting at 12:00 o'clock, the second most important is next, through to the 15th most important*.

Finally, colours and shadings indicate the direction of influence of the stakeholder and whether the stakeholder is internal or external to the organisation.

---

*   The design constraint in the *Stakeholder Circle* to plot the top 15 stakeholders does not mean these are the only important stakeholders or that every activity should always manage all 15. The number of important stakeholders that need active management is entirely dependent on the nature of the activity. The choice of 15 stakeholders for the *Stakeholder Circle* display was based on empirical observation of 'who mattered' during the development of the tool.

Figure 1.4   Reading the *Stakeholder Circle*

Colours can[10] indicate the stakeholder's *influence category* relative to the activity:

- Orange indicates an *upwards* direction – these stakeholders are senior managers within the performing organisation that are necessary for ongoing organisational commitment to the activity;

- Green indicates a *downwards* direction – these stakeholders are typically members of the project team or suppliers of services needed by the activity;

- Purple indicates a *sideways* direction – peers of the activity manager either as collaborators or competitors; and

- Blue indicates *outwards* – these stakeholders represent those outside the activity such as end users, government, the public and shareholders.

Colour intensity differentiates stakeholders *internal* to the organisation (dark hues and patterns) and light hues and patterns for those *external* to the organisation.

Some changes within a stakeholder community are to be expected. For example, the degree of importance attached to the end users of a new airport terminal may be relatively low during the early phases of the work where the key focus is on obtaining design approvals and funding. However, as the opening day approaches, the expectations and actual experiences of both airline staff and passengers (the end users) will become increasingly important and this should correspond to a higher ranking in the next iteration of stakeholder community as shown in the *Stakeholder Circle*.

STEP 4: ENGAGE

The team must understand the expectations of all stakeholders and how those expectations can be managed to maintain supportive relationships and to mitigate the consequences of unsupportive stakeholders. The process of documenting stakeholder *attitude* is developed through application of *step 4.*

---

10 Colours are not shown here: for a full colour representation refer to www.stakeholder-management.com or Bourne (2009).

A stakeholder's *attitude* towards an organisation or any of its activities can be driven by many factors, including:

- Whether involvement is voluntary or involuntary;

- Whether involvement is beneficial personally or organisationally; and

- The level of a stakeholder's investment either financial or emotional in the activity.

If the individual's or group's stake in the activity is perceived to be beneficial, or potentially beneficial to them, they are more likely to have a positive attitude to the activity and be prepared to contribute to the work to deliver it. If on the other hand they see themselves as victims, they will be more likely to hold a negative attitude to that activity. Any assessment of *attitude* will need to take into account the following elements:

- Culture of the organisation doing the activity and a stakeholder organisation;

- Identification with the activity and its outcomes or purpose;

- Perceived importance of the activity and its outcomes; and

- Personal attributes, such as personality or position in the organisation.

Engagement profiles are developed by assessing the actual *attitude* of selected stakeholders and the target *attitude* of these stakeholders necessary for success of the activity. The steps in this process are (Bourne 2010):

- Identify the current level of *support* of the stakeholder(s) at five levels: from *active support* (committed – rated as 5), through neutral (rated as 3), to *actively opposed* (antagonistic – rated as 1).

- Analyse the current level of *receptiveness* (to information about the work) of each stakeholder to messages about the activity: from *eager to receive information* (direct personal contacts encouraged – rated as 5), through *ambivalent* (rated as 3), to *completely uninterested* (rated as 1).

- Identify the optimal engagement position: the level of *support* and *receptiveness* that would best[11] meet the needs of both the activity and the stakeholder. If an important stakeholder is both actively opposed and will not receive messages about the activity, they will need to have a different engagement approach from stakeholder(s) who are highly supportive and encourage personal delivery of messages.

The result will be a matrix that compares the current and target *attitude* of any particular stakeholder. The first of these matrices will provide a baseline for measuring the effectiveness of any communication planned to engage a stakeholder. It will also indicate which stakeholders will require additional information (communication) beyond the regular reports and meetings.

Figure 1.5 shows the results of this *step* for three different stakeholders. Stakeholder 1 has been assessed as being *ambivalent* about the activity, *neither supportive nor unsupportive* (3), and not really interested in receiving any information about the activity (2). These results are shown by 'X' in the appropriate boxes in the matrix. However, the team has decided that the *target attitude should be neutral* (3) and *ambivalent about information* (3); this is shown with a bold circle. In this assessment there is only a small gap between the stakeholder's current *attitude* and the *attitude* the team has agreed is essential for the success of the activity: the engagement profile is shown as being close to optimal.[12]

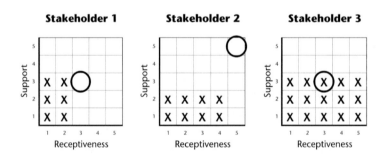

Figure 1.5   An example of stakeholder *attitude*

---

11 'Best' involves balancing what is realistically achievable against the importance of the stakeholder moderated by the amount of effort that team can allocate to the communication process.

12 It is not essential that all stakeholders have a high level of support and receptiveness toward the activity: part of the key decision the team has to make is whether the stakeholder in question is important enough to warrant any additional work to achieve this high level of support.

Stakeholder 2 has been assessed as *passive unsupportive* (2) and at a *medium level of interest* in receiving information about the activity (4). The engagement profile should be *actively supportive* (5) and *eager to receive information at any time* (5). In this case, the gap between the current engagement profile and the optimal profile indicates that a high level of effort will be required to develop communication strategies for this stakeholder, to encourage their support and interest in information about the activity: generally this level of support is only needed from key stakeholders such as the sponsor, steering committee, or a member of the steering committee.

Stakeholder 3 has been assessed as being *neither supportive nor unsupportive* (3), but *eager to receive information any time* (5). The team has assessed that this stakeholder *should be* at a level of receptiveness of *ambivalent*: neither supportive nor non-supportive (3). This is a situation where the current profile is quite different from the optimal profile and will require careful handling from the team to avoid alienating the stakeholder.

Based on the overall level of engagement and the *mutuality* factors identified in *step 1*, a targeted communications plan can be developed focusing on the important stakeholders and stakeholders with a significant gap between their current *attitude* and the target attitude.

Communication

A project's major constraint will be availability of resources, both human and financial. The time frame for completion of the work will usually provide an additional constraint. For these logistical reasons alone, the team will need to consider how best to manage its communication activities for maximum efficiency and effectiveness. This is assisted by a structured approach to:

- Understanding which stakeholders are most important;

- What their expectations and *attitude* to the activity are; and

- Understanding potential conflicts between different stakeholders' expectations of the activity that should be exposed and addressed early.

The basis for an effective communication plan is defining for each stakeholder:

- The *purpose* of the communication: what do the team need to achieve through the communication.

- The most *appropriate* information: most effect *message* format and delivery method.

- *Targeted* to meet the expectations and requirements of the stakeholder and the capacity and capability of the team.

PURPOSE

The purpose of the message will affect the format, content and frequency of its delivery, as well as the decision about who should deliver it. To prepare a purposeful message the question must be asked: *What does the team want to achieve through the distribution of this information?* Is it:

- Raising the profile of the project?

- Providing stakeholders with information to maintain credibility or to build credibility for the team?

- Improving support of important stakeholders?

- Reducing resistance to change resulting from the work?

THE MOST EFFECTIVE MESSAGE

Mutuality (from *step 1: identify*) will define the focus of the message. If the message is crafted to give the stakeholder information that shows that his requirements are known and being considered, this will sustain a perception that the activity is well-managed.

THE MOST EFFICIENT METHODS

The following guidelines provide the team with an understanding of where to focus their communication efforts. It is based on the analysis of engagement profiles described earlier (*step 4: engage*), and by defining different levels of communication activities depending on whether the current engagement position:

- Is *equal to* the optimal position – the current and target *attitude* are the same;

- Is *less than* the optimal position (see stakeholder 2, Figure 1.5); or

- Is *greater than* the optimal position (see stakeholder 3, Figure 1.5).

In the first instance where the current *attitude* is *equal to* the target *attitude* communication can be maintained at its current level: the defined level and frequency of regular reports, meetings and presentations can be safely maintained. For the situation where the current engagement position is *greater than* the target position, two possible approaches need to be considered, depending on the results of the engagement matrix. Stakeholder 3 is rated as being well above the level of *receptiveness* to messages necessary for success of the activity, but at the appropriate level of support of the activity to ensure success of the activity. The decision the team has to make regarding stakeholder 3 is whether to reduce the level of information flowing to this stakeholder (and risk a reduction in their support) or to maintain the current level of communication. The decision can only be made in the light of the knowledge the team has gained during the preceding steps of the stakeholder analysis.

In the third category the current engagement position is *less than* the target position; if the stakeholder is important, the team needs to focus communication efforts on *heroic* communication; stakeholders 1 and 2 are in this category. *Heroic* communication is generally needed for only a small percentage of stakeholders, but any effort expended on increasing the levels of support and receptiveness to the optimal position will significantly benefit the work of the team, and its potential for success.

THE COMMUNICATION PLAN

Based on each stakeholder's unique engagement profile, a communication plan can be developed. The communication plan should contain:

- Mutuality:

  - How the stakeholder is important to the activity; and
  - The stakeholder's *stake* and expectations.

- Categorisation of influence (*upwards, downwards, outwards, sideways, internal and external*).

- Engagement profile preferably in graphical form:

  - Level of support for the activity;
  - Level of receptiveness to information about the activity; and
  - Target engagement: target levels of support and receptiveness.

- Strategies for delivering the message:

  - *Who* will deliver the message?
  - *What* the message will be: regular activity reports or special messages?
  - *How* it will be delivered: formal and/or informal, written and/or oral, technology of communication – emails,[13] written memos, meetings?
  - *When*: how frequently it will be delivered; and over what time frame (where applicable)?
  - *Why*: the purpose for the communication: this is a function of mutuality – why the stakeholder is important for activity success, and what the stakeholder requires from the activity.
  - *Communication item:* the information that will be distributed – the content of the report or message.

EFFECTIVE COMMUNICATION

Irrespective of how well the communication strategy and plan are crafted, other factors must be considered:

- The different levels of power or influence between the team and the stakeholder: it may not be considered appropriate for an individual from the team to communicate with a stakeholder at a higher level in the organisation or the community outside the organisation.

---

13 *Beware of how you use email!* Too many conflicts have been exacerbated by unplanned, intemperate use of email as a primary means of communication. A good rule of thumb is this: will you be prepared to say directly to the recipient what you have written in your email? If the answer is NO then you will need to rewrite it!

- Role of the stakeholder:

  - Sponsor or other political activity supporters may require exception reports, briefing data sufficient to be able to defend the activity; and *no surprises*.
  - Middle managers who supply resources need time frames, resource data and reports on adherence to resource plans and effectiveness of resources provided; more comprehensive information.
  - Staff working on the activity and other team members need detailed but focused information that will enable them to perform their activity roles effectively.
  - Other staff need updates on progress of the work, particularly information on how it will affect their own work roles.
  - External stakeholders will also require regular planned and managed updates on the activity, its deliverables, its impact, its progress.

- Credibility of the messenger and the message: the more the team has worked to build trust and a perception of trustworthiness and competence the more readily a stakeholder will receive, and act on, information. Credibility of this nature takes time to develop and is often the result of previous positive experiences, a reputation for being trustworthy, or through being seen by stakeholders as delivering information in a proactive and timely manner, even if it is bad news.

- The relevance of the information to the recipient: The team must ensure that information is of interest to the stakeholder and delivered in a manner that is most easily read and absorbed.

- The format and content of the message: the most appropriate level of detail and presentation style will also assist in ensuring that information is received and responded to in the most suitable way.

OTHER BARRIERS

Other factors may act as barriers to effective communication: some of those listed below can be managed through accessing information already available through data collection within the *Stakeholder Circle* methodology itself, other factors, such as environmental and personal distraction, may be temporary. Awareness of these factors and their consequences may drive the timing and context of the communication activity.

- Personal reality: conscious and unconscious thought processes will influence how individuals receive and process any information they receive.

- Cultural differences: differences in communication requirements may be caused by cultural norms influencing the preferred style of presentation, content, or delivery of information. These differences may be national, generational, professional and organisational.

- Personal preferences: personality differences may also dictate the how and what of effective communication. A senior manager with limited available time and a preference for summary information will have no patience for information delivered as a story, whereas a team member or a stakeholder with a different personality style may find the delivery of facts not interesting enough.

- Environmental and personal distractions will include noise, lack of interest, fatigue, emotions – if either the sender or the receiver is known to 'have had a bad day', or is feeling unhappy, it is better to postpone any face-to-face communication until another occasion.

Measuring Communication Effectiveness

STEP 5: MONITOR THE EFFECTIVENESS OF THE COMMUNICATION

The process of monitoring the effectiveness of communication involves:

1. Review of the stakeholder community to ensure that the membership is current – the right stakeholders for the current phase or time; and

2. Review of the stakeholder engagement profile.

MAINTENANCE OF THE STAKEHOLDER COMMUNITY

The process of identifying, prioritising and engaging stakeholders cannot be a once-only event. The work of managing relationships with stakeholders does not stop with planning. The nature and membership of the stakeholder community changes as stakeholders are reassigned or leave the organisation, assume different levels of relative importance to the activity, or experience fluctuations in their power, interest or influence.

The key to managing stakeholder relationships is in understanding that the stakeholder community is a network of people. It is not possible to develop relationships that will never change, just as it is not possible to make objective decisions about people. At best, a methodology should aim to reduce the subjectivity inherent in people making decisions about how to develop and maintain robust relationships with other people.

Because relationships are not fixed, it is necessary to review the membership of the stakeholder community regularly and continuously. Regular reviews should be programmed when the work of the activity moves from one stage of its implementation to the next: that is from planning to build, or build to implement; at regular intervals within a particular phase, if that phase is intended to go for a long time. A typical interval for this type of review would be three months.

The team also needs to continuously scan their stakeholder community for unplanned occurrences that may trigger a review when the activity moves from one stage of its implementation to the next or new personnel join the team. Each time the dynamics of the stakeholder community change, membership of the community must be reassessed.

REVIEW OF THE STAKEHOLDER ENGAGEMENT PROFILE

Each time the stakeholder community is reassessed and the *Stakeholder Circle* updated, the corresponding engagement profile should also be reviewed, any movement in the gap between the stakeholder's current *attitude* and the target *attitude* must be considered. This movement will provide an indicator of the effectiveness of the communication. Additional ad hoc reviews are triggered when the team observes an unexpected change in *attitude* in a key stakeholder.

The process of review is a reassessment of the ratings for *attitude*, consisting of assessing the current level of *support* and *receptiveness*. The new ratings are compared to the defined target *attitude* and any previous assessment, to measure any changes in the gaps between the current assessment and the target assessment and the current and previous assessment.

Some Examples of Results of Reviews

Stakeholder 1 fits the profile of a government agency that is significant through its power to provide approvals (Figure 1.6). Like most government bodies it is neutral in *support* but requires more information (regular reports, other regulatory requirements). The first assessment of stakeholder 1 showed that there was not a large gap between the current attitude and the target *attitude*. To maintain this relationship the team must provide any and all information necessary to meet the agency's requirements, and meet the team's needs for the approvals. On the next scheduled review, the *attitude* of stakeholder 1 has reached the target. No new action will be necessary as a result of this review. The third assessment shows that the engagement profile is still at the target level: no additional communication effort is necessary under the current conditions.

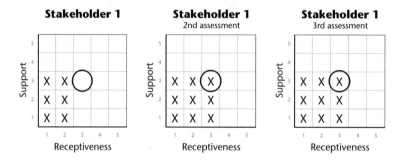

Figure 1.6   Measuring communication effectiveness (stakeholder 1)

Stakeholder 2 (Figure 1.7) fits the profile of a senior manager in the organisation, perhaps the sponsor or a group such as the senior leadership team. It may also describe a stakeholder outside the organisation, such as a government minister, or a powerful lobby group. For stakeholder 2, the first assessment shows that *heroic* communication efforts are required to close the gap between current and target *attitude*. In this case, the intention of any communication must be to increase the stakeholder's level of *support* and *receptiveness*. The second assessment reveals that some progress had been made, but more work is necessary to achieve the desired level of engagement. The decision the team needs to make at this point is whether to continue at the same level of communication, expecting a steady growth in this stakeholder's *attitude*, or to include additional techniques and messages to raise the levels of support and receptiveness to the desired level.

In the case of stakeholder 2, whatever the team decided to do, their efforts (measured after a defined period of time) were moderately successful: the stakeholder was rated as *passively supportive*, where the target had been defined as *actively supportive*. The decision the team must make at this stage is whether to aim for the highest level of support, or be satisfied with the result achieved to date. This decision must be made in the context of the needs of the activity, the amount of available time and personnel that can be devoted to this task and whether the team can actually gain any more of the stakeholder's time and attention. The team may need to seek advice from others with more knowledge and experience of the politics of the organisation, to better understand the expectations of the stakeholder under consideration.

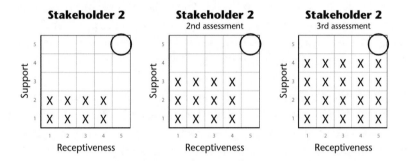

Figure 1.7   Measuring communication effectiveness (stakeholder 2)

MONITORING TRENDS

As noted earlier, it is not possible to develop a methodology that is able to measure the relationships between an activity and its stakeholders objectively. The process of this methodology and every other methodology that attempts to define relationships depends on one group of people making decisions about the needs, requirements and attitudes of other people. There are two issues: first, peoples' needs, requirements and attitudes do not remain fixed and secondly we cannot read the hearts and minds of others no matter how empathetic we believe we are, or how close our relationship is with them.

Rather than attempt to measure absolutes, trend reporting is commonly used for measuring intangible or unmeasurable data, through measuring progress, such as actual against planned or other changes usually assessed against the first record – the baseline. Through a comparison of each new set of data against the baseline or previous sets of data, the changes or differences will provide an indication of the success or otherwise of what is being measured.

Advising Upwards

Senior managers in an organisation have usually attained those positions by displaying aptitude for surviving in the corporate jungle. This aptitude for survival includes the ability to recognise potential 'enemies', use 'pre-emptive strikes' to neutralise competition and use the precepts of *command and control* to ensure the required outputs are delivered. When these senior managers become executives and are appointed to the senior leadership team, their skills and behaviours need to be more focused on motivation, support and leadership rather than command and control. Many newly promoted executives find changing the habits of a working lifetime difficult to achieve.

To understand more about what it means to be an executive in a large organisation, it is important to explore the nature and culture of organisational leadership: what it takes to reach an executive position, and the demands of decision-making in today's competitive environment.

Newly appointed executives struggle to make the transition to the ranks of the senior leadership team. The Watkins (2003) study of Fortune 500 organisations identified four broad categories of challenges for new executives:

- Letting go of 'hands on' detail and thinking/acting more strategically *(the big picture);*

- Develop new and unfamiliar skills and behaviours in an environment with new rules *(learning on the job);*

- Managing upwards *(they have to do it too!)*; and

- Balancing early wins with realistic goals *(getting 'runs on the board').*

The transition strategies that these new executives reported as being successful included:

- *Managing upwards* through clarifying expectations of key stakeholders on objectives, goals and leadership styles;

- Building alliances and support structures through establishing personal credibility with stakeholders and understanding the culture (of the organisation, but also of the leadership team – the peers of the executive); and

- Focus on personal reinvention – substituting skills, values and behaviours not appropriate to the new role with those that were now appropriate.

It is interesting to note that the challenges and transition strategies that the new executives recognised they needed to address are exactly the same as the challenges and strategies that managers within the organisation must use to manage the relationships with these same executives (senior management stakeholders)!

THE PARADOX OF LEADERSHIP

Leadership can be defined simply as a relationship with two major components: leaders must have followers; and these followers must be inspired or motivated to achieve a joint vision. To maintain the loyalty of followers and continue to inspire them requires flexibility and credibility. Personal styles and characteristics defined by traditional leadership theory as promoting leadership success include a combination of:

- creativity;

- analysis and judgement; and

- resilience and persuasiveness.

The expectations that organisations and their people have of their leaders requires a combination of left brain and right brain activities, such as control and creativity or analysis and judgement. This paradox of an organisation's expectations of their leaders goes even further: it is the contradiction of requiring their leaders to be *heroes*, the lone symbolic embodiment of the organisation, while at the same time expecting them to empower their people and delegate tasks.

Building robust and trusting relationships between the team and senior management starts with the establishment of the team's professional credibility through a track record of success and achievement. The second building block is the building of social connections and networks, within and around the environment of the activity and the organisation. Credibility and capability to operate at a senior level and understanding that their responsibilities and drivers are different is critical to building rapport with senior business managers.

Managing a senior manager's optimistic expectations needs a strong relationship between the team and its stakeholders. Consistency, perseverance and determination are important in building respect. The development of stakeholders' perceptions of the individual's personal credibility, wider personal and professional relationships, contacts and networks are all essential elements that go towards building the respect needed to change senior stakeholders' perceptions. These wider relationships must be built not just for the project but maintained long term.

Advising Upwards at T5

The project to open T5 suffered the same issues that many activities and projects face:

- One stakeholder (the CEO) was more demanding (and had more power) than others;

- His expectations were in conflict with the expectations of other important stakeholders;

- The aggressive time frame he imposed caused the project team to operate in 'urgent' mode, believing that there was no time to properly analyse the stakeholder community and negotiate the conflicting expectations; and

- Staff morale was already low, there had been ongoing issues between staff (and the unions) and management, so management's request for volunteers was ignored.

These issues alone would be enough to prevent the team from fully defining their stakeholder community and applying any structure to their approach. Before the team could think strategically about the best way to identify and engage all stakeholders, they would have to manage the CEO's unrealistic expectations.

INFLUENCING THE CEO

Managing upwards (or *advising upwards*) is a universal problem for teams. The actions and reactions of a stakeholder such as the CEO of BA will be familiar to countless project managers and teams as they strive to deliver outcomes for organisations. Some aspects that project managers and their teams need to consider are:

- The drivers for management 'deadlines': what does the stakeholder expect to achieve through meeting these deadlines (*expectations*)?

- *Being heard* – being able to discuss these expectations with a senior stakeholder and being listened to takes time. The manager needs to act strategically and build credibility with stakeholders (*credibility bank*).

- The manager may also need to develop a network of allies: influential stakeholders who are supportive of the work and are prepared be an advocate for the work and the team (*influence networks*).

- Using the approach of a methodology such as the *Stakeholder Circle* to understand who all the important stakeholders are and how best to engage them through purposeful, targeted and appropriate communication.

USING THE METHODOLOGICAL APPROACH

Using the approach of the methodology described in the previous sections, the project manager and team responsible for managing the opening of T5 could have identified the following stakeholders as most important:

- travelling public;

- front-line staff;

- baggage handlers;

- sponsor (Willie Walsh);

- BA management team;

- infrastructure development teams;

- the media; and

- BA marketing and PR teams.

There were probably many more stakeholders whose requirements needed to be acknowledged, but from the transcripts of the report of the House of Commons Transport Committee (2008), this list identifies the most important. As is often the case, the requirements of the sponsor to meet a particular timeframe overwhelmed and conflicted with the requirements of other equally important stakeholders – the staff and the travelling public. The project manager and team were not able to convince the CEO and BA's management team of the importance of the expectations of these stakeholders. The results of this situation speak for themselves.

The minimum application of the methodology would have been to work with the list of stakeholders described above and using the *step 4: engage* processes develop an understanding of the *attitude* of each of these stakeholders – how supportive were they of the objectives of management and the opening, and how willing were they to receive and respond to the information about the importance of the new terminal and its opening at that particular time. If the project team and BA's management team had not informed them properly of the benefits to the organisation and themselves, BA's staff and their unions would not be prepared to meet the requests of management to volunteer their time and their services to meet the management drivers.

MAKING STAKEHOLDER MANAGEMENT WORK

There are other factors that contribute to successful stakeholder relationship management. First, the *team approach* was essential to the task of developing knowledge about the stakeholder community. Many teams and individuals believe that if they are working within time constraints that they don't 'have enough time' to assemble and brief a team or to reach a decision. Research (Bourne 2009) has shown that even though working with teams may take a little extra time, the decisions that result are more robust and sustainable. Secondly, many teams will have concerns that using a structured methodology such as the *Stakeholder Circle* will be too complex and too time-consuming. Using aspects of the methodology according to the needs of the team and the maturity of the organisation supports a flexible approach that enables the team to focus on the parts of the methodology that matter.

Finally, projects such as the opening of T5 show what happens when the stakeholder community is not understood. In the tradition of continuous improvement (Deming 1982; Tague 2004) the benefit of the reduction of rework far outweighs the cost of using appropriate processes and practices in the first place.[14] For stakeholder relationship management it is better to take a little extra time to better understand the stakeholder community and how best to engage important stakeholders, than to have to deal with the aftermath of the uninterest or lack of support of neglected stakeholders.

Conclusion

Communication is itself a human endeavour, and the complex communication that may be necessary for managing stakeholder relationships within an organisation or around its activities requires planning, monitoring and also leadership. The team must apply analysis, skills and experience to succeed in communicating to engage stakeholders. The structured approach offered by the five *steps* of the *Stakeholder Circle* methodology in tandem with proactive communication approaches and willingness to operate in the power structures of the organisation are the keys to successful delivery of outcomes through projects or other organisation activities.

---

14   This could be described as the 'zero cost of stakeholder engagement', a direct analogy to the concept of 'zero cost of quality' from the quality movement of the 1980s.

The T5 construction project team used the principles of the Egan report to radically reduce the time and cost of delivery and to produce a safety record far superior to the culture of construction in UK at the time. Its success was based on acknowledgement of the importance of people (stakeholders) to its success, and understanding and developing appropriate relationships with these stakeholders. BA's CEO and management team, on the other hand, placed management objectives foremost: to open despite the risks of unfinished infrastructure and inadequate preparation of staff. BA failed to properly engage its important stakeholders – staff – yet expected them to be able to offer service to BA's other important stakeholders – the travelling public. BA failed because it failed its stakeholders, and paid the price of a tarnished reputation.

Case studies such as the opening of T5 show what happens when the stakeholder community is not understood and the long-term principles of advising upwards are not considered. Rather than being recognised for its customer-oriented approach to travel in the innovative T5 infrastructure and practices, it is still remembered for the lost baggage and disaffected travellers when it first opened in 2008. Managing stakeholder relationships is difficult and takes more time than expected, but the costs of not engaging stakeholders, particularly senior management stakeholders, are significantly higher.

References

Bourne, L. 2010. *Stakeholder Relationship Management and the Stakeholder Circle*. Saarbrücken: Lambert Academic Publishing.

Bourne, L. 2009. *Stakeholder Relationship Management: A Maturity Model for Organisational Implementation*. Farnham: Gower.

Crane, A. 2010. Rethinking Construction and Making Change Happen: Proceedings of CIOB Global Construction Summit. Shanghai, China, conference paper.

Deming, W.E. 1982. *Out of the Crisis*. Melbourne: Cambridge University Press.

Egan, J. 1998. *Rethinking Construction*. London: HMSO, Dept of Trade and Industry.

Granovetter, M.S. 1973. The strength of weak ties. *American Journal of Sociology* 78(6): 1360–1380.

House of Commons Transport Committee 2008. *The Opening of Heathrow Terminal 5*. London: House of Commons

McGrath, J.E. 1984. *Groups: Interaction and Performance*. Englewood Cliffs, NJ: Prentice Hall.

Mitchell, R.K., Agle, B.R. and Wood, D. 1997. Toward a theory of stakeholder identification and salience: defining the principle of who and what really counts. *Academy of Management Review* 22(4): 853–888.

Potts, K. 2006. *Project Management and the Changing Nature of the Quantity SURVEYING profession – Heathrow Terminal 5 Case Study: Proceedings of COBRA 2006*. London: The RICS.

Rowley, T.J. 1997. Moving beyond dyadic ties: a network theory of stakeholder influences. *Academy of Management Review* 22(4): 887–910.

Tague, N.R. 2004. *The Quality Toolbox*. Milwaukee, Wisconsin: ASQ Quality Press.

Watkins, M. 2003. *The First 90 Days*. Boston, MA: Harvard Business School Press.

2

Enterprise Risk Management: Managing Uncertainty and Minimising Surprise

David Hillson

Introduction

Many of the most important decisions made within an organisation relate to risk, because anything that is innovative or competitive or worth doing is likely to be risky. However, risk exists at various levels within an organisation, from top to bottom. As a result the effective organisation needs to be able to communicate about risk between levels in a way that enables it to manage uncertainty and minimise surprises. Unfortunately it is all too common for organisations to suffer the effects of unmanaged uncertainty and to be reacting to surprises rather than responding proactively. This is usually because risks remain hidden within the organisation at levels where they cannot be managed appropriately or effectively. In order to counter this tendency risk information must be advised upwards to ensure that it reaches the right level where it can be used to influence the overall performance of the organisation.

This chapter explains how risk relates to the most fundamental purposes of any organisation through its inherent link to objectives, and presents the case for an integrated and hierarchical approach to risk management across the organisation, known as Enterprise Risk Management (ERM). After defining the main concepts and outlining the basics of the risk process, we consider the two key aspects of ERM that are often least well addressed, namely how to manage risk across boundaries within an organisation, and how to report risk upwards to the appropriate level for both attention and action.

Key Definitions

Risk is everywhere, influencing all aspects of human endeavour, from personal to professional, affecting individuals, groups, organisations and nations. No-one would disagree with the statement that life is risky, or that it is important for us to try to respond to risk effectively. This explains the increasing prominence of risk management in all areas of life, and the growth in risk-based approaches to many disparate tasks (risk-based auditing, remuneration, regulation, legislation, pricing, testing, oversight, decision-making, etc.). It is of course axiomatic that the purpose of risk management is to manage risk. In order for risk management to be effective however, we must first be clear about what is meant by the word 'risk', so that we know precisely what risk management is supposed to manage.

This is not a trivial task: the word 'risk' has varying interpretations in different settings, and it has changed its meaning over time. The definition debate has been rehearsed by many authors in recent years, Hulett et al. (2002) provides a useful summary. An interesting illustration of the various ways in which the word 'risk' and the term 'risk management' are used in different risk disciplines is presented by Hillson (2007), with perspectives from a wide range of approaches including the management of strategic, financial, operational, legal, contract, project, technical, reputation, environmental and fraud risk, as well as corporate governance, business continuity and counter-terrorism.

Across all of these different application areas, there are a number of common themes which reveal important characteristics about risk. Understanding these factors is essential if risk management is to be effective, especially within complex organisations.

The first universal element of risk about which all are agreed is that it is something to do with *uncertainty*. All risks are uncertain, because they are future events or conditions or sets of circumstances whose occurrence is not guaranteed. A risk may or may not happen. This characteristic is vital to the effective management of risk, because risk management seeks to identify risks before they happen and to create management space and time during which an appropriate response can be developed and implemented. There are many causes of uncertainty (including ambiguity, variability, complexity etc.), but the key point here is that risk is a type of uncertainty. If it is not uncertain then it is not a risk.

Secondly, although all risks are uncertain, not all uncertainties are risks. When considering what should go in a risk register or what needs to be identified and managed proactively, some filter is required otherwise risk registers would be infinitely large. We need to know which uncertainties matter, which ones we need to know about, record and tackle. Clearly not all uncertainties qualify for our attention or action. The filter used to distinguish risks from uncertainties is to determine whether a particular uncertainty has the potential to affect achievement of one or more of our *objectives*. In every area of human endeavour there are objectives to be met, and we need to be concerned about anything that might have an influence on them. The task of risk management is to find and address those uncertainties that could influence objectives. If it does not matter then it is not a risk.

Combining these two characteristics allows us to produce a proto-definition of risk as *'uncertainty that matters'*. This simple phrase captures the essence of risk as something future which may or may not occur, but which if it does occur would influence achievement of one or more objectives. The concept of 'uncertainty that matters' can be expanded into more precise definitions, and Table 2.1 illustrates how some of the more prominent risk standards and guidelines follow this pattern when defining risk.

One further characteristic of risk is important in the definition debate. This relates to the type of effect that uncertainty might have on objectives if it occurs. Until fairly recently it was common for risk to be defined in exclusively negative terms, representing only those uncertainties that could have an adverse or harmful effect on achievement of objectives, leading to delay, additional cost, reputation damage, lost value, accidents etc. Under this perspective, the word risk was seen as synonymous with 'threat'. This position has been challenged by the latest thinking and practice in risk management across a number of application areas, where it is recognised that 'uncertainty that matters' can include the possibility of positive impacts. There are uncertainties that if they were to happen would result in time or cost savings, enhanced reputation, improved productivity or benefits etc. These upside risks can also be called 'opportunities', leading to a double-sided definition of risk that includes *both threat and opportunity*. This broader definition is then reflected in an extended risk-management process that tackles both upside and downside risks in an integrated approach (Hillson 2002a, 2004). This position has gained widespread (though not universal) acceptance in the past decade and is reflected to a greater or lesser degree in the standards and guidelines included in Table 2.1.

Table 2.1   **Definitions of risk as uncertainty that matters (adapted from Hillson 2009)**

Standard	Definition of risk	
	Uncertainty ...	**... that matters**
British Standard BS6079-3:2000 (British Standards Institute, 2000)	Uncertainty inherent in plans and the possibility of something happening (i.e. a contingency) ...	... that can affect the prospects of achieving business or project goals.
British Standard BS IEC 62198:2001 (British Standards Institute, 2001)	Combination of the probability of an event occurring ...	... and its consequences on project objectives.
A Risk Management Standard (Institute of Risk Management et al., 2002)	The combination of the probability of an event ...	... and its consequences.
Risk Analysis and Management for Projects [RAMP] (Institution of Civil Engineers et al., 2005)	A possible occurrence ...	... which could affect (positively or negatively) the achievement of the objectives for the investment.
APM Body of Knowledge (Association for Project Management, 2006)	An uncertain event or set of circumstances ...	... that should it or they occur would have an effect on achievement of one or more project objectives.
Management of Risk [M_o_R]: Guidance for Practitioners (Office of Government Commerce, 2010)	An uncertain event or set of events ...	... that should it occur will have an effect on the achievement of objectives.
A Guide to the Project Management Body of Knowledge [PMBoK® Guide] (Project Management Institute, 2008)	An uncertain event or condition ...	... that if it occurs has a positive or negative effect on a project's objectives.
British Standard BS31100:2008 (British Standards Institute, 2008); ISO31000:2009 (InternationalOrganization for Standardization, 2009)	Effect of uncertainty ...	... on objectives.

Bringing these thoughts together allows us to produce a generic definition of risk: 'Any uncertainty that, if it occurs, has a positive or negative effect on achievement of one or more objectives.'

The link between risk and objectives is essential if we are to understand how risk should be managed across an organisation in the way necessary to advise upwards appropriately. But first we need to be clear about the place of objectives in the organisation.

Objectives exist at many levels within the typical organisation, ranging from strategic to tactical. The vision and mission of the organisation exist at the highest level and these are expressed in strategic objectives which define how the vision and mission will be achieved. Strategic objectives are then decomposed into more detailed statements of what needs to be done in order to achieve them. This progressive decomposition leads to a *hierarchy of objectives* across the organisation from top to bottom, which can then be used to structure the management and control of the various functions and activities (as discussed below). The concept of a hierarchy of objectives has been understood for many years (Granger 1964), and is illustrated in Figure 2.1, which shows the general case with a variable number of intermediate levels of objective between strategic and tactical. In the simplest case there may be no intermediate levels, but it is most common to have several steps of decomposition in order to elaborate strategy into something that can be implemented practically at the working level.

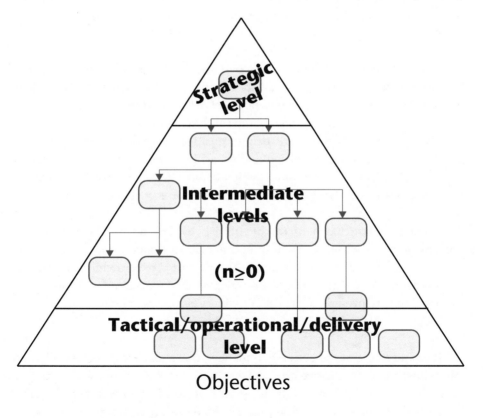

Figure 2.1   Illustrative hierarchy of objectives

Within a particular organisation the hierarchy of objectives can be constructed top-down and validated bottom-up, using an integrated How–Why approach:

- *Top-down*: starting with each of the overarching strategic objectives, repeatedly ask '*How can we achieve this?*' This will generate lower-level, measurable objectives that help to accomplish the higher-level objective.

- *Bottom-up*: take lower-level activities and repeatedly ask '*Why are we doing this?*' It should be possible to fit all lower-level activities and objectives into existing high-level objectives, although the exercise may expose hidden objectives that need to be tested and approved.

Once an organisation is understood as a hierarchy of objectives, the link with risk management becomes clear, since risk is defined as 'any uncertainty that, if it occurs, has a positive or negative effect on achievement of one or more objectives'.

At each level in the organisation where there are objectives, there will also be uncertainties that matter because they could influence those objectives. The hierarchy of objectives leads to a *hierarchy of risk*. Indeed the generic definition of risk derived above can be instantiated in a wide range of ways, simply by specifying which objectives are being considered. Thus strategic risks are defined as uncertainties which could affect achievement of strategic objectives, operational risks are uncertainties which could affect operational objectives, project risks are uncertainties which could affect project objectives, and so on.

Having constructed a hierarchy of risk by linking uncertainty to the multiple levels of objectives within and across an organisation, it is a small step to recognise that risk management also needs to be hierarchical. Wherever risk exists it must be managed, from strategic risk management at the top of the organisation through to tactical or delivery risk management at project and operational levels.

It would of course be possible to manage risk at each level independently and without reference to the other levels. Indeed this is currently the practice in many organisations, where there is little or no communication or linkage between different types of risk process. In these organisations there is no way of connecting management of financial risk by the treasury function to business-as-usual risks at operational level, or using project risk exposure to inform corporate governance decisions, or understanding how attempts to generate portfolio risk efficiency might influence reputational risk. Clearly the most efficient way to address risk management within an organisation would be to have an approach that was integrated across the hierarchy. This is the realm of ERM – also known as Enterprise-Wide Risk Management (EWRM) or Integrated Risk Management (IRM). There are however a number of ways in which ERM is understood, and it is important to be clear about the way we are using it here. Table 2.2 presents a range of current ERM definitions from several of the major professional associations in the risk field.

Table 2.2   Definitions of enterprise risk management (adapted from AIRMIC 2008)

Organisation	Definition
Association of Corporate Treasurers (ACT)	ERM is designed to enhance corporate decision-making with tools being developed and implemented to support actions ranging from optimisation of the insurance programme to analysis of overseas expansion plans, business mix or capital allocation.
Association of Insurance and Risk Managers (AIRMIC) Institute of Risk Management (IRM)	Risk management is the process whereby organisations methodically address the risks attaching to their activities with the goal of achieving sustained benefit within each activity and across the portfolio of all activities.
Committee of Sponsoring Organizations of the Treadway Commission (COSO) Institute of Chartered Accountants in England and Wales (ICAEW)	ERM is a process, effected by an entity's board of directors, management and other personnel, applied in strategy setting and across the enterprise, designed to identify potential events that may affect the entity, manage risk to be within its risk appetite and to provide reasonable assurance regarding the achievement of entity objectives.
HM Treasury	All the processes involved in identifying, assessing and judging risks, assigning ownership, taking actions to mitigate or anticipate them, and monitoring and reviewing progress.
Institute of Internal Auditors (IIA)	A rigorous and coordinated approach to assessing and responding to all risks that affect the achievement of an organisations' strategic and financial objectives.
International Organization for Standardization (ISO)	Coordinated activities to direct and control an organization with regard to risk (ISO31000).
Risk and Insurance Management Society (RIMS)	A strategic business discipline that supports the achievement of an organization's objectives by addressing the full spectrum of its risks and managing the combined impact of those risks as an interrelated risk portfolio.
The Public Risk Management Association (ALARM)	The culture, processes and structure that are directed towards effective management of potential opportunities and threats to the organisation achieving its objectives.

There are four distinct alternatives for how the term ERM may be used, each of which is current in different settings. These four definition options for ERM relate to the type of risk that is considered to be in scope for ERM, summarised as follows:

1.   Risk *to* the enterprise;

2.   Risk *of* the enterprise;

3.   Risk *within* the enterprise; and

4.   Risk *across* the enterprise.

RISK TO THE ENTERPRISE

Here the goal for ERM is to manage any uncertainty that has the potential to affect the organisation as a whole. The word 'enterprise' is taken to refer to the entity, so ERM is management of risks to the entity. This leads to an exclusively high-level strategic and corporate view of ERM, and it is the clear responsibility of the organisation's senior leadership to implement risk management at this level.

RISK OF THE ENTERPRISE

With this interpretation the scope of ERM is seen as being limited to the risk that the enterprise poses to its stakeholders. As for the first definition, this view of ERM leads to a high-level implementation, focused only on those uncertainties that could directly influence the major stakeholders. It tends to address the uppermost layer of risks, plus any which have filtered up from below because they have the potential for strategic impact.

RISK WITHIN THE ENTERPRISE

This perspective sees 'enterprise risk' as being the total of all risk exposure at all levels within the organisation, summed up to some aggregate amount. Again management of this type of risk requires action at senior levels within the organisation, with the leadership attempting to use ERM to address the overall risk exposure of the whole enterprise.

RISK ACROSS THE ENTERPRISE

A fourth option is for the term ERM to be used to describe an integrated and hierarchical approach to management of risk across the enterprise at every level. Here ERM has wide applicability at all levels and describes the combined effort of all staff to manage the risks that they face at their level, but to do this in an integrated way.

Although each of these variants of ERM is used by some organisations and risk practitioners, the last is the most widely accepted and seems to be gaining ground as a best-practice definition. For example Chapman (2006) provides a more formal statement of this definition of ERM as 'a comprehensive and integrated framework for managing company-wide risk in order to maximise a company's value'.

This is the understanding and definition of ERM used in the remainder of this chapter.

Prerequisites for Effective ERM

Before discussing the details of how ERM should be implemented within an organisation to support effective communication of risk at all levels, there are four essential prerequisites which must be in place for ERM to work properly, namely:

1. Clearly defined objectives;

2. An organisational structure that is aligned to these objectives;

3. Unambiguous boundaries between hierarchical levels; and

4. A risk-aware culture at all levels in the organisation.

DEFINED OBJECTIVES

We have defined risk in terms of objectives and shown that without clearly defined objectives it is not possible to identify or manage risk. Consequently the primary prerequisite for implementing ERM across an organisation is the existence of a set of layered objectives across the organisation that is clear, aligned and coherent. Each of these characteristics must be in place before ERM can work. Organisational objectives must be:

- *Clear*: vague objectives which are not understood unambiguously by all will lead to a confused and unfocused risk process. It is vital that objectives are fully comprehensible to those who are charged with achieving them, as well as by those who receive the benefits from them. Clear objectives will meet the SMART criteria: Specific, Measurable, Achievable, Relevant and Time-bound.

- *Aligned*: objectives at all levels in the organisation must be pointing in the same direction, not working against each other. Alignment of objectives ensures that the organisation is focused on a common overall goal and that the efforts of all are working in synergy without waste, duplication or omissions.

- *Coherent*: this refers to the need for organisational objectives to fit together as a set and to form a cohesive whole. Given the hierarchical nature of organisational objectives, it is essential for each higher-level objective to be fully expressed and contained in the lower-level objectives derived from it. Similarly coherence means that achievement of all lower-level objectives in a particular area will result in fully obtaining the benefits of the higher-level objective to which they contribute.

MATCHING ORGANISATION TO OBJECTIVES

Once the full set of organisational objectives is properly defined, the organisation itself should reflect them. The most effective organisations have structures that mirror the hierarchy of objectives, with clear mapping between levels. It should be obvious which layer in the organisation is responsible for achieving strategic objectives for example, and where responsibility lies for operational objectives. This mapping should cover a number of important organisational characteristics, including definition of roles and responsibilities, lines of communication and reporting across the organisation, decision-making thresholds etc.

Figure 2.2 illustrates the correspondence between the ideal hierarchy of objectives and the optimal organisational structure that would best deliver these objectives. The figure shows the highest and lowest levels of each hierarchy, with the top leadership of the organisation (board-level executives and directors) being responsible for achieving strategic objectives, and front-line staff (project teams, operational groups, supply chain and delivery partners) tackling operational and delivery objectives. The number of intermediate levels is variable, ranging from zero for small organisations to many for the largest and most complex, with middle management being responsible for these levels. It is often in this middle area that organisational objectives lose clarity, alignment and coherence, and middle management should play a vital role in maintaining the integrity of the hierarchy of objectives.

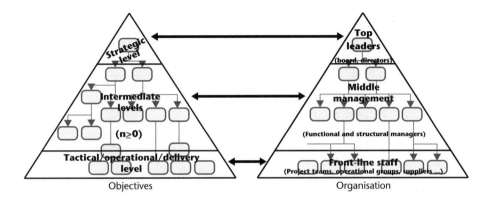

Figure 2.2   Mapping hierarchies of objectives and the organisation

CLEAR BOUNDARIES

The third prerequisite for effective ERM which arises from the structure of an organisation as a hierarchy of objectives is a set of clear boundaries and interfaces for both objectives and the organisation. It must be unambiguous and obvious to all where one level ends and another begins. There should be no discussion or debate about whether a particular objective belongs at a particular level or whether it belongs to the level above or below. Similarly the comparable organisational hierarchy must be equally clear, with no uncertainty over lines of responsibility, communication or decision-making authority.

RISK-AWARE CULTURE

Finally, if ERM is to work properly the organisation needs a fully mature risk-aware culture at all levels, with a commitment to act to manage risk wherever it is found, and for such action to be properly resourced and supported. ERM cannot operate effectively if any level within the organisation denies the existence of risk or refuses to take responsibility for managing risk in their area of authority.

REALITY CHECK

Many managers and leaders may recognise that one or more of these four elements are missing or incomplete in their organisations. It is typical to find businesses without clear objectives, either strategic or tactical, and even more common for links between different levels of objectives to be missing, unaligned or incoherent. Organisational structures have often evolved over time, representing responses to challenges that no longer exist, or reflecting turf wars or power plays by key figures. A clear correspondence between the way the organisation is structured and its various objectives is often missing, and boundaries and thresholds between layers are fuzzy or inconsistent at best. Finally the risk culture of many organisations is often unmanaged or reactive, not actively set and managed by the top leadership or implemented consistently throughout the organisation in all its activities.

If these four characteristics are prerequisites for effective ERM, and if they are often missing or only partially present in organisations, does this mean that implementation of ERM must remain an unrealistic aspiration for most, until or unless they can develop and establish all of the prerequisites? Is it possible to make progress on managing risk across the enterprise in their absence?

Obviously the ideal scenario is for an organisation that recognises itself to be deficient in one or more of the attributes to take steps to develop them. Some of these prerequisites can be put in place quite quickly and painlessly, such as objective-setting at the various levels across the business. It might take some time to design and implement structural changes to the organisation to achieve a close mapping between layers of management and levels of objectives, but this need not be a long-term activity. Clear boundaries and thresholds can be designed into any new or evolving organisational structure. The longer-term task is to develop a risk-aware culture across the business, because any culture change can take a number of years to become fully embedded. This might require a focused initiative including education and training, process and skills development, pilot risk studies and regular communications. Details of how to develop and establish these four attributes within an organisation are outside the scope of this chapter, but a wide range of advice and support is available to any organisation wishing to address the necessary changes.

In the meantime, where one or more of these prerequisites is missing, how can ERM be addressed? As we will see below, the key activities are the management of risk across boundaries and the communication of risk information between levels. Even where a full hierarchy of objectives or matching organisational structure are absent, or where the overall risk culture is unsupportive, it should be possible to implement these two key activities in patches within the organisation. If a particular middle manager or functional leader or programme director understand the main principles, they should be able to manage the risks within their own layer in the organisation, and communicate upwards and downwards to their interfacing layers, even if this is not occurring consistently across the whole business. In this way they are treating their section of the business as a mini-enterprise, and implementing a cut-down version of ERM within the scope of their own authority. Where this is successful, these pioneering managers should communicate and celebrate their success, telling their peers and colleagues what they have discovered about how to manage risk more effectively. Such success stories should encourage others to follow in their footsteps and build momentum towards a wider take-up of the principles and practice of ERM. The main driver in this situation is the courage and determination of insightful leaders to act as pioneers for the organisation, breaking new ground and enabling others to follow.

Basic Risk Management

Enterprise Risk Management is one particular type of risk management with an area of application that covers the whole enterprise, as discussed above. However, the process for managing risk across the organisation is not significantly different from any other risk management process. This has been covered widely elsewhere, for example in the major risk standards such as ISO31000:2009 (International Standards Organization, 2009), BS31100:2008 (British Standards Institute, 2008), or the OGC *Management of Risk* guidelines (Office of Government Commerce, 2010), and the process does not need to be detailed here. It would nevertheless be useful to summarise the risk process so that readers are clear about what needs to be implemented at each level within the organisation in order to manage risk.

The elements of a common risk process can be described using eight key questions:

1.   What are we trying to achieve and how much risk can we take?

2.   What could affect us achieving this?

3.   Which of those things are most important?

4.   What shall we do about them?

5.   Who needs to know about them?

6.   Have we done what we decided to do?

7.   Having taken action, what has changed?

8.   What did we learn?

These eight questions represent the simplest expression of a risk-management process. They can be expanded into a more detailed and formal risk process with the following steps (illustrated in Figure 2.3).

GETTING STARTED (RISK PROCESS INITIATION)

Risks only exist in relation to defined objectives. We cannot start the risk process without first clearly defining its scope and clarifying which objectives are at risk. It is also important to know how much risk key stakeholders are prepared to accept, since this provides the target threshold for risk exposure. The balance between worthwhile and achievable objectives and the associated level of risk should be designed to offer a risk-efficient solution as far as possible.

FINDING RISKS (RISK IDENTIFICATION)

Once the scope and objectives are agreed, it is possible for us to start identifying risks, including both threats and opportunities. We should use a variety of risk identification techniques, each of which has strengths and weaknesses.

SETTING PRIORITIES (RISK ASSESSMENT)

Not all risks are equally important, so we need to filter and prioritise them, to find the worst threats and the best opportunities. When prioritising risks, it is common to use qualitative assessments of their various characteristics, such as how likely they are to happen, what they might do to objectives, how easily we can influence them, when they might happen, and so on. We may also decide to use quantitative risk analysis methods where these are considered appropriate.

DECIDING WHAT TO DO (RISK RESPONSE PLANNING)

Once we have prioritised individual risks, we can think about what actions are appropriate to deal with individual threats and opportunities, in order to maintain our risk exposure below the acceptable threshold. Each risk needs an owner who should decide how to respond appropriately.

TELLING OTHERS (RISK REPORTING)

It is important to tell people with an interest in the activity about the risks we have found and our plans to address them, especially if we need their help in managing the risk.

TAKING ACTION (RISK RESPONSE IMPLEMENTATION)

Nothing will change unless we actually do something. Planned responses must be implemented in order to tackle individual risks and change the overall risk exposure, and the results of these responses should be monitored to ensure that they are having the desired effect. Our actions may also introduce new risks for us or others to address.

KEEPING UP TO DATE (RISK REVIEWS)

We have to come back and look again at risk on a regular basis, to see whether our planned actions have worked as expected, and to discover new and changed risks that now require our attention. Reviews can be undertaken at various levels, for example with more frequent minor reviews and occasional major reviews.

CAPTURING LESSONS (RISK LESSONS-LEARNED REVIEW)

When we have finished our activity or project we should take advantage of our experience to benefit future similar tasks. This means we will spend time thinking about what worked well and what needs improvement, and recording our conclusions in a way that can be reused by ourselves and others.

The generic risk process outlined in these eight steps can be applied at any level within an organisation, targeting uncertainties that might affect achievement

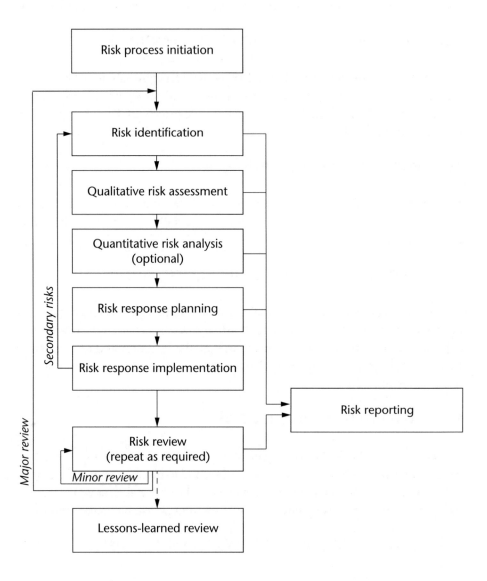

Figure 2.3   A typical generic risk management process (adapted from Hillson, 2009)

of the relevant objectives at that level. In terms of ERM, this generic process is replicated at all the different levels across the organisation, but it needs to be conducted in a way that is consistent, coherent and aligned, as discussed above.

There are however two important key additions to this generic risk process that are required for the implementation of ERM across the organisation in an integrated and hierarchical manner. It is not enough to ensure that risk is identified, assessed and managed at each individual level. As well as this single-level risk management, ERM focuses on interfaces between the levels, to ensure that the overall management of risk within the enterprise is managed in an integrated and hierarchical way. This inter-level interfacing requires two specific areas to be addressed.

1. It is necessary to have a mechanism for passing risks across boundaries within the hierarchy, so that they are managed at the most appropriate level.

2. There needs to be a way of communicating upwards about risk so that managers, decision-makers and other stakeholders have the risk information they need at their level, based on what risks exist and are being managed (or not) elsewhere in the organisation.

These two aspects are discussed in the following two sections.

Managing Risk across Boundaries

We have seen that a generic risk process can be applied at any level within an organisation in order to address any type of risk. However, this multilevel approach to risk management is not sufficient to ensure that the overall management of risk will be effective across the enterprise. This requires risks to be communicated between the various levels, to ensure that they are addressed at the most appropriate level.

In principle there are three potential sources of risk that could affect any particular level of an organisation (Hillson 2008). Risks can arise from three directions, as illustrated in Figure 2.4, namely up from lower levels, down from the levels above, or sideways at the particular level itself. Risks can come up from below by escalation or aggregation, and risks can be passed down from above via delegation, as outlined below.

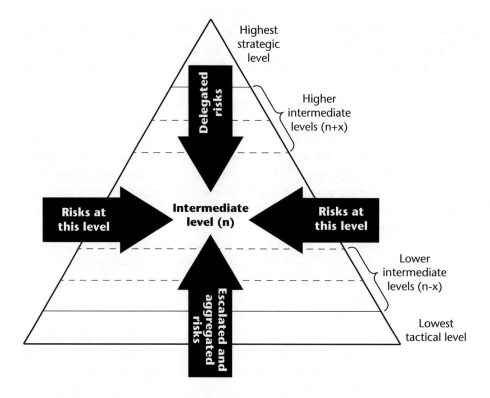

Figure 2.4   Sources of risks at intermediate levels

RISKS FROM BELOW

There are two main ways in which any intermediate level can be affected by risks from lower levels:

- *Escalation*. Some lower-level risks are so large that they can affect the achievement of higher-level objectives. The word 'large' needs to be defined of course, since not all lower-level risks are relevant at the higher level. Escalation criteria which will define the thresholds at which a lower-level risk should be passed up to the next level are therefore required. This is discussed below. These criteria need to include risks which impact higher-level objectives, as well as risks requiring responses or action at the higher level.

- *Aggregation*. It is also necessary to be able to aggregate lower-level risks, where a number of similar and related risks might combine to create a higher-level risk, either by simple summation (ten insignificant lower-level risks may equal one significant higher-level risk), or as a result of synergy (the whole overall risk exposure may be greater than the sum of the parts). Suitable risk categorisation schemes are required to facilitate such aggregation by identifying commonalities and possible synergies, and a generic Risk Breakdown Structure (RBS) may be used for this purpose (Hillson 2002b, 2003). When a group of aggregated risks becomes sufficiently significant it is escalated in the same way as an individual large risk.

RISKS FROM ABOVE

Organisational strategy is delivered by decomposing strategic objectives into lower-level objectives, as discussed above, creating an essential link between intermediate levels and those above them. There are strategic risks associated with the overall direction of the organisation, and many of these can and should be addressed wholly by the senior leadership of the organisation. However, some strategic risks will have implications for those lower levels that are used to deliver the strategy and create the business benefits. Strategic risks which can significantly affect lower-level objectives or which require specific action at a lower level will need to be delegated. This requires well-defined delegation criteria and thresholds, as well as clear channels of communication to ensure that management of strategic risks delegated to lower levels is reported back to senior management. The goal is to achieve delegation without abdication.

RISKS AT THE SAME LEVEL

In addition to risks escalated and aggregated from below or delegated from above, each level in the organisation is affected by specific uncertainties arising at that level. These include both threats and opportunities across the full range of risk types, including technical, management, commercial and external risks. These need to be managed by application of the generic risk process previously discussed.

An essential prerequisite for escalation or delegation of risks is clear definition of the boundaries and thresholds between the different levels in the organisation. This is necessary so that everyone knows where each risk belongs, without confusion or ambiguity. Regardless of where a risk is identified, it needs to be managed at the right level, and this is defined by the level of the objective(s) which would be affected if the risk occurred. This can easily be translated into quantitative measurable terms, based on a range of characteristics of the risk, including:

- Total maximum impact of a single risk, not weighted by probability, monetised where possible;

- Total aggregated unweighted impact of related risks, monetised where possible;

- Impact on corporate reputation; and

- Impact on one or more higher-level objectives.

A particular organisation may wish to add to these characteristics, depending on the type of business or the nature of the risks faced. For example some organisations may wish to define thresholds based on safety or regulatory compliance or share price etc.

An example of escalation/delegation criteria is presented in Table 2.3, showing application of four criteria at three levels to create quantified inter-level risk thresholds. A risk is escalated from a lower level to the next level up if any one of the criteria exceeds the threshold value. A risk is delegated down to the next level below if all criteria are below the threshold values. For example, where a functional manager identifies an opportunity to create additional value of >$250m for the business, this must be escalated for divisional-level management attention. Similarly if an individual threat is discovered in a project which has the potential to have a serious effect on programme-level objectives it should be escalated. Conversely if a divisional manager finds a threat which has a low-value monetary impact, with no possibility of affecting reputation and no effect on divisional objectives but only affecting tactical objectives, this can safely be delegated to the appropriate tactical level for management.

Table 2.3   **Example threshold values for escalation/delegation criteria**

Criterion	Threshold values		
	Tactical–functional	Functional–divisional	Divisional–corporate
Monetary maximum value of impact	US$50m	US$250m	US$1bn
Monetary aggregated value of impact	US$50m	US$250m	US$1bn
Reputational impact	Local	National	International
Impact on higher-level objective(s)	Significant	Serious	Critical

Of course whenever a risk is escalated or delegated between levels, this must be followed by allocation of an agreed 'risk owner' at the new level for the risk, who accepts accountability for management of the risk. Effective handover of escalated and delegated risks is essential to ensure that such risks are managed properly, and that a risk does not fall between the levels with each assuming that the other will handle it.

This generic scheme for escalation and delegation of risks to the appropriate level for management can be applied at any intermediate level in the organisation. There are however two places in the organisational hierarchy where the situation is slightly different, namely the top and the bottom. Referring back to Figure 2.4, 'Sources of risks at intermediate levels', it is evident that risks cannot be escalated to the lowest tactical, operation or delivery level. Similarly delegation of risks is not relevant at the highest strategic level. This implies some distinctive features of risk management at the top and bottom of an organisation, since both represent the end of the line in different ways. For example in the project-based organisation, project risk management is used to manage the potential impact of uncertainty on the creation of project deliverables that generate benefits to the business. The project risk process is the last resort to ensure that projects optimise their ability to achieve objectives. Similarly at strategic level there is no higher place to which risks can be referred for attention or action by someone else. The senior leadership of the organisation need to take responsibility for managing strategic risks plus any other major risks escalated to them from lower levels. In a real sense, risk management at the top strategic level and at the bottom tactical level is what counts most, since there is nowhere else to go. Risks at each intermediate level could be escalated or delegated to another level, but the buck stops at the top and bottom of the hierarchy. This is why organisations need to pay attention to their approaches to strategic or corporate risk, as well as ensuring a robust and effective way of managing risks to projects, operations and delivery.

Reporting Risk Upwards

In order to be effective, ERM must facilitate the passing of risks across boundaries within the organisational hierarchy so that they are managed at the most appropriate level, and this is achieved using escalation and delegation criteria which define inter-level thresholds, as discussed above. In addition the organisation must be able to communicate upwards about current risk exposure in order to provide appropriate risk information to decision-makers at every level. This is the realm of 'advising upwards' in the context of risk management across the enterprise.

There are two reasons for communicating upwards about risk:

1. *For attention and information*: there may be some lower-level risks where the potential impact on other levels is sufficiently significant that those who might be affected must be informed. In addition managers and leaders higher in the organisation should be supplied with the necessary information on risk status to enable them to make effective risk-based decisions.

2. *For action and involvement*: some risks may be identified at a lower level that requires the active involvement of others elsewhere in the organisation to ensure that they are managed effectively.

In order to communicate appropriately about these risks, a structured approach should be adopted. The key is to identify those stakeholders who need risk information, and to define their information needs. Outputs from the risk process can then be designed to meet those needs specifically and precisely. This requires four steps:

1. Identify stakeholders;

2. Analyse stakeholder risk information needs;

3. Design and validate risk communications; and

4. Implement and review.

Each of these four steps is discussed in turn below.

IDENTIFY STAKEHOLDERS

A stakeholder is defined as any person or party with an interest or 'stake' in the project. By implication, most stakeholders are also able to influence the project to some degree. All stakeholders should be defined, together with their level of interest and degree of influence, using one of the standard stakeholder analysis frameworks such as the Stakeholder Cube (Murray-Webster and Simon 2006; Hillson and Simon 2007) or the Stakeholder Circle (Bourne 2007, 2009).

ANALYSE STAKEHOLDER RISK INFORMATION NEEDS

Requirements for risk management information should be determined for each group of stakeholders, linked to their interest or stake, by answering the following questions:

1. What risk information is required?

2. How will it be used?

3. What level of detail and precision is required?

4. When must risk information be supplied?

5. What time delay is acceptable (if any)?

6. How frequently are updates needed?

7. How should information be delivered?

This information should be recorded in a stakeholder risk information needs analysis, such as the example shown in Table 2.4.

Table 2.4   **Stakeholder risk information needs analysis, with sample entry (from Hillson 2004)**

Stakeholder	Interest ('stake')	Information required	Purpose	Frequency	Format
Project sponsor	Meet business case	Project status summary	Project monitoring	Monthly	Two-page hard-copy report
		Risk status summary	Manage key risks	Monthly	Two-page hard-copy report
		Problems outside project control	Assist project manager	Immediate	Verbal plus email

DESIGN AND VALIDATE RISK COMMUNICATIONS

Based on the stakeholder risk information needs analysis, outputs from the risk process should be designed to meet the identified requirements. This should

include consideration of content and delivery method, as well as defining
responsibilities:

- *Content*: a range of outputs may be required at different levels
  of detail, delivered at different frequencies. It is more efficient to
  design outputs in a hierarchical manner if possible, for example
  to allow high-level reports to be generated as summaries of low-
  level reports, in order to avoid the overhead of producing multiple
  outputs.

- *Delivery method*: alternative methods of delivering risk management
  outputs to stakeholders should be identified, and the appropriate
  means to be used for each. These might include written reports in
  hard copy or electronic format (email, intranet, website, accessible
  databases), verbal reports (briefings, presentations, progress
  meetings), graphical or numerical outputs (tables, charts, posters).

- *Responsibilities*: each output should have a defined owner responsible
  for its production, and a designated approval authority. It may also
  be helpful to identify those whose contributions will be required,
  and who will receive the output for information. A RACI analysis –
  responsible, approval, contributor, information – might be used to
  document this.

Proposed risk outputs should be documented as shown in Table 2.5.
Information in this table should be cross-referenced with Table 2.4 to ensure
that all stakeholder requirements are met by the proposed outputs. The design
process should also include a validation step, checking with each group of
stakeholders that the proposed communication meets their need.

Table 2.5   Risk outputs definition, with sample (from Hillson 2004)

Title	Content	Distribution	Frequency	Format	Responsibility
Risk status summary	Summary of risk status Key risks Changes since last report Recommended actions	Project sponsor Project manager Programme review board Corporate risk manager	Monthly	Two-page hard-copy text report, including 'Top risks' table, risk trend graph, and Action table	Project manager (with input from key team members)

IMPLEMENT AND REVIEW

The agreed risk communication strategy and outputs should be documented and implemented, delivering agreed outputs to stakeholders as defined. After one or two cycles of risk reporting, the communications process should be reviewed with key stakeholders to check whether their needs are being met, or whether adjustments are required. Periodic reviews of the risk communications process should also be planned, as the risk information needs of stakeholders are likely to change with time.

Each stakeholder has a different requirement for risk-related information, and the risk process should recognise this and deliver timely and accurate information at an appropriate level of detail to support the needs of each stakeholder. It is not adequate to simply take raw risk data and pass it on or make it available to the project stakeholders. *Data* needs to be analysed and structured to transform it into *information*, and then actively communicated to create *knowledge* which can form the basis for *action*, as illustrated in Figure 2.5 (which also shows the transformations necessary to generate *understanding* and *wisdom*, as well as the feedback loops to the internal and external environments).

The risk process typically generates a number of standard outputs, including:

- Risk register;

- 'Top risks' list;

- Individual and aggregated risks for escalation;

- Risks for delegation;

- Risk distributions; and

- Metrics and trend analysis.

It is likely that these various outputs will be combined into an information package for delivery to stakeholders, most commonly as some form of risk report. The level of detail supplied to different stakeholders will of course vary, and three levels of risk report may be considered.

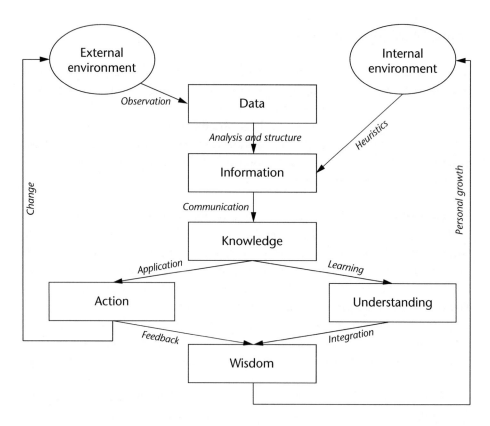

Figure 2.5   Transforming data into information, knowledge and wisdom

RISK LIST

This is the minimal level at which risk information can be reported, presenting nothing more than a simple list of identified risks, perhaps prioritised by probability and impact, and perhaps filtered to show only those risks currently active. Threats and opportunities may be listed separately or combined into a single report.

SUMMARY RISK REPORT

At this level the risk report is likely to contain only basic information. An executive summary should be used at the start of the report to present the overall risk position in a few concise paragraphs. This should be followed by details of the key risks, describing their main features and the planned responses. The remaining risks may not be discussed in detail, but could be presented using graphical analyses and pictures. Key changes since the last report should be summarised. The report should end with conclusions and recommendations, briefly assessing the current situation and summarising those actions which are required to keep risk exposure within acceptable limits. The risk register or 'top risks' list may be supplied as an appendix to the summary risk report.

DETAILED RISK REPORT

This type of report will contain full details and analysis of all identified risks, with supporting information. The report should start with a brief executive summary, then summarise the overall risk position. A review of current risks may follow, highlighting the top threats and opportunities. A detailed analysis of individual risks may be presented, covering changes in the status of identified risks, and listing any new risks identified since the last report. Risk distribution data can be presented and discussed, identifying common sources of risk, hotspots of exposure in the project, etc. Quantitative analytical results may also be presented and discussed where quantitative risk analysis has been undertaken. Key risk themes will be identified and discussed, as well as a trend analysis addressing changes in risk exposure. Similar to the summary risk report, the more detailed report will also end with conclusions (what does it mean?) and recommendations (what should be done?), though these are likely to be more comprehensive in the detailed risk report. Supporting information will also be presented in appendices, including the risk register, other detailed assessment results and supporting data.

One of the key issues in communicating about risk is to identify when stakeholders require information to be supplied, and timeliness is as important as content. There is no advantage in getting the right information too late to use it. It is therefore important to consider when risk reporting should be undertaken in the risk process. Risk methodologies tend to include risk reporting as one of the last steps in the process. In reality however risk information becomes available incrementally throughout the risk process. For example it is possible to list the risks immediately after risk identification, and to start compiling the risk register using output from the qualitative risk assessment. A preliminary risk report could therefore be produced early in the risk process, without waiting for all the details, and then reissued when more information becomes available.

Given the need to inform stakeholders promptly about risks requiring their attention or action, it is recommended that risk reports should be generated as soon as possible, even if some of the information is preliminary and will require updating later. Early reporting maximises the time available for consideration of options, development of effective responses and implementation of planned actions. One purpose of the risk process is to generate management space, allowing a proactive approach to dealing with uncertainty. Any delay in communicating risk information reduces the available time in which it is possible to be proactive.

Why Bother?

This chapter has explored the importance of understanding and managing risk at all levels within and across and organisation. Linking risk to objectives ensures that effective risk management will contribute to successful benefits delivery and value creation. The existence of multiple levels of objectives in a hierarchy throughout the organisation leads to the need for a matching hierarchical and integrated approach to risk management, known as enterprise risk management (ERM). However, the true power of ERM lies in its ability to make connections between the various levels across the organisation, allowing risk to be managed across boundaries and communicated between levels. The outcome should be seen in effective management of risk wherever it manifests in the organisation, with each risk being addressed at the appropriate level where it can best be tackled. In addition ERM provides a framework for ensuring that risk information reaches the right levels where it can be used to support informed risk-based decision-making.

To return to the beginning, this chapter has a two-part title, suggesting that ERM can be used to *manage uncertainty* and *minimise surprise*. These two phrases summarise the goals of ERM, and particularly relate to its dual role in ensuring that risk is communicated across the organisation to the appropriate level. As we have seen, risk needs to be advised upwards to provide higher-level managers and leaders with the accurate and timely tailored risk information they need to manage and lead. The first purpose of ERM is to bring risks to the attention of the people who need to know about them. But knowledge is not sufficient; there are some risks which require action and involvement at a higher level to ensure that they are properly managed, and these risks also need to be advised upwards to the appropriate people. The second purpose of ERM is therefore to ensure that action to manage risk is taken at the appropriate level in the organisation. These two purposes of ERM can be summarised as follows:

1. Managing uncertainty (action and involvement); and

2. Minimising surprise (attention and information).

In conclusion, it is self-evident and axiomatic that an organisation will only succeed and thrive if its objectives are consistently and completely met at all levels. Risk management identifies and manages proactively those future uncertain events and influences that could affect achievement of objectives either positively or negatively, and ERM provides a framework to support this across the organisation at all levels in an integrated and hierarchical manner. This strong positive correlation between organisational success/failure and risk management success/failure explains why ERM is a critical success factor that distinguishes winning organisations from the rest, through their ability to manage uncertainty and minimise surprise.

References

AIRMIC. 2008. *Research into the Benefits of Enterprise Risk Management*. London: AIRMIC.

Association for Project Management. 2006. *APM Body of Knowledge*, 5th edn. High Wycombe: APM Publishing.

Bourne, L. 2007. *Avoiding the successful failure. Proceedings of PMI Global Congress Asia–Pacific 2007*, Hong Kong, January 2007, conference paper.

Bourne, L. 2009. *Stakeholder Relationship Management*. Farnham: Gower.

British Standards Institute. 2000. *British Standard BS6079–3:2000. Project Management – Part 3: Guide to the Management of Business-related Project Risk*. London: British Standards Institute.

British Standards Institute. 2001. *BS IEC 62198:2001. Project Risk Management – Application Guidelines*. London: British Standards Institute.

British Standards Institute. 2008. *British Standard BS31100:2008. Risk Management – Code of Practice*. London: British Standards Institute.

Chapman, R.J. 2006. *Simple Tools and Techniques for Enterprise Risk Management*. Chichester: Wiley.

Granger, C.H. 1964. The hierarchy of objectives. *Harvard Business Review*, 42(3), May–June, 55–66.

Hillson, D.A. 2002a. Extending the risk process to manage opportunities. *International Journal of Project Management*, 20(3), 235–240.

Hillson D.A. 2002b. The risk breakdown structure (RBS) as an aid to effective risk management. *Proceedings of Fifth European Project Management Conference (PMI Europe 2002)*, Cannes, France, June 2002, conference paper.

Hillson, D.A. 2003. Using a risk breakdown structure in project management. *Journal of Facilities Management*, 2(1), 85–97.

Hillson, D.A. 2004. *Effective Opportunity Management for Projects: Exploiting Positive Risk*. Boca Raton, FL: Taylor and Francis.

Hillson, D.A. (ed.) 2007. *The Risk Management Universe: A Guided Tour*, revised edn. London: British Standards Institute.

Hillson, D.A. 2008. Towards programme risk management. *Proceedings of PMI Global Congress North America 2008*, Denver, Colorado, October 2008, conference paper.

Hillson, D.A. 2009. *Managing Risk in Projects*. Farnham: Gower.

Hillson, D.A. and Simon, P.W. 2007. *Practical Project Risk Management: The ATOM Methodology*. Vienna, VA: Management Concepts.

Hulett, D.T., Hillson, D.A and Kohl R. 2002. Defining risk: A debate. *Cutter IT Journal*, 15(2), February, 4–10.

Institute of Risk Management (IRM), National Forum for Risk Management in the Public Sector (ALARM), and Association of Insurance and Risk Managers (AIRMIC). 2002. *A Risk Management Standard*. London, UK: IRM/ALARM/AIRMIC.

Institution of Civil Engineers, Faculty of Actuaries and Institute of Actuaries. 2005. *Risk Analysis and Management for Projects (RAMP)*, 2nd edn. London: Thomas Telford.

International Organization for Standardization. 2009. *ISO31000:2009. Risk Management – Principles and Guidelines on Implementation*. Geneva: International Organization for Standardization.

Murray-Webster, R. and Simon, P. 2006. *30 Lucid Thoughts*. Hook: Project Manager Today.

Project Management Institute. 2008. *A Guide to the Project Management Body of Knowledge (PMBoK®)*, 4th edn. Newtown Square, PA: Project Management Institute.

UK Office of Government Commerce (OGC). 2010. *Management of Risk: Guidance for Practitioners*, 3rd edn. London: The Stationery Office.

3

Conversations that Engage: The Challenge of Advising Senior Managers

Jürgen Oschadleus

Giving advice, defined as 'an opinion given about what should be done' (Oxford English Dictionary) or a 'recommendation regarding a decision or course of conduct' (Merriam-Webster Dictionary), is one of the most natural of human impulses; we enjoy solving other people's problems or telling them what they should do. In the business world it is one of the inherent roles of middle and senior-level management. As project and programme managers or subject matter experts we are expected to advise our stakeholders on options and solutions they should take, either because they ask us for our input, or because we have spotted an issue of which they are not aware.

Unfortunately the annals of project and organisational failures are littered with examples in which solid, well-intentioned advice fell on deaf ears or was rejected. The relevant information was available, even known, but was not acted upon. The captain of the Titanic ignored numerous messages warning him of unusually heavy iceberg activity in the path of his 'unsinkable' ship. The warnings of engineers that the USS Challenger's o-rings could fail on launch went unheeded. Concerns expressed about the ultimately fatal damage to the heat deflection tiles on the USS Columbia were dismissed. The employee who approached Enron's new CEO with evidence of financial misdemeanours was fired. Kennedy deliberately avoided Schlesinger's contrarian opinion before embarking on the Bay of Pigs fiasco. These are but a few of the more commonly cited examples in a litany of poor decisions in the face of good advice.

How many project managers, when attempting to demonstrate the risks inherent in unrealistic schedules and budgets, are told to 'just get on with it' and deliver a solution?

Why is good advice often ignored or rejected by higher levels of managers? Why do projects (and organisations) keep failing, when the people on the ground know the issues, but either don't communicate them to management, or find the information they *do* present is ignored or rejected? Why do we sometimes feel in our gut we have the right answer, even though we may not be able to explain why or even support the assertion with numbers? More importantly, how do we communicate with stakeholders in such a way that we maximise the likelihood of our advice being received and acted upon?

The simple truth is that we make decisions based on experience, instinct, intuition and emotion. Even good advice given to (or by) the wrong person, presented at the wrong time, or delivered in an incorrect manner or context could nullify the quality of the information being transmitted. Mental blindspots, emotions and ego contribute to errors of judgement which, when accompanied by groupthink or fear, lead to the flawed decisions we see around us.

In this chapter we will briefly consider how our brain processes information and aids us in making rapid decisions, both good and bad. We will then utilise this knowledge to challenge our own thinking processes, and to outline some principles for how to deliver advice in such a way that it can be received and acted upon by others.

THE CHALLENGE WITH GIVING ADVICE

Many years ago I represented a vendor working on a global travel and expense management programme for a major multinational company. Our specific project was aimed at tailoring the global system to suit the needs of the Asia-Pacific market, and then deploying it into Australia, New Zealand and progressively into the remaining countries in the region. Several months into the project I approached the local sponsor with an idea that would effectively reduce the cost of the project by a third, largely through eliminating a costly and time-consuming middle layer. Rather than invoicing the US-based head office, I proposed a local invoicing structure which would eliminate foreign exchange costs, streamline the layers of oversight and reduce the actual cost of consultants, while also speeding up the invoicing and billing cycle, and all of it possible without impacting the level of service or support available to the project team. It seemed a logical decision, a win–win approach, a classic no-brainer.

Imagine my surprise when my advice was rejected!

After several unsuccessful attempts to help the sponsor work through the numbers and the facts, I eventually threw up my hands. 'You just don't get it; you would save your company a lot of money.'

'Maybe,' the sponsor replied. 'But right now the project costs me nothing. I don't think head office even realises they're paying for it. If I accepted your proposal it would draw attention to this project, and they might ask me to fund it out of my department's budget. So, sorry, but no!'

The more I tried to reason (he called it 'argue') with him about the need to place the corporate good above that of his department, the more adamant he became that he could not, and would not, heed my advice.

Decision-Making is Not a Rational Process

As business people we like to consider ourselves to be logical and rational beings. However, increasing evidence from research into the neurosciences demonstrates that many, if not most, critical decisions are made intuitively, and are driven largely by emotion and instinct (also termed 'gut feel', intuition or even a sixth sense), rather than by logical analysis. We then employ 'rational' thinking to justify why our decisions were the correct, logical ones to make.

Logic is largely dependent on the worldview of the individual. The more neuroscientists discover about the operation of the brain, the more we recognise that the thinking process consists of a spaghetti bowl of chemical connections in the mind, which through time and experience have developed into a myriad of belief systems and mental maps, many of which lie buried deep within the subconscious mind. The wiring of each person's brain, the flow of information within it, and therefore the concept of 'logical' or 'rational' thought is unique to each individual. This makes the human decision-making process both extraordinarily complex – and yet very simplistic.

My project sponsor's decision made perfect sense – when seen from his perspective. I had focused on logic from my perspective, without addressing his interests. Despite all the hours spent crafting my rational argument and supporting it with facts, figures and benefits, I had not taken the time to understand him or his needs. I had assumed – as many would-be influencers do – that the numbers would speak for themselves.

Most texts on improving decision-making suggest a classical model of laying out the options, defining the objectives and assessing each option against each objective. If that approach works in decision-making, then it holds that advice presented as a series of options, objectives and assessments should also be accepted as being valid.

However, this is not the way our brains naturally work. Instead, we analyse the situation using what Campbell, Whitehead and Finkelstein (2009) refer to as *pattern recognition*, and simultaneously arrive at a decision on how to act by using *emotional tags* associated with those patterns. When faced with a decision or a new situation, our brain integrates information from up to 30 different areas, based on assumptions and mental models created from our memories of prior decisions and experiences. These mental patterns and their related emotions enable us to rapidly, even intuitively, assimilate information, ascribe meaning to it and make decisions.

Pattern Recognition

THE DEVELOPMENT OF MENTAL MODELS

The brain's ability to create patterns is an essential part of the sense-making and learning process. Most learning and development occurs in the brain through a continual process of creating and either strengthening or weakening a series of synaptic connections between the 100 billion neurons that exist in each brain. Each neuron can establish up to 10,000 connections to other neurons, with each set of connections becoming a mental model that represents new ways of interpreting or making sense of the world around us.

Throughout life neurons compete to be part of meaningful circuits. While genetic factors shape the early development of the brain, every subsequent event and decision we make (including activities we engage in, our exercise, diet and sleep patterns and the friends we interact with) affects its future development, either reinforcing existing connections, or creating new ones.

The more useful a particular circuit – in other words, the more frequently it is used – the stronger that neural path becomes. We could compare it with creating a path through a forest. Clearing a path requires considerable effort. However, the more frequently subsequent travellers follow that path, the more well-defined it becomes, the less energy it consumes and the more likely it will be that future travellers utilise the existing path. In like manner, the more established a set of neural connections is, the more likely the brain will be to reuse that mental map.

Consequently, people who work extensively in a particular realm are likely to have developed a strong set of mental models which enable them to make intuitive decisions, without always knowing the reasons why. They have a strong gut feel for what works and what does not. In fact, research by psychologist Gary Klein suggests weighing options generally makes sense for novices, who need a decision-making framework to help them think their way through a problem, but that this framework would slow down experienced decision-makers (see, for example, Breen 2000).

PATTERN RECOGNITION – THE PROBLEM OF MENTAL SHORTCUTS

Along with all its benefits, pattern recognition also leads to mental blindspots that can cause us to miss critical information or to dismiss advice which may have improved the quality of our decisions. When dealing with seemingly familiar information, our brains are quick to leap to conclusions and are reluctant to consider alternatives.

Given the high volume of internal and external signals the brain has to process and compare against existing knowledge each waking minute, our brains develop filters to generalise, distort (adapt) or even delete signals. At the simplest level, the filtering process assesses an incoming signal to determine whether it poses a threat (in which case the fight or flight response is activated) or requires immediate attention. If not, the brain will compare it against its vast databank of maps and will try to identify a matching known mental map. If a close enough match is found, the brain can access the appropriate shortcut and deal with the signal at a subconscious level.

For example, you could sit at a table in a crowded restaurant and follow the conversation at your table. You might be aware of the hum of conversation at surrounding tables, but the content of those messages would not penetrate your conscious mind. However, your subconscious brain continues scanning all the incoming signals, and when it detects what it interprets as an important signal – such as someone mentioning your name – it automatically attempts to engage in that conversation.

The brain's tendency for selective processing of signals is clearly illustrated by Professor Daniel Simon's 1999 experiment, in which people were shown two groups of basketball players and were asked to count the number of times people wearing white shirts passed the ball to each other. By focusing on the white-shirted players, many people's brains filtered out all the black-shirted players – and the gorilla that walks across the playing area.[1]

Project managers regularly accuse sponsors and senior managers of selective hearing when it comes to our list of assumptions, risk assessments, cost or time requirements, and so on. Given what we now know about pattern recognition in the mind, we should not be surprised. When information does not fit the mental patterns of the stakeholders concerned, their brains may well have deleted, distorted or generalised what they have heard against what their intuition, experience or preconceived ideas tells them.

The danger is that in the highly adaptive world of the twenty-first century, the experiences on which we rely may no longer be relevant; what's worked in the past has in many cases been superseded. Knowledge is accumulating at such a rapid rate that the methods utilised by senior managers as they moved up through the ranks are often no longer applicable. This was true half a century ago, when Peter Drucker (1954) identified one of the major obstacles to organisational growth: managers' inability to change their attitudes and behaviour as rapidly as their organisations require. It is even more relevant today.

Emotional Tags – Decision-making Requires Emotion

When we rely on instinct to make decisions, we frequently cannot quite explain why that's the decision, other than that it 'feels right'. The use of that specific word is not accidental, because our feelings and emotions are a critical part of decision-making.

---

1   A video demonstration is available at http://viscog.beckman.illinois.edu/grafs/demos/15.html.

The terms emotion and motivation are both derived from the Latin term *movere*, meaning 'to move'. Logic gets us thinking, but *emotion* gets us moving. Neurological research by Damasio (2005) and Lehrer (2009) discovered that brain damage in the areas controlling emotions can make us slow or even incompetent decision-makers, even though we may retain our capacity for objective analysis. The emotional information we attach to the thoughts and experiences stored in our long-term memory guide our brain in determining where to pay attention and the urgency of any related action.

The brain is designed to deal with perceived threats before it deals with rational thought. The limbic system, and specifically the amygdala, our brain's emotional response centre, continually scans the environment for perceived threats to our physical or mental well-being. When such threats are detected, it prepares us for a fight or flight response by shutting down all non-vital functions, including rational thought (over-stimulating the senses, such as when overwhelming the brain with options or choices, can also lead to a freeze response).

For example, if you touch a hot plate, your brain will automatically send out signals to the hand to withdraw from danger. The conscious decision to remove your hand comes after the hand has *already* moved away. In like manner, when our self-worth comes under perceived attack, our brain automatically reacts to defend and protect us.

EMOTIONAL TAGS – EGO AND FEAR GET IN THE WAY

As with pattern recognition, the emotional tags we associate with specific mental maps can also mislead us. When we speak of 'pushing someone's buttons' we are in effect activating a set of habitual responses (patterns) which have strong emotional meaning to the person in question. The stronger the emotional link to a particular mental model, the more likely we are to allow an emotional response (either positive or negative) to cloud our judgement.

The stronger the emotion at the time the connection is formed, the deeper the impact – either because of traumatic experience or because of strong bonds to the issue at hand. For example, initiating or supervising a project can bring with it an emotional investment and a subconscious commitment to seeing it through; any advice that threatens the continued existence of the project could equally be interpreted as an attack on the initiator. It is this emotional investment that makes 'sacred cow' projects so hard to kill.

Neuroscientists have discovered through the use of functional magnetic resonance imaging (fMRI) that mental threats can impact our brains as much as physical threats do, and have identified four common triggers which are likely to cause a reaction in the brain which has all the hallmarks of physical pain (Rock and Schwarz 2006). The four threats are:

1. Uncertainty;

2. The perceived lack of autonomy;

3. Perceived loss; and

4. The perceived lack of fairness.

UNCERTAINTY

A lack of certainty generates mental stress. While we all need a degree of stress and tension to produce the adrenaline and cortisol required to facilitate thinking and other mental functions, too much uncertainty overwhelms the brain; people revert to habit, while memory, planning and creativity fall by the wayside. Ultimately, this leads to poor decision-making. The ambiguity inherent in project management exacerbates the high degree of uncertainty that already exists in the modern workplace; consequently, if we approach stakeholders with uncertain estimates or what they may perceive as a lack of confidence, we may well be contributing to their stress levels, while also undermining the believability of the advice we're offering them.

THE PERCEIVED LACK OF AUTONOMY

The degree of control we exercise over our environment or situation shapes our perception of it (this principle underpins the work of Dr William Marston, which will be addressed later in the chapter). Organisational life continues to be dominated by a 'command and control' attitude and a fear that 'employee empowerment' will undermine the power of managers, particularly those who lack security or confidence in their own positions. The need to exert control and show others who the boss is can lead to the undervaluing of advice given by subordinates.

PERCEIVED LOSS

This threat is closely aligned to the preceding one. Numerous studies such as Rock and Schwartz (2006) and Ariely (2008) have shown people to be largely risk-averse and more motivated by the prospect of loss than the potential for gain. The threat of loss extends beyond financial matters to include perceived loss of control or loss of social status. It is particularly this last element which is very pertinent for advice-givers, and will be explored in greater detail in the next section of the chapter.

THE PERCEIVED LACK OF FAIRNESS

The fourth threat is the perceived lack of fairness, which can impact our emotional response to advice. The fairness aspect comes into play in a myriad of ways every day. One of the common topics of conversation at present is on the changing demographics of the workplace, and particularly the generation gap between Gen-X and Gen-Y. Generation X, who have grown up in the late twentieth century and have looked forward to their time at the senior levels of organisations once the baby boomers retire, become disgruntled that the inexperienced, brash young Gen-Ys expect everything to be handed to them. The Gen-Y ability to adapt more readily to the rapidly changing demands of modern life and the speed of technological innovation make it all the harder for more traditional Gen-X managers to accept advice and input from the young upstarts.

All these threats contribute towards creating an emotional response in the listener, which causes the brain to shut down the rational prefrontal cortex in favour of preparing the body for a fight or flight response.

Receiving Advice can Spark Fight or Flight Behaviour

When we give someone advice it is often construed as us *telling* them what they should do. It is widely accepted that this is not a good leadership style for persuading subordinates because it can spark resistance, and stifle creativity and ownership of the ideas being generated (Rock 2006; Hamlin 2006). In short, it has the capacity to diminish people's self-worth and perceived social standing within that group.

Our social status is a powerful driving force that goes well beyond the organisational hierarchy. It touches on our experiences and conversations, and how these make us feel. Even seemingly innocuous interactions – for example, giving inappropriate feedback or solving other people's problems for them – may trigger a subconscious feeling of inadequacy within the recipient of the advice, particularly in cases where the person is under pressure, lacks confidence, or has a low emotional maturity.

This is even truer when managing upwards. Even senior leaders of organisations are still fallible human beings, who are subject to the same (at times seemingly irrational) workings of the human mind. The pace of change, the uncertainty of the modern business environment and the immersion of technology into every aspect of corporate life can easily disorient executives who rose to the top in more stable times, who had a better understanding of a broader range of organisational issues and who worked their way up the organisational ranks in a time when managers were expected to know the answers.

The leadership competencies demanded in this new environment can present an enormous challenge to the self-esteem of less confident managers. To mask our perceived failures or shortcomings, we often over-compensate, either in over-utilising our strengths (Kaplan and Kaiser 2006), or through an intense adherence to bureaucracy and process. This principle is summed up in the classic 'Peter Principle', which posits that we are promoted to our highest level of incompetence (Peter and Hull 1969). We work in areas in which we have expertise, and are promoted. However, at some point we may be promoted to a role that requires a set of skills or competences we do not possess, and we become overwhelmed by the demands of the job. When we reach this level it is easy to become defensive, all the more so when we deal with people we perceive – for whatever reason – to be a threat to our own career, self-worth or even to ideas or projects in which we have a significant emotional investment.

At the other end of the scale, senior managers have achieved their position by virtue of their knowledge and experience, and have a far greater investment in maintaining the status quo which got them to where they are. In either case, we either ignore solid advice, or fail to seek it to begin with. Our fear and ego get in the way.

Given all the neurological and emotional reasons for rejecting advice, we now turn our attention to the question of how we can provide senior stakeholders with sound advice which they can take on board and put into practice. There are two aspects to this – understanding and challenging the biases in our own thinking, and then practising techniques to help others through the same process.

CREATE A PLATFORM OF CREDIBILITY

Before attempting to advise others, we should create a platform of trust from which we can offer advice. This entails understanding our own influence base, developing a reputation for what Maister and Green (2001) refer to as being a 'trusted advisor', and continually being open to challenging our own thinking.

DEVELOP INFLUENCE AND TRUST

Some 2,500 years ago the Greek philosopher Aristotle (350BC) identified three broad approaches we could adopt when seeking to influence others. He termed them *ethos, pathos* and *logos*:

> *Of the modes of persuasion furnished by the spoken word there are three kinds. The first kind depends on the personal character* [ethos] *of the speaker; the second on putting the audience in a certain frame of mind* [pathos]; *the third on the proof or apparent proof* [logos], *provided by the speech itself.*

> *Persuasion is achieved by the speaker's personal character when the speech is so spoken as to make us think him credible. We believe good men more fully and readily than others; this is true generally whatever the question is, and absolutely true where exact certainty is impossible and opinions are divided.*

ETHOS = CHARACTER AND COMPETENCE

Ethos, typically translated as 'character', could also be translated as 'credibility', 'competence', and possibly even 'ethics'. This is the foundation of influence. The degree of value or trust we place in a message depends in large part on the source from which it is obtained. What we believe about another person's character, competence and credibility directly influences how readily we allow ourselves to be influenced by what that person says or does. The more we respect and trust the person delivering the message or advice, the more likely we are to accept it. Recognising that someone has credibility, a track record and a solid reputation in an area gives far greater weighting to that person's advice.

It is worth emphasising at this point the importance of perception. Credibility, like beauty, is in the eye of the beholder. We ascribe levels of trust to people based on our experience of them, and on our perception of reality, rather than on 'the facts'. Having a persona of trust and credibility is important (hence the desire to build rapport, which is a hallmark of confidence tricksters, politicians and sales people alike), but it must be rooted in reality.

PATHOS = EMOTIONAL APPEAL AND RELATIONSHIP

The second core persuasive technique described by Aristotle is the ability of the speaker to put the listener in 'the right frame of mind'. *How* we transmit a message (the medium used, the delivery and timing, even the person selected to communicate the content) has a significant impact on whether a message will even reach its intended audience, and how it will be interpreted if it does.

Effective, influential communication is not simply a matter of what we say, but of how, why, when and to whom we do so. Our believability is linked to the passion we have for our subject and our people, and to our ability to evoke an emotional response in our listeners. Ultimately, it's about how we make them feel.

Many texts on communication cite the Mehrabian and Ferris (1967) model of persuasive communication, which suggests that content accounts for only 7 per cent of the overall impact of a message. The remainder is made up of non-verbal cues, notably vocal delivery (38 per cent) and body language (55 per cent).[2] When the words are not aligned with the listeners' interpretation of non-verbal cues the latter take precedence, and the impact of the message is destroyed. Consequently, when attempting to influence or advise others, we need to ensure that our non-verbal message is congruent with the verbal.

Closely aligned with this is the relationship we foster with the people around us. Cohen and Bradford (2005) devote a considerable portion of their book, *Influence without authority*, to building relationships through reciprocity and the exchanging of favours (termed 'influence currencies') with diverse

---

2   A Stanford University study subsequently revised the figures to 35, 20 and 45 per cent respectively. But the import remains the same: persuasive communication is about far more than the words we speak.

people within the organisation and beyond. Cialdini (1984), one of the world's experts on social influence, also identified reciprocity as one of the six universal laws of influence. And Dale Carnegie, whose 1936 best seller *How to win friends and influence people* (Carnegie 1989) started a whole new focus on the subject of influence, cites numerous examples of some of the world's great leaders taking an active interest in the personal lives of their subordinates, thereby building a loyalty far more powerful than could be achieved through logic or words alone.

We are more likely to respond positively to people who reinforce our perception of self. As Aristotle noted, we are more likely to believe the best about people we like, and less about those we dislike. This is also one of the six universal laws of influence posited by Cialdini. At the end of the day, the degree of influence we wield over people has a direct correlation to the relationship we have with them and how we make them feel.

LOGOS = USE OF LOGIC AND REASON

The third component of persuasion identified by Aristotle is the logic of the actual argument being presented. This is the part we love focusing on in the business world, because surely if we present a logical argument, with all the relevant facts and figures to support our view, then they will have to believe us.

If only ...

As my interaction with the sponsor illustrates, logic is based on an individual's mindset. Our upbringing, our experiences and our thought patterns determine our *Weltanschauung* or worldview. What appears completely logical and rational to us may not, in fact, appear logical or rational to someone viewing the same situation from a different perspective and with a different mental model. To us people may appear to be making irrational and illogical choices. To them, we may be guilty of the same thing. The challenge is to identify the worldview of our listeners or audience, and to present our reasoning in terms that would be meaningful and reasonable in their minds, not ours. This requires us to identify and understand the interests, needs and perceived options of the specific people we're seeking to advise.

INFLUENCE IS ABOUT BALANCING THE THREE DIMENSIONS

Ethos, pathos and logos are all techniques that can be utilised in persuading others, but as outlined in *Heart of Influence* (Oschadleus 2004) it is the *overlap* of these three components which develop what I call Influence Equity™ – that is our ability to consistently influence those around us.

Financial equity is a measure of the financial resources available to a person or organisation. The greater the positive difference between financial assets and liabilities the greater the owner's equity, and the more capable the owner is of utilising that equity towards attaining organisational or individual objectives. Influence Equity™ is similar in concept, but the value is of an intangible nature. Rather than focusing on financial capital, we are interested in the degree of the influence we wield over the people in our world. Covey (1989) refers to this as an Emotional Bank Account, into which people can make deposits or withdrawals, utilising their 'currencies' of choice – finances, recognition and satisfaction.

The greater the equity we build up in our account, the higher the levels of trust, and the greater the degree of reciprocal influence we exert over each other. Every interaction we undertake should establish our character and credibility at the outset, understand the impact of that communication on the listener and ensure that it addresses the logic or world view of the other party.

Understand Your Own Information-processing Style

Giving advice is about effective communication and how we make people feel, which requires understanding how we process information.

GETTING THE SEQUENCE RIGHT

Consider the simple example of telephoning another person. By dialling ten digits in a particular sequence we are able to establish a connection to a specific individual and engage them in a conversation. Mix any of them up, or replace even one digit with another, and the connection fails.

To further complicate matters, the set of numbers dialled depends on the country we're in and the country we're trying to reach. We may have to dial more or fewer digits, and adhere to specific protocols about prefixes or suffixes.

For people we call often we might create shortcuts through the use of contact cards or speed dials, but these would be unique to a particular set of people and the communication devices we use.

Our endeavours to communicate with others depends on the same principle of pushing the right numbers in the right sequence. We have our own unique ways of processing information, and the manner in which data is presented will influence how it is received, interpreted and acted upon. This is particularly true when the topic of our communication pertains to sensitive or emotional material, or potentially requires people to re-evaluate their own thoughts, beliefs or desires.

UNDERSTANDING BEHAVIOUR

In the early 1920s, well before the advent of the neurosciences, researcher Dr William Marston started observing students on campus, and tried to define why they behaved in specific manners. Using the same Jungian theories that gave rise to assessment tools such as the Myers–Briggs Type Indicator (MBTi), the Kiersey's Temperament Sorter and more recently the 4-D System used at NASA, amongst others, Marston developed a theory which underpins the various flavours of modern DiSC® behavioural profiles.

Marston (1928) believed our behaviour is the visible response to our perceived environment in two dimensions. The first dimension relates to the perceived safety of the environment (that is whether it is safe or hostile) and the second to our perceived ability to control that environment. This gives rise to a matrix of four primary style-types that represent which motivators are more intense in people, described in Table 3.1.

Table 3.1   Information processing and communication preferences

	Task-oriented focus	Social- or people-oriented focus
Extroverted (Assertive)	Dominance – refers to control, power and assertiveness. Active in dealing with problems and challenges, and can be described as demanding, forceful, egocentric, strong-willed, driving, determined, ambitious, aggressive and pioneering. People with low 'D' scores want to do more research before committing to a decision, and are described as conservative, low-keyed, cooperative, calculating, undemanding, cautious, mild, agreeable, modest and peaceful.	Influence (inducement in Marston's terminology) – relates to social situations and communication. Talkative and active, with a tendency towards emotion; can be described as convincing, magnetic, political, enthusiastic, persuasive, warm, demonstrative, trusting and optimistic. People with low 'I' scores influence more by data and facts, and not with feelings, and are described as reflective, factual, calculating, sceptical, logical, suspicious, matter of fact, pessimistic and critical.
Introverted (Passive)	Conscientiousness (caution or compliance in Marston's time) – relates to structure and organisation. Adhere to rules, regulations and structure, like to do quality work and do it right the first time. They are careful, cautious, exacting, neat, systematic, diplomatic, accurate and tactful. People with low 'C' scores challenge the rules and want independence. They are described as self-willed, stubborn, opinionated, unsystematic, arbitrary and unconcerned with details.	Steadiness (submission in Marston's time) – relates to patience, persistence and thoughtfulness. People who seek a steady pace and security, and do not like sudden change. They tend to be unemotional, and be described as calm, relaxed, patient, possessive, predictable, deliberate, stable and consistent. People with a low 'S' score are those who like change and variety, and could be described as restless, demonstrative, impatient, eager, or even impulsive.

As with all the profiling assessments, none of the quadrants represents inherently right or wrong behaviour; rather, these tools illustrate how differently we perceive and process information. We all exhibit elements of behaviour from each quadrant, but have a preference for one or two of the quadrants. Marston's theory has several implications for our approach to communicating advice. As we review the core characteristics of each, it is also easy to see how miscommunication can occur when interacting with individuals from other quadrants.

GUARDING AGAINST UNWARRANTED CONFLICT

Being aware of our own preferences gives us a greater ability to understand why we do the things we do, and enables us to guard against undervaluing or misunderstanding the communication styles of others. It also suggests to us potential areas of what Porter (1996) calls 'unwarranted conflict', in other words conflict that results from unintentional miscommunication or incorrectly interpreting the other party's behaviour (as opposed to conflict resulting from fundamental differences in goals or objectives).

People who operate primarily from diagonally opposite quadrants are likely to unknowingly create conflict in the way they approach communication. For example, if I have a strong orientation towards D-type behaviours, my fast, task-oriented style would cause considerable stress to a typically S-type manager who values relationships, harmony and a slower pace. The more pressure I exert on my manager to make a decision, the more reluctant they would be to commit, and the more I forcefully I would demonstrate what I perceive to be my strength. This cycle of misunderstanding and conflict spirals downwards in a vicious circle. Remember that the moment one party in a conversation feels threatened, the defensive walls go up and the brain prepares for fight or flight. By becoming more aware of our own physical, emotional and behavioural traits we start recognising in ourselves (and in others) the signs that one or both parties are becoming emotionally charged and at risk of engaging in fight or flight behaviour.

Some common behavioural indicators of both are highlighted in Table 3.2 (based on Patterson et al. 2002). If we can spot the signs in ourselves and others, we can utilise conversational techniques to re-establish a safe zone of dialogue, rather than confrontation or unwarranted conflict.

Table 3.2   Differences in fight and flight behaviour

Approach	Fight	Flight
Impact	Forcing our view on to everyone else.	An attempt to avoid potential problems, either by playing verbal games or by withdrawing from the issues.
Common behaviours:	*Controlling*: forcing our views on others, or dominating the conversation (interrupting, overstating facts, speaking in absolutes, changing subjects, using leading questions). *Labelling*: placing a label on people or ideas so that they can be dismissed under a general stereotype or category. *Attacking*: verbal (or even physical) abuse to make the person suffer (belittling, threatening).	*Masking*: understating or selectively showing true opinions; includes the use of sarcasm, sugar coating and couching. *Avoiding*: steering away from sensitive subjects (that is refusing to address the real issues). *Withdrawing*: no longer contributing to the conversation, or even leaving the room altogether.

DEVELOP A HABIT OF REFLECTION AND LEARNING

Not only do we need to develop our influence skills and a greater awareness of how we process information, but we also need to create an environment in which we continually challenge our own thinking and perceptions in order to spot potentially incorrect patterns or emotional tags identified earlier. In particular, we need to guard against blindspots caused by self-interest, emotional attachments or misleading memories. This involves both becoming more reflective of what we do, as well as identifying trusted third parties to act as sounding boards for our thinking. In short, we need to become better at lifelong learning.

Argyris (1991) notes that it is often the smartest people in an organisation who have not learned how to learn, simply because they have not mastered the art of critical self-examination. He and others (Senge, 1990; Daudelin 1996) contend that as leaders we need to become more reflective in learning about how our own behaviour contributes to organisational problems, and that the very manner in which we go about defining and solving problems can be a source of problems in their own right. They suggest we should regularly take time to reflect on an event, mull it over in our mind and make connections to other experiences, filtering out biases in the process, and then start asking questions of a wide audience.[3]

Asking questions forces the brain to seek answers. At the more conscious and semi-conscious levels, we interpret the data to make it fit with existing knowledge and preconceived ideas. The brain hates dissonance and will attempt to resolve seemingly contradictory information, either by forcing us to think about the data, or by subconsciously continuing to compare the information against what we already know. This is why certain ideas may continually come back into memory as our brain seeks to resolve the disconnect.

It is when we take the time to reflect and to quieten the conscious mind that our subconscious mind can search out new connections and generate the insight and mental change we and our organisations require (Rock 2006; Winston 2003).

GIVING ADVICE THAT CAN BE HEARD, BELIEVED AND ACTED UPON

And so we come back to our key question – how do we give advice in such a manner that our stakeholders will be able to hear it, accept and believe it

---

3   The concept of 'learning organisation' is a critical aspect in this context, but is outside the scope of this discussion. The works cited here provide a good starting point for readers interested in pursuing this topic. A good practical application of the power inherent in a more questioning approach to leadership is provided by Captain D.M. Abrashoff, former commander of the USS Benfold, in his book *It's Your Ship* (2002).

and then act on it? As with effective communication, giving good advice is not just about the information being presented. It's about *how* the information is presented, *why* it is being presented, *when* it is presented, in *what* manner, *to whom* and *by whom*. All of these factors influence how information is received and processed. This is part of traditional stakeholder management, and is addressed in various chapters of this book.

It is important to recognise that it is not purely about the content that we convey, nor even our intent in communicating it, but also the *perceived intent* that the recipient ascribes to us, the intent with which they listen and the political realities confronting the decision-maker. As this chapter has shown, the existing knowledge, beliefs and preconceptions of the listener, coupled with subtle cues conveyed by (or perceived in) our delivery, and by the relationship that exists between us, combine to shape how our advice will be received and what will be done with it.

In order to communicate effectively with other people, we need to format our message in a manner appropriate to them. We need to understand their communication and information-processing preferences, tailor our message to accommodate those preferences and adapt our engagement strategy to the people we are advising. This is particularly important when we are dealing with potentially contentious matters, areas in which those stakeholders have strong beliefs or opinions, or those where they have a considerable emotional investment. In all of these cases we are likely to elicit a defensive reaction if we approach the subject incorrectly or a dismissive attitude if the advice does not align with their preconceived ideas.

Not only do we have to dial their number in the right sequence (as per our earlier telephone analogy), but once we have them on the line we have to keep them engaged in dialogue, and influence their thinking without activating their fight or flight responses.

BUILD RELATIONSHIPS

Our first response, therefore, is to develop with these stakeholders a solid relationship based on influence and credibility. As Cialdini, Carnegie and others have noted, we prefer doing business with, and are more likely to listen to, people we trust and respect, and people who we believe have the knowledge and expertise to offer advice in the area under discussion.

FRAME ADVICE BASED ON THEIR DECISION-MAKING STYLE AND INTEREST

Part of the relationship-building process involves getting to know and appreciate the preferred information-gathering and decision-making styles of the people we're advising. This ensures that we are able to present information and concepts to them in a manner appropriate to their style. The more we learn about their mental models and hot buttons and their needs and interests, the more effective we become at framing messages in ways that will resonate with them.

We also need to understand how they prefer receiving advice and making decisions, and for this it is useful to examine stakeholder preferences against a model such as the DiSC® Profile outlined previously. For some it means providing a quick summary of key issues, along with a clear recommendation. For others we may need to provide extensive background or detailed technical information, along with the time they need to study the arguments and arrive at their own conclusions.

ASK GOOD QUESTIONS

In many cases it entails refraining from offering advice, and rather framing a series of questions that enable the stakeholders to examine their *thinking* on a particular topic, and in this manner to plant seeds which their subconscious mind can continue to process and search for connections. Questions are at the heart of all major innovations and revolutions throughout history – *why are we doing this? Why don't we try that? What would happen if…?*

Questions cause neurons to fire and seek out new mental connections in the brain. The right questions asked of the right people at the right time are powerful tools for delivering new insight and changing mindsets.

PERSEVERE

We also need to keep at it, in spite of opposition or seeming lack of progress. Helping people see things in a different light may require lengthy interventions based on how those specific people see the world and process information. We may have to provide them with a series of messages utilising a variety of channels (direct communication from various people, formal conference proceedings, quiet conversations, formal or informal meetings, and so on) that reinforce a consistent message over time.

Luc de Brabandere (2005) suggests we need to help people change twice, first by changing the reality of our constantly changing physical environment, and then in our *perception* of that reality. It is this second change which requires creating new mental connections and new systems-oriented thinking. But as he, Senge (1990) and May (2006) note, getting people to adopt a systems-view of the world requires time and effort.

SPEAK UP AGAINST CONVENTIONAL WISDOM

One of the dangers is that the advice being offered flies in the face of conventional wisdom. Various research has demonstrated the power of peer pressure or groupthink in affecting decision-making. The Abilene Paradox (Harvey 1974) is a commonly cited story illustrating the ease with which we can fall in with the perceived desires of other people when we don't actually want to do the activity. The story is about four Texan adults who spend a hot day driving into Abilene on an excursion that nobody really wants to undertake.

Even earlier, Solomon Asch (1951, 1955) conducted a well-known experiment in which people were asked questions about a set of cards they were shown. When the collaborators Asch had planted in the group gave deliberately wrong answers, there was a high tendency for the 'independent thinkers' to also give the wrong answer. Sobering as these findings are, the study also revealed two additional truths we should keep in mind when advising others:

1. Some people proved to be consistently impervious to the influence of others. However, their rationale for doing so differed. For one group the resistance was related to a strong belief in their own judgement; these people had the courage to confront opposition and go with their own intuition – a commendable trait, which also means in instances where they *are* wrong (such as when they have a deep emotional attachment to one view, or misleading memories of past actions or beliefs related to the issue), it will be much harder to convince them differently. The second (smaller) group of

'independent' thinkers acknowledged they were probably wrong, but insisted on their right to 'call it as we see it'.

2.   A second key observation for advice-givers is the impact that other dissenting voices have in swaying the decision. In the experiments Asch found the number of erroneous group decisions dropped significantly when even one of his collaborators gave the correct answer, rather than the majority answer. The implication is that when dealing with inherently right or wrong answers where the majority wish to pursue the wrong course of action, we should ensure we have at least one dissenting voice who will speak out and offer 'correct' advice.

This principle was illustrated in the lead up to the disastrous Bay of Pigs invasion in 1961. Soon after becoming President of the USA, John F. Kennedy learned of a CIA-inspired raid to overthrow Fidel Castro in Cuba. A number of Latin American experts from the State Department, amongst them his advisor Arthur Schlesinger, objected to what they saw as an ill-conceived and poorly formulated plan. However, when it came to the crucial cabinet meeting at which Kennedy made his decision, Schlesinger was not asked and did not offer his dissenting opinion. His silence contributed to the poor decision and the deaths of numerous soldiers.

Conclusion

Even highly experienced executives have been guilty of overlooking the obvious, getting emotionally attached to an idea or project and rejecting sound advice from subordinates who were in a better position to understand the dynamics of what is happening on the ground.

Before we can expect to give advice which challenges the thinking of our stakeholders we must learn to receive and accept advice, even if – or especially when – it challenges our own thinking. Unless we are willing and able to listen to the opinions and insights of others, we will not be able to give advice to others effectively. Only when we understand the need to balance our intuition and gut feel with other perspectives (obtained through reflection and listening to others) will we become aware of the blindspots in our thinking, and develop the maturity to identify and deal with blindspots in the thinking of our stakeholders.

And because we become more aware of our information gathering and processing styles, we develop an appreciation for the unique decision-making styles of others. Once this happens, we are able to frame our advice in terms which others can hear, believe and act upon.

References

Argyris, C. 1991. Teaching smart people how to learn. *Harvard Business Review*, May–June, 99–109.

Ariely, D, 2008. *Predictably Irrational*. New York: HarperCollins.

Aristotle (350BC). Rhetoric. *The Complete Works of Aristotle. Vol. 2*, translated by J. Barnes. Princeton, NJ: Princeton University Press.

Asch, S.E. (1951). Effects of group pressure upon the modification and distortion of judgment. In H. Guetzkow (ed.), *Groups, Leadership and Men*. Pittsburgh, PA: Carnegie Press, pp. 177–190.

Asch, S. E. (1955). Opinions and social pressure. *Scientific American*, 193: 31–35.

Breen, B. 2000, *What's Your Intuition?* 31 August. Available at http://www. fastcompany.com/magazine/38/klein.html, accessed 19 September 2010.

Campbell, A., Whitehead, J. and Finkelstein, 2009. Why good leaders make bad decisions. *Harvard Business Review*, February, 60–66.

Carnegie, D. 1989. *How to Win Friends and Influence People*. New York: Pocket Books.

Cialdini, R. 1984. *Influence: The Psychology of Persuasion*. Melbourne: The Business Library.

Cohen, A. and Bradford, D. 2005. *Influence Without Authority*. New York: Wiley.

Covey, S. 1989. *The Seven Habits of Highly Effective People*. New York: Free Press.

Damasio, A.R. 2005. *Descartes' Error: Emotion, Reason, and the Human Brain*. Putnam, 1994; revised Penguin edition, New York: Penguin.

Daudelin, M.W. 1996. Learning from experience through reflection. *Organisational Dynamics*, Winter, 24(3): 36–48.

De Brabandere, L. 2005. *The Forgotten Half of Change: Achieving Greater Creativity Through Changes in Perception*. Chicago, IL: Dearborn Trade Publishing.

Drucker, P.F. 1954. *The Practice of Management*. New York: Harper and Row.

Hamlin, S. 2006. *How to Talk so People Listen*, 2nd edn. New York: HarperCollins.

Harvey, J.B. 1974. The Abilene paradox and other meditations on management. *Organizational Dynamics*, 3(1): 63–80.

Kaplan, R.E. and Kaiser, R.B. 2006. *The Versatile Leader: Make the Most of Your Strengths – Without Overdoing It*. San Francisco, CA: Pfeiffer.

Lehrer, J. 2009. *How we Decide*. Orlanod, FL: Houghton Mifflin Harcourt.

Maister, D. and Green, C. 2001. *The Trusted Advisor*. New York: Free Press.

Marston, W.M. 1928. *Emotions of Normal People*. Torquay: Devonshire Press.

May, M.E. 2006. *The Elegant Solution: Toyota's Formula for Mastering Innovation*. New York: Free Press.

Mehrabian, A. and Ferris, R. 1967. Inference of attitudes from non-verbal communication in two channels. *The Journal of Counselling Psychology*, 31: 248–252.

Oschadleus, H.-J. 2004. *Heart of Influence: Assertive Communication as a Lifestyle*. Sydney: Act Knowledge.

Patterson, K., Grenny, J., McMillan, R. and Switzler, A. 2002. *Crucial Conversations: Tools for Talking when Stakes are High*. New York: McGraw Hill.

Peter, D.L. and Hull, R. 1969. *The Peter Principle*. New York: William Morrow and Company.

Porter, E.H. 1996. *Relationship Awareness Theory. Manual of Administration and Interpretation*. Carlsbad, CA: Personal Strengths Publishing.

Ratey, J.J. 2001. *A User's Guide to the Brain: Perception, Attention and the Four Theaters of the Brain*. London: Little, Brown.

Rock, D. 2006. *Quiet Leadership: Six Steps to Transforming Performance at Work*. New York: Collins.

Rock, D. and Schwartz, J. 2006. The neuroscience of leadership. *strategy+business*, 43: 1–10, reprint 06207.

Schwartz, J.M. and Begley, S. 2002. *The Mind and the Brain: Neuroplasticity and the Power of Mental Force*. New York: Harper.

Senge, P.M. 1990. *The Fifth Discipline: The Art and Practice of the Learning Organisation*. Currency Doubleday.

Winston, R. 2003. *The Human Mind and How to Make the Most of it*. London: Transworld Publishers.

4

From Commander to Sponsor: Building Executive Support for Project Success

Randall L. Englund and Alfonso Bucero

Introduction

In the action and historical drama film *Master and Commander,* Captain Jack Aubrey (played by Russell Crowe) of the British frigate *HMS Surprise,* faces the problem of how to make his ship appear invisible in pursuit of the French privateer *Acheron*, a cutting-edge vessel both heavier and faster than his own.

His mission is to 'burn, sink or take her a prize'. He walks into the cabin where the ship's doctor Stephen Maturin (played by Paul Bettany) studies strange creatures that reside on the isles of the Galapagos Islands. The doctor and his young assistant describe the rare phasmid, stick insects whose natural camouflage makes them resemble a stick, difficult to spot, and able to confuse their predators. The captain gets an idea. The next scene shows the doctor coming up on deck and seeing the warship being disguised as a whaling ship. The privateer, in greed, would come in close to capture the ship rather than destroy it outright. Captain Aubrey says:

> *A nautical phasmid, Doctor. It's amazing how much one can learn about naval warfare by observing nature. I intend to take a greater interest in the bounty of nature from now on. I had no idea that the study of nature could advance the art of naval warfare. Now to bring this predator in close and spring our trap.*

The doctor corrects him, 'Jack, you're the predator.'

Several points from these scenes demonstrate how the captain transitioned from commander to sponsor. Faced with a clear-cut mission to accomplish, he practiced *management by wandering around* (MBWA). He sought out advice from people on his team and listened to what they were working on. He applied an organic approach to solving problems, realising that nature and natural living systems have much to offer when applied to work situations. The captain did not need to have all the answers or take the credit; solutions are present in the people, process, or environment wherein we reside. Innovative ideas can come from anywhere. Finding solutions requires inquiry, adoption, adaptation and application. In becoming a *predator*, he assumes the role of an aggressive, determined, or persistent person, all the while maintaining his role as a sponsor and leader. The captain has the authority to implement the creative solution and complete the mission.

While military models often portray a command and control approach, they also depict times when sponsorship is the desired role. Many people find themselves wanting to contribute more within their organisations but feel constrained by the limits of *commander* leadership. This chapter addresses both the role of sponsorship and how to advise upwards when a sponsorship culture is weak, ineffective, unfamiliar, good but not great, or missing. Much of the discussion draws from the discipline of project management and the world of projects, as that is where the authors live and breathe on a daily basis. The concepts and practices apply, however, to all forms of work, disciplines and industries.

This chapter is organised to first discuss the need for sponsors, followed by attitudes and steps to follow to manage upwards, and then summarises lessons learned to facilitate the transition from commander to sponsor.

The Need for Sponsorship

Why do we need sponsorship? Everybody does … on every activity worth pursuing. Chief Information Officers and other executives oversee a vast array of projects of which many, to their dismay, provide disappointing results. Who do you turn to for relief? How about the sponsors?

A compelling case can be made for raising the capabilities of sponsors. Terry Cooke-Davies (2005) and Human Systems International conducted research worldwide to find approximately 26 per cent of the variation in project success is accounted for by variation in governance or sponsor capabilities. The capabilities that matter most: 50 per cent improvement in effectiveness when sponsors ensure strategic options are largely considered, projects are fully resourced and project teams have the authority necessary to accomplish project goals; 70 per cent improvement in efficiency when sponsors support proven planning methods, fully develop the business case, staff capable and effective teams and identify clear technical performance requirements that achieve business goals. Cooke-Davies (2005) concludes that 'the sponsor does indeed play a pivotal role. It is time for project management professional organizations to provide help and guidance to executive sponsors!'

CASE STUDY 4.1   CHANGING A SPONSOR'S SUPPORT

When I (Bucero) was assigned as project manager for a government project that was considered a strategic project for the company, the Spanish CEO was assigned as project sponsor. At that time I lacked knowledge about sponsorship but did observe dysfunctional behaviours. My project sponsor was not confident in me; he duplicated many of my activities. He wanted to act as a 'super project manager'. He used his high-level contacts at top management level in Europe to accelerate equipment delivery, and he also micromanaged me. That created a lot of stress for me. However, I discovered one thing that worked very well. Every time we had a customer executive meeting, I made the effort of travelling with him the day before, having dinner together, talking about my vision for the project and providing him a wide variety of project details. Six months later his behaviour changed to a very positive attitude towards me. This situation illustrates how executives (sponsors) and project managers need to spend time talking, discussing and getting to know each other better to achieve successful projects and positive business impact.

The Problem

Many executives are assigned as sponsors, but their organisations do not spend time training them in preparation for the role, explaining their expected roles and responsibilities during project life cycles. The accidental project manager role is well known, and the same applies to sponsors. Case study 4.2 depicts the challenges created by poor sponsors.

Recognise that the 'sponsor' is a universal role and has application for all activities that an organisation undertakes. Moving from a state of poor sponsorship to excellence in sponsorship is the goal set out by this chapter. The sponsor role can have a tremendous impact on organisational success. However, effective implementation in reality is quite different. The sponsor role appears confused in many organisations: sometimes the sponsor is not very involved in the work. On the other hand, sometimes a sponsor is too involved and acts or tries to act as a super project manager, generating more conflict and problems. Managing upwards involves shifting roles.

CASE STUDY 4.2   AN EXAMPLE OF POOR SPONSORSHIP

An example of poor sponsorship appeared when I (Bucero) was assigned as a project manager to a large customer project in the financial industry in Spain; my general manager was assigned as project sponsor. He never came to talk to me or asked me about project progress. Periodically, I kept him informed. He only visited the customer twice in a three-year period. When I talked to him, he said it was my responsibility to take care of the customer. He had never been trained in project sponsorship; in fact, he believed it was my role as project manager to assume most responsibilities of the sponsor. I spent a lot of time treating him to coffee in order to let him know about my expectations and the customer's expectations of him.

In that particular project, I played two roles (the project manager role and the project sponsor role), and it did not work. I always believe that communication is more effective when project managers talk to project managers, technical people talk to technical people and executives (project sponsors) talk to customer sponsors.

For me as project manager it was very difficult to wear two hats at the same time, but I did my best. I spent time, effort and passion to do that. Finally, I was considered a trusted advisor to my customer and was invited to attend customer executive committee meetings on a monthly basis. But the customer was unhappy about the situation and complained to the project provider organisation. The lack of effective sponsorship created ill feeling all around.

Invest in Relationships

One of our insights is that the project manager and sponsor should invest in *relational chemistry*. The key to developing chemistry with leaders is to develop relationships with them. By learning to adapt to the boss's personality while still being yourself and maintaining your integrity, you will be in a better position to *advise upwards*.

To begin investing in relationships, be aware of cultural characteristics. For example, these characteristics have been observed as representative of European culture:

- inordinate sense of reality;

- a belief that individuals should be at the centre of life;

- a sense of social responsibility;

- a mistrust of authority; and

- a desire for security and continuity.

We asked a number of professionals in Europe the question: 'Was the chemistry between your project team, your executives and yourself working properly throughout the work cycle?'

Adriano Brilli from Ericsson (Italy) says:

> *The key is to mediate. Different interests can converge into a project, functional workload and project work. The solution of this is always in the ability to find mediation between needs, priorities and understanding the approach from both sides. If the project manager is able to find the best mediation, and the parties involved assume a proactive and cooperative approach, then the compound is stable.*

Gregorio Tierno from HP (Spain) says:

> *I believe good chemistry can be achieved dealing with people as human beings, not only as employees. Being confident, respectful, sincere,*

creating a team spirit in the project, clarifying the common objective.
These attitudes should generate enthusiasm itself.

We believe the job of leaders, no matter what their level in the organisation, is to connect with the people they lead. In an ideal world, that's the way it should be. The reality is that some leaders do little to connect with the people they lead. Leaders need to take on the responsibility to connect not only with the people they lead, but also with the person who leads them (manager, sponsor). In order to lead up, it is necessary to take the responsibility to connect up.

Apply Best Practices

Here are a variety of practices that work for the authors in leading work efforts across organisations:

1.   Listen to your leader's heartbeat;

2.   Know your leader's priorities;

3.   Catch your leader's enthusiasm;

4.   Support your leader's vision;

5.   Connect with your leader's interests;

6.   Understand your leader's personality;

7.   Earn your leader's trust; and

8.   Learn to work with your leader's weaknesses.

LISTEN TO YOUR LEADER'S HEARTBEAT

You need to listen to your leader's heartbeat to understand what makes them tick. That may mean paying attention in informal settings, such as during hallway conversations, at lunch, or in the chance encounter that often occurs informally before or after a meeting. If you know your leader well and feel the relationship is solid, you may want to be more direct and ask questions about what really matters to them on an emotional level.

If you're not sure what to look for, focus on these three areas:

1. What makes them laugh? This is very important.

2. What makes them cry? This is what touches a person's heart at a deep emotional level.

3. What makes them sing? These are the things that bring deep fulfilment.

All people have dreams, issues or causes that connect with them. Those things are like the keys to their lives. Think about it from your own point of view for a moment. Are you aware of the things that touch you on a deep emotional level? What are the signs that they 'connect' for you? Do you see those signs in your leader? Look for them, and you will likely find them.

KNOW YOUR LEADER'S PRIORITIES

The priorities of leaders are what they have to do, and by that we mean more than just to-do lists. All leaders have duties that they must complete or they will fail in fulfilling their responsibility. It's the short list that the boss's boss would say is do-or-die for that position. Make it your goal to learn what those priorities are. The better acquainted you are with those duties or objectives, the better you will understand and communicate with your leader.

CATCH YOUR LEADER'S ENTHUSIASM

It is much easier to work with someone when you share an enthusiasm. If you can catch your leader's enthusiasm, it will have a similarly energising effect and it will create a bond between you and your leader. If you can share in that enthusiasm, you will pass it on because you will not be able to contain it.

SUPPORT YOUR LEADER'S VISION

When top leaders hear others in their organisation articulate the vision they have cast for the organisation, their hearts sing. It's very rewarding. It represents a kind of *tipping point*, to use the words of author Malcolm Gladwell (2002). It indicates a level of ownership by others in the organisation that bodes well for the fulfilment of the vision. Leaders in the middle ranks of the organisation who are champions for the vision become elevated in the estimation of a top leader. They get it: they are on board. And, therefore, they have great value.

Never underestimate the power of a verbal endorsement of the vision by a person with influence. As a leader in the middle ranks, if you are unsure about the vision of your leader, then talk to them. Ask questions. Once you think you understand it, quote it back to your leader in situations where it's appropriate to make sure you are in alignment. If you have got it right, you will be able to see it in your leader's face. Then you can start passing it on to the people in your own sphere of influence. It will be good for the organisation, your people, your leader and you. Promote your leader's dreams, and they will promote you.

CONNECT WITH YOUR LEADER'S INTERESTS

One of the keys to building relational chemistry is knowing, and connecting with, the interests of your leader – both work-related and personal interests. It is important to know enough about your leader to be able to relate to them as an individual beyond the job. If your boss is a golfer, you may want to take up the game or at least learn something about it. If the boss collects rare books or porcelain, then spend some time on the Internet finding out about these hobbies. Just learn enough to relate to your boss and talk intelligently about the subject.

UNDERSTAND YOUR LEADER'S PERSONALITY

Two staff members were discussing the president of their company, and one of them said, 'You know, you cannot help liking the guy.' To which the other replied, 'Yes, if you don't, he fires you.'

Leaders are used to having others make allowances for their personalities. As you lead down from the middle of the organisation, don't you expect others to conform to your personality? We don't mean that in an unreasonable or spiteful way that you would fire someone who didn't like you, as in the joke. If you are simply being yourself, you expect the people who work for you to work with you. But when you are trying to lead up, you are the one who must conform to your leader's personality. It is a rare great leader who attempts or even considers accommodating to the people who work for them.

It is wise to understand your leader's style and how your personality styles interact. Most of the time, personality opposites get along well as long as their values and goals are similar. Using temperament theory from the ancient Greeks, *cholerics* (doers) work well with *phlegmatics* (self-content and kind); *sanguines* (extroverted) and *melancholics* (ponderer) appreciate each other's strengths. Trouble can come when people with similar personality types come together. If you find that your personality is similar to your boss's, then remember that you are the one who has to be flexible. That can be a challenge if yours is not a flexible personality type.

EARN YOUR LEADER'S TRUST

When you take time to invest in relational chemistry with your leader, the eventual result will be trust, in other words, *relational currency*. When you do things that add to the relationship, you increase the change (surplus currency) in your pocket. When you do negative things, you spend that change. If you keep dropping the ball, professionally or personally, you harm the relationship, and you can eventually spend all the change and bankrupt the relationship.

LEARN TO WORK WITH YOUR LEADER'S WEAKNESSES

You cannot build a positive relationship with your boss if you secretly disrespect him because of his weaknesses. Since everybody has blindspots and weak areas, why not learn to work with them? Try to focus on the positives and work around the negatives. To do anything else will only hurt you.

People can usually trace their successes and failures to the relationships in their lives. The same is true when it comes to leadership. The quality of the relationship you have with your leader will impact your success or failure. It is certainly worth the investment.

NEED FOR MANAGEMENT SUPPORT

Management support is always needed on every activity. In fact, the sentence: 'we need more management support' is very common in most organisations. In every project, the project manager and team needs management support. Each project needs a single sponsor: avoid multiple sponsors because that usually equals no sponsorship. To give effective management support, managers need to know what is expected from them. Many sponsors do not know very much about the projects they are sponsoring, and no one has explained the meaning of project sponsorship to them.

According to a study of change management research, the number one contributor to project success is visible and effective sponsorship. Participants cited:

> *The top changes they would make regarding project communications in the future would be to incorporate more frequent communications earlier in the project, conduct more face-to-face communications, offer more communications from executive sponsors and senior managers, and deliver more information about the impact of the change.*

And:

> *Many managers spend the better part of their time focusing on technology or system issues surrounding organisational changes, rather than creating a comprehensive plan to facilitate critical communications with all the sponsors and target audiences that will be impacted.*

Also required is the need to '*promote visible support from executives*' (Urban 2004).

Many organisations focus on key initiatives that may be different at various times in the life of the organisation. Some examples would be:

- The improvement of project management processes and practices in the organisation.

- The implementation of specific project management methodologies.

- The development of a project management career path for the organisation's project management personnel.

However, few organisations are aware of how to develop the skills of their managers and top executives to enable them for understand and better exploit the influence they can have on overall success. Graham and Englund (2004) target this audience, Dinsmore joined them to document how to implement a project-based organisation, (Englund, Graham and Dinsmore 2003). New work by Englund and Bucero (2006) focuses on the role of project sponsors within the guidelines established by the previous work. The goal is to help generate excellence in project sponsorship.

Few professionals in organisations have a clear idea of what sponsorship entails. We find different degrees of understanding and different behaviours from sponsors across the vast variety of organisations with whom we have made contact or worked. Some professionals and managers think that sponsorship is just work authorisation, signing up contracts, funding the activity and deciding to go on or not go on to the next phase. Provision and guarantee of funding are essential roles of sponsorship, but there is much, much more.

Sponsor Definition

There are common definitions of the role of sponsor that apply to a multitude of work situations:

1. One who assumes responsibility for another person or a group during a period of instruction, apprenticeship, or probation;

2. One who vouches for the suitability of a candidate for admission;

3. A legislator who proposes and urges adoption of a bill;

4. One who presents a candidate for baptism or confirmation: a godparent;

5. One who finances a project or an event carried out by another person or group, especially a business enterprise that pays for radio or television programming in return for advertising time.

Another definition of sponsorship more useful in the context of this chapter is 'a commitment by management to define, defend and support major activities from the start to the end'.

Sponsorship needs to be an active role during the life cycle of an activity or project.

Obviously, the types of sponsor roles and activities may vary, but there are some things all sponsors have in common, including:

- obligation;

- devotion;

- achievement;

- in other words, *commitment*.

Making the Commitment

Sponsorship means commitment to people in organisations. Sponsors are managers who need to be committed to active involvement throughout the activity. These are professionals who meet regularly to track progress. One basic characteristic of good sponsors is that they are clear about the objective for the activity and at the same time consistent, acting as a *parachute* for the project team. Project sponsorship does not mean doing project planning or work directly.

Sponsorship means dealing with people. The sponsor is both a supplier and protector of resources and the focal point of escalation for the project manager. During product or project life cycles, the sponsor acts as a high-level decision-maker because they are usually more knowledgeable about the business context in which the work is happening. Case study 4.3 provides an example.

CASE STUDY 4.3   AN EXAMPLE OF THE SPONSORSHIP ROLE

When I (Bucero) was assigned as a project manager for a software development project in an insurance organisation, I started running into problems with a third party. That third party did not follow the project procedures – the established methodology – and missed some key meetings. I talked to his manager but the manager did nothing. So, I talked to my sponsor to ask him to substitute that third party with another company to benefit the project. I was surprised when my sponsor's answer was 'No'. He explained to me that the third party had an intimate relationship with the customer and was also involved in five more projects with my delivery organisation. Strategic information such as this may be known to an executive but not be known by project managers.

Sponsorship means owning the objective, determining priorities and keeping the work going. Many problems with a particular activity can be avoided if it has a sponsor who defends the priority of the work, the task manager and team members. For example, it is very common in organisations that provide information services to have conflicts in terms of resource assignments among various activities. The sponsor plays a key role in keeping the project priority as established at the very beginning of the project. Success often comes from a sponsor who gives teams the benefit of the doubt and supports the project manager and the team. The sponsor also guides change when business priorities dictate change in the work that supports the business.

Proactive People

Sponsorship means dealing with a variety of people. Unfortunately, many project and organisation professionals operate without a clear definition of sponsorship. Sponsorship requires taking an active role during the whole project. Serving as the sponsor requires making a commitment to define, fund, defend and support major activities from the start to the finish. The task continues to ensure the benefits that the intended outcomes offered are realised.

The ideal situation is *proactive sponsorship* – getting a sponsor who is committed, accountable, serious about the work, knowledgeable, trained and able not only to talk the talk but also to walk the walk. Such people are trustworthy in all respects. Their values are transparent and aligned with the organisation and its strategy. Such sponsors protect the team from disruptive outside influences and back the team up when times are tough. It is far better to start out with the right sponsor rather than having to correct a bad sponsorship situation down the road. That is why it is so important to select the right sponsor and train the person for the role. Do not be surprised by this reaction:

WHO ME? A SPONSOR?

We find a number of cases where executives do not believe they need training on sponsorship. Usually this is because nobody has spent adequate amounts of time with them explaining how critical their participation and teamwork with project managers and their teams is in order to achieve better business results. Explaining the strategic impact of project management to executives is still a real challenge – difficult but not impossible. An organisational culture committed to a proactive approach is a desired goal. It represents a well-developed, mature organisation. *Do it right the first time and save grief later on.* The best way to sustain good sponsorship is to start out with good sponsorship. Anything less is remedial.

Achieving Role Transformation

Coaching and mentoring are desired characteristics of a good sponsor. Many sponsors have not managed projects or other task-oriented work, making it difficult for them to be effective mentors. Furthermore, they allow themselves to remain woefully ignorant about daily project obstacles, issues and problems.

Usually, the sponsor is a professional with a higher level of authority than the project manager and team in the organisation. It is preferable for the sponsor to be an experienced executive. The person's experience is crucial to ensure that activities execute organisational strategy because the sponsor is aware of the strategy and can affect resources to support it.

Probability of greater success is massively increased through better sponsorship. Sometimes executives are unable to pull the plug on troubled projects. Yet all the resources, energy and passion not poured into those activities could substantially improve the organisation's bottom line. Sponsors fulfil a crucial role by guiding right decision-making throughout every development life cycle. Sponsorship means commitment and assuring alignment to objectives from the beginning to the end of every project.

CASE STUDY 4.4   GAINING MANAGEMENT SUPPORT

To illustrate the extent to which executives may be ignorant regarding the value of sponsorship, when I (Bucero) was a consultant for a multinational company in the oil and gas industry in Barcelona one goal of the company was to develop a culture of sponsorship in the organisation. The current project culture was poorly understood and poorly developed. I organised a meeting with all of the management team in order to explain the importance of project sponsorship. Before that meeting, I asked them to do some homework. I asked every one of them to prepare a list of the projects they were sponsoring. When I asked them to present the required list, more than 75 per cent of them had very little information about project status, customer relationship, or potential future

---

business. As the senior manager was in the room, he said to the attendees, 'Do you really believe that with so little data about the projects your people are managing we will be able to make the right decisions and maintain a successful business relationship with our customers?'

I then had the opportunity to explain very clearly what they, as sponsors, might do in order to improve. The sponsorship and presence of the upper manager were key to moving forward. They established goals to achieve and measures to be applied. Executive commitment started that day, and now they are moving forward.

Support is Required

Executives are advised to support project management in organisations in order to reap the benefits. This means they need to spend time understanding their roles and responsibilities during project life cycles. Case study 4.4 provides an example of an encounter that helps clarify these responsibilities. The sponsor has a relationship with all stakeholders, especially the project manager. The sponsor performs various roles (such as seller, coacher and mentor) during all phases of each project. Many of these roles require new skills that need to be developed and different behaviours to be adopted (see Figure 4.1). That development process takes time.

When the sponsor role appears confused, making changes and speaking the truth to those in power may not always appear viable.

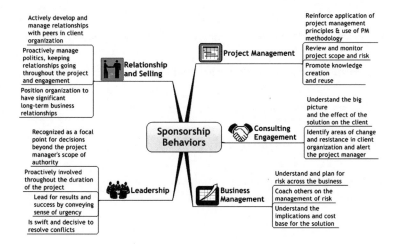

Figure 4.1   Roles and behaviours of sponsors

**CASE STUDY 4.5   IT IS NOT ALWAYS POSSIBLE TO GET THROUGH
                    TO MANAGERS**

One of my (Englund) clients in a government setting worked for a director who
took a commander approach to roles and responsibilities. The director thought
he could resolve the issues on his own between his people in headquarters
and others out in the field. But interviews with a cross-section of key people
revealed that while they were willing and able to perform at higher levels, lack
of resolution around roles and responsibilities hindered them from doing so.
The client manager had an uncanny ability to protect and manage his director.
But we were unable to get through to the director how engaging his people in
discussions about the issues might be more productive.

Results are difficult to achieve when emphasis appears to be on controls.
Some managers want to do everything themselves. What can you do when
support is not present or adequate or politics appear to rule? Take the initiative!

Surveys and data gathering are useful tools to establish awareness of a
problem. Here is a simple benchmark quiz to get started. Which one of the
following answers to the question 'Describe your sponsor's behaviour?' most
accurately describes the current reality?

   A. What sponsor?

   B. The sponsor started the project but then disappeared until…

   C. The sponsor was too distant to be helpful.

   D. The sponsor tended to micromanage the project.

   E. The sponsor was moderately helpful.

   F. The sponsor made it clear what was needed and assisted in every way
      to make that happen.

G. The sponsor defined the project, identified constraints, funded the project with adequate resources, made timely decisions, resolved conflicts and supported the project team.

Obviously, the preferred answer is to be close to response G. In almost all groups where we've conducted this quiz, we get a normal distribution with the peak in the middle between slightly negative and slightly positive responses. Often there will be one or two who reach the ideal definition described by G. Those people describe environments where very enlightened managers successfully transitioned from commander to sponsor. Moving from A to G takes awareness and explicit commitments to make changes and continuously improve the sponsorship role. Invoke a quiz like this to measure progress. Use positive examples and dialogue, coupled with patience and persistence, to stay the course.

Clarifying Roles and Responsibilities

Get clear understanding about roles and responsibilities to ensure that all projects achieve successful outcomes. Do this by developing a plan to work with sponsors on a regular basis and seek a better outcome from this interaction. Project managers need to manage their sponsors as well as how sponsors do their jobs to optimise project success. Case studies (Englund and Bucero 2006) illustrate how people can (and have!) successfully managed upwards. Another (Englund) client, again in a government setting, was able to muster support across a variety of sponsoring departments when he drew support from his own sponsor and then actively recruited support from sponsors in other departments. He systematically met with them one on one, starting first with those from his stakeholder analysis who were most supportive, progressing then through others who were perceived as less supportive. This process created a critical mass of support. He educated them about their roles as sponsors at the same time as he 'sold' them on the value of the initiative and cajoled them into operating differently than in the past. The programme achieved its objectives due to this manager's initiative, belief in the programme and active recruiting of sponsors.

Often a positive attitude in the relationship between executive and project manager helps: this is a critical pairing for project success. Executives do not like complaining project managers – it is not the right attitude for good business results. Executives like action- and business-oriented people and need project managers who are leaders. The desired end result is to dramatically and sustainably increase the probability of success, especially in political yet innovative environments. The bottom line message is … take the initiative.

Expectations

It is also important to understand expectations that sponsors have of the people working for them. Here is a recent example for an employment opportunity posted by a PMI chapter for a local organisation: 'The position requires a hands-on, get-the-job-done, attitude.'

1. You understand the theory of project management principles, but even better, you know how to adapt them to the situation at hand;

2. You're a fan of process, but only the right amount;

3. You understand and drive issues to conclusion;

4. You're a great communicator, even the people you pester like having you on the team; and

5. You love the Web, how it works, how sites are developed, and where it's going. If you have a track record for delivering customer-facing Web projects in a fast-paced, constantly changing environment, we'd like to talk to you.

This somewhat unorthodox set of requirements nonetheless helps potential candidates know what is expected of them. Expectations are a double-edged sword. They serve well when clear, articulated and congruent with organisational goals. They are problematic when vague, unexpressed and out of alignment. Put in the effort to bring expectations and assumptions to the surface and engage in dialogue until mutual understanding is achieved.

Applying Lessons Learned

In thinking about applying lessons learned while working in high-tech new product development, here are lessons distilled from the authors' experiences that assist the transition to becoming a more effective leader and advisor.

SUCCESS MEANS TAKING THE INITIATIVE

It is important for managers and leaders in general to lead and manage all stakeholders, often requiring them to manage up the organisation. Successful managers are the ones who take the initiative ('This *is* my job'), realising they still do not have control over stakeholders, but nevertheless they seek to influence and guide them for the sake of the project and the good of the organisation.

ENCOURAGE SENIOR MANAGERS TO WORK AS A TEAM

A suggestion for an action step that starts at the top and ripples throughout all the components of an action plan to create an environment for successful projects is to get upper managers working together as a team. Ask them to document strategic goals, establish criteria for prioritising and selecting projects and communicate this information among all stakeholders. By asking these questions, you demonstrate initiative to mentor upwards and your interest in helping the organisation to perform better. Inevitably you can reach the conclusion *I realise that stakeholders need to be managed, which was something I always thought was not my job, or beyond my control.*

GOOD QUESTIONING TECHNIQUES

When probing for status, a sponsor or project manager may ask a project team member a 'Yes/No' question. However, open-ended and probing questions are more effective. To better understand what is going on, for example, ask, 'What preparations have you made for the inspection?' or 'How have other team members helped prepare for the upcoming review?' Likewise, ask open-ended questions when managing upwards, such as 'What is your vision for this department?', 'What are our strategic goals for this year?' and 'What are the criteria for selecting projects?'

PRESENTING LESSONS LEARNED

To increase the power of knowledge management dissemination, ask for a *'what I learned from previous projects'* presentation by each project manager when assigned a new project. That presentation can be made to the sponsor, an upper manager business team, and/or to the project team at a project start-up event.

BUILD ON STRENGTHS

While it's laudatory to improve weaknesses in any performance challenged situation, the real pay-off – and opportunity for extraordinary results – is to build upon strengths. These are areas that are more natural, take less energy to do and are easier – all recipes for greater success. It's also good to start any review or plan with strengths. For example, if strategic planning is quite good but the environment for execution is not, suggest that upper managers include a strategic goal to improve project manager selection and development, organisation support for projects and the project management culture. Use data from surveys to help make the case.

STORYTELLING

A good lesson to apply when faced with the oft-experienced challenge of contributing something of value in a tense setting, is to tell a personal story. Nobody else can tell the same story, so by its nature it is unique. Of course, it's important that the story is relevant and contributes some way to better understanding the human condition, even if it's your own admonition to keep or stop doing certain behaviours. Participating in discussions is a great catalyst for storytelling and learning. The authors experienced this in writing business management books. While talking about the material, stories inevitably popped up that could be used in the text. We cherish these collaborative moments.

SCOPE CREEP

With regards to scope creep, demonstrate to stakeholders the consequences of their actions. Find a creative way to itemise the delays, impact on costs, or resource challenges: just the data. No judgements, emotional outbursts, or accusations. Workers are very close to this information – make it publicly visible and let people come to their own conclusions.

INTIMIDATING BEHAVIOUR

Apply a negotiating rule about not rewarding intimidating behaviour. Invoke tit for tat. When the other party is aggressive, ignore their behaviour, take a time out, or withdraw your concessions. When the other party is conciliatory, make generous offers, acknowledge the good behaviour, smile. You train other people through your own behaviour.

THE RULE OF EXCHANGE

Don't forget this rule: always get something in exchange for every concession you make, especially when being asked to do more, do it sooner, or at lower cost. Failing to get something in return creates regrets, bad feelings and poor outcomes. Creativity or ingenuity or good plain business sense may decide on what that 'something' is, but never, ever, violate the rule.

FAST-PACED ENVIRONMENTS

A suggestion for getting responses from stakeholders in a fast-paced environment is to address a process for short-term requests or changes up front at a work start-up meeting. Solicit suggestions from team members about how they want to operate. When you come up with a 'solution', ask team members or stakeholders to commit to rapid responses. For example, people will read the website or emails daily and respond within 24 hours to all questions, reviews, or requests for changes. Then your job as leader is to enforce this expected behaviour (instead of having to beg for responses or do it all yourself).

USING DEFAULT RESPONSES

A technique when sending out time sensitive material to be reviewed is to say, 'If you do not respond within XX days/weeks, then your default response will be logged as [accepted or rejected]'. Pick a default response that will be most detrimental to the person or department; this way you get their attention. The fact that you log default responses means the responses become public record. If people complain, your response is to say you are only the reporter; people have full control over their choice and what gets logged by simply responding to your request. This process helps to engender more accountability, especially when dealing with busy people. This approach is not a case of offending people; it's expressing leadership on a time-critical activity to keep an important process moving and completed on time. Explain the process up front to people and state it's a condition of participating on the project. You can always give more time on a case-by-case basis if necessary, but you've set the expectation that people need to be accountable and meet commitments.

BUT ABOVE ALL: FOLLOW YOUR BLISS

Most of all, life is too short to spend precious time in a miserable job, regardless of the pay or benefits. Find a way to be happy, 'follow your bliss', and believe finding purpose and meaning in your job is important. The only thing you'll regret about moving on or making a change is that you didn't do it sooner.

Managing the Transition

Sponsor activities and behaviours vary with the organisation. The lack of good sponsorship is a major cause of difficulties and problems. Well-executed sponsorship by senior executives brings better results.

In our research on sponsorship (Englund and Bucero 2006), we found a number of examples of how people can successfully manage upwards. What are some common steps?

- Sell the features to upper managers about their roles as sponsors.

- Emphasise the value of sponsorship and the advantages that accrue to the organisation when it is done well.

- Ask sponsors what they know and what they do not know about the projects they are involved in. This question is not meant to reveal ignorance but to get their attention. This questioning process may also demonstrate to senior executives that their sponsors are not as active and knowledgeable about their activities as they should be.

- Create a training programme on sponsorship.

- Ask for the order: get executive commitment to engage fully in the sponsorship role.

- Establish agreements about next steps (action plan).

Any sales process needs to focus on features, benefits and advantages. To sell sponsors on accepting their role, first recognise the rewards for sponsorship.

THE REWARDS FOR SPONSORS

- An improved standing and profile within the organisation: important projects may empower project sponsors to success (while also being aware of the attendant risks to their reputations from failed projects).

- Being linked with an exciting and very successful project: exciting projects have high visibility in organisations.

- An opportunity for project sponsors to promote their professional background and prestige: marketing potential and image selling.

- Media opportunities: at official launches, presentation evenings and mentions in local newsletters or news.

- Get an agenda implemented: sponsorship represents an opportunity to turn a vision into reality through a set of assigned resources.

A complete manager develops the aptitude, attitude, and skills to manage up, down and across the organisation (see Figure 4.2 which is an outline of forthcoming material from the authors).

Figure 4.2   Developing a complete skill set

Achieving a state of completeness[1] involves:

- Focusing on your strengths;

- Reframing your attitude;

- Assessing your environment;

- Developing action plans, targeted at the environment, to increase management commitment;

- Integrating skills from multiple disciplines; and

- Applying learning to get better results.

Realise that a command and control leadership style is the *old story* of applied leadership; the *new story* is a focus on coaching and mentoring, engaging people to do their best work, learning from each other and from experiences, both good and bad, and doing it faster than competitors. Create a political plan that accesses the power to do good and get results. If necessary, become a *project office of one* (POO). Be the instigator of a learning organisation. Motivate others to join in the quest to create a greater good. Throughout this process, have fun!

Summary

Key lessons are these:

- Illustrate where the absence of thoughtfully assigned sponsors with well-defined and clearly understood responsibilities is a major cause of difficulties and frustrations in many types of work.

- Complex programmes that cross internal and external organisations require a structured approach to sponsorship.

- Senior executives are more effective when they understand their role as sponsors and do not delegate this responsibility to lower levels.

---

1   See the assessment tools and action plan templates in the 'Offerings' tab of www.englundpmc. com.

- Publicise how well-executed sponsorship brings financial results, increases motivation and participation and improves the productivity of the organisation.

- Accept managing upwards as part of your purpose as an effective leader, regardless of where you are in the organisation or what work you do.

- Know that sponsors need followers who urge them to be better sponsors and care enough to help them move forward.

- Workers at all levels, for the own well-being as well as for the organisation, have both an obligation and the means to manage upwards.

- Both sponsors and leaders of work need to convey a positive attitude that extends across the team and all stakeholders.

A good sponsor needs to deal with resource availability, minimise functional barriers, get help from senior management and be sure the right tools are used. A key obligation of every sponsor is to create the right environment for success. Problems and issues that arise from people at work are greatly eased when effective sponsors are fully present and skilled in fulfilling their roles.

Success starts with a strong commitment to improve. Leaders become better prepared as sponsors of work by taking inventory of their talents, skills and behaviours and putting appropriate action plans in place. They need to acquire skills and knowledge to transition from commander to sponsor.

Knowledge management encompasses the ascent of a stairway from data to information to knowledge and wisdom: this is shown in Figure 4.3. One objective is to unlock and open the doors to effective sponsorship. Reaching the doors at the top of the stairway represents enlightenment – eyes are fully open about why, what and how to invoke excellence in sponsorship. The reader has choices: ignore the opportunities the open door represents, approach it cautiously, or pass through it eagerly. As you stand before an open door, you can spend time and energy on non value-adding activities or embrace sponsor and management commitments that achieve greater success … and take on attendant responsibilities to manage upwards.

Figure 4.3   Ascending steps to excellence in sponsorship

Sponsorship is a required and critical success factor for all projects and almost all work, in all industries and disciplines. Executives need training, experience and practice to be effective sponsors. Most of all, they need followers who urge them to be better sponsors and care enough to help them move forward. Believe that every day is a good day for change. Excellence in sponsorship needs to be every manager's mantra for achieving more within the organisation.

References

Cooke-Davies, T. 2005. The executive sponsor: the hinge upon which organisational project management maturity turns? *Proceedings of PMI, EMEA Congress, Edinburgh, Scotland*, conference paper. Newtown, PA: Project Management Institute.

Englund, R. and Bucero, A. 2006. *Project Sponsorship: Achieving Management Commitment for Project Success*. San Francisco, CA: Jossey-Bass.

Englund, R., Graham, R. and Dinsmore, P. 2003. *Creating the Project Office: A Manager's Guide to Leading Organizational Change*. Jossey-Bass Business and Management Series. San Francisco, CA: Jossey-Bass.

Gladwell, M. 2002. *The Tipping Point: How Little Things Can Make a Big Difference*. Boston, MA: Back Bay Books, Little Brown and Company.

Graham, R. and Englund, R. 2004. *Creating an Environment for Successful Projects*, 2nd edn. San Francisco, CA: Jossey-Bass.

Urban, C. 2004. The human factor of change management. *Training*, 22 December. Available at http://www.trainingmag.com/article/human-factor-change-management, accessed May 2001.

PART II
The Effects of Culture

5

How Groups Shape Information and Decisions

Ruth Murray-Webster

The starting premise of this chapter is that groups of people working in teams are central to organisational life. Although individual stakeholders are important and influential to some degree, there are not many individual people who have the structural and moral authority to lead an organisation alone. Groups of people, working to achieve shared objectives, are the organisational unit that this chapter focuses on. The role of groups in their 'advising upwards' endeavour is explored; from the perspective of the group as the 'advisor', and the group as the 'advised'.

The chapter starts with an exploration of the notion of information and decision quality – it works from an assumption that to be successful in advising upwards, it is important to have a clear understanding of what constitutes information that is fit for purpose and 'decision-ready'.

Next, the chapter looks at how teams shape:

- information that is constructed and passed on, and

- decisions that are taken as a result of this information.

A range of influences on collective behaviour are explored. The notion of groupthink (Janis, 1971) is discussed; what it is, why it occurs and its impact on information and decisions. Then other influences – 'beyond groupthink' – are highlighted.

But so what? What can teams do differently to provide better-quality information to enable better-quality decisions? What can individuals working within teams do to facilitate overall improvement? The implications for advising upwards are highlighted and discussed.

The objective of this chapter is to give people usable information about the influences on the provision of quality information and what the impacts on decision-making can be. The chapter also aims to provide practical guidance on how to overcome communication and decision-making barriers in order to improve the performance of working groups and teams as they attempt to engage and influence stakeholders.

The content of this chapter has drawn heavily on earlier published work by the author and David Hillson (Murray-Webster and Hillson, 2008; Hillson and Murray-Webster, 2007).

Information and Decision Quality

There can be little argument with the idea that 'good' decisions rely on the timely availability of 'good' information. But what is a good decision? And what constitutes good information?

There is an extensive body of research related to decision-making, both in general, and under uncertainty. In its simplest terms, a decision is an allocation of resources (time, money and goodwill) made in order to achieve an objective. The decision-maker is the person or party with control over the resource allocation. They decide whether to make an allocation of resources depending on their objectives and the values and motives that underpin those objectives.

Every decision situation has three core features:

1. The articulation of the objective or decision to be made (the framing of the challenge);

2. The uncertainties that could affect the outcome (the risks); and

3. The outcome itself.

The majority of decisions are made without the aid of specialist decision analysis or models to represent the relationships between these three core features, and this is entirely appropriate and necessary. However, sometimes the decision-maker needs to use more structured tools to compare alternative courses of action and their consequences before deciding what to do.

Clearly, decision-making is more than just the decision itself. Decisions are reached through a process that can be implicit or explicit, simple or complex. As a result, there are two distinct elements to consider when determining whether a decision is 'good' or not, namely:

- The quality of the decision-making process adopted; and

- The effectiveness of the decision outcome in achieving objectives.

These two distinct aspects of decision-making are not necessarily correlated. While people would hope that a good decision-making process would result in a good outcome, this may not be the case. It is entirely possible to have a perfectly good decision-making process that results in an unsuccessful outcome. Many people invest in stocks and shares but do not realise a profit. This does not necessarily mean that the original investment decision was poor based on the information available at the time – sometimes people take a chance based on the available information and are just unlucky.

Conversely, it may be expected that a poor decision-making process would result in a suboptimal outcome, but this may not be the case and a deficient decision-making process can end up with a good outcome. For example, you and your children may arrive safely at your destination after driving down the motorway above the speed limit and with your children unrestrained in the back seat. This successful outcome does not mean that the original decision was good. You were lucky!

These two aspects of decision-making – process and outcome – are relevant in all decisions made by all decision-makers, whether individuals or groups, regardless of the complexity of competing objectives, the inherent risks in the situation, or the multiplicity of alternative courses of action that could be adopted. However, defining and measuring the characteristics of a good outcome is almost impossible. There are undoubtedly some situations where a decision-outcome could be mathematically modelled and predicted with some certainty, assuming all the variables are understood and can be clearly defined. In most situations, this is not the case. Even if the variables can be defined in principle, and the interdependencies between them mapped, most decisions are taken under uncertainty where information is best represented in ranges that reflect that uncertainty rather than in precise, but maybe 'precisely incorrect' values. It is not practical to think about the quality of decision outcome. However, research and experience agree that considerable value *can* come from improved decision-making processes.

It is easier to define and measure the characteristics of a good process, as opposed to measuring the optimality of a decision outcome. For example, a good decision-making process is likely to be characterised by most or all of the following:

- The right people are involved;

- All objectives are clearly understood as far as possible;

- Uncertainties that could affect achievement of objectives (both damaging threats and beneficial opportunities) are identified, assessed and managed;

- Communication processes and values exist that allow perspectives to be shared openly;

- Hidden agendas are exposed and dealt with openly;

- Differences in perspective that different people bring to the table are explored and valued;

- People are willing to resolve any conflicts in the interests of making the optimal decision;

- Data are collected and analysed as rationally as possible; and

- A range of alternatives is considered, not just the obvious one, and alternatives are compared and traded-off against each other.

Several models exist to define and calibrate the appropriateness of a decision-making process. One of these models, from Strategic Decisions Group., a company affiliated to Stanford University in the United States, is described below. The model uses the language of quality management to determine whether the decision-making process was 'fit for purpose' in the circumstances.

This model assesses the quality or fitness for purpose of the decision at the point at which it is being made. It examines six main features of the decision-making process used to get to that point. The list below summarises the main decision quality criteria (adapted from Strategic Decision Group) which are then discussed in more detail.

- Appropriate frame;

- Creative, feasible alternatives;

- Meaningful, reliable information;

- Clear values and trade-offs;

- Logically correct reasoning; and

- Commitment to action.

The first question to ask is, 'Is the decision framed appropriately?' This question addresses whether there is a clear purpose and defined scope that has been agreed upon following discussion. It requires conscious exploration of assumptions, issues, concerns, perspectives and other sources of bias. The decision problem is then phrased in such a way to present the decision-maker with as neutral a choice as possible. A quality decision has a shared perspective of scope and the decisions to be addressed by all the relevant decision-makers and stakeholders.

The second question asks, 'Have a number of creative and valid alternatives been identified that span the solution space?' Most decisions have more than two possible options, but often groups will offer up only one alternative to business as usual, missing or ignoring other possibilities. When coming up with a number of alternatives there is often no clear winner, but it should be possible to identify the best attributes of each alternative. Work may also be needed to confirm the feasibility of different alternatives. A quality decision chooses the feasible alternative that combines as many of the best attributes from other alternatives as possible.

Third, 'Has the right amount of appropriate information been gathered to support each alternative?' Meaningful, reliable information makes clear what is important, and is explicit, correct and based on appropriate facts, whilst taking into account all knowable risks (threats and opportunities). A quality decision is linked to a structured risk-management process where uncertainty is quantified and the limits of knowledge are known.

The fourth question to be answered is 'Have clear criteria been established that represent the value being sought by the decision-makers and enable optimal trade-offs to be made?' Wants and needs are discussed and translated into clear attributes that represent success. This involves engaging stakeholders, understanding their value drivers and being explicit about important preferences and expectations as far as possible. A quality decision has clear and explicit attributes, and the relevant priority between these attributes is articulated allowing trade-offs to be made.

Fifth, 'Is the logic underpinning the decision clear and correct?' This question examines links and dependencies so that models can be created with explicit logic. This assumes that logically correct reasoning cannot exist if decision-makers rely on single-point, deterministic information instead of using a probabilistic approach. Deterministic thinking is common in Western societies, with the conviction that there is 'one right answer'. This leads to rejection of possible optimal solutions. Probabilistic approaches, supported by simulation models, can address multiple possible outcomes based on source data, allowing more feasible options to be considered. Accordingly a quality decision has clear, explicit, correct logic where dependencies are clearly mapped and probabilistic analysis has been performed.

Finally, the test of a quality decision asks 'Is there commitment to action from key players?' Lack of active interest by key decision-makers is likely to lead to insurmountable organisational hurdles. Active participation is needed by the right people. For a quality decision to exist there needs to be buy-in and commitment to action from the decision-makers as well as the groups that are required to implement the decision.

Decision-making groups can take each of these six questions in turn and decide the degree to which the decision-making process has satisfied the criteria. Results can be plotted on a simple radar plot (as illustrated in Figure 5.1), to determine whether the process has been appropriate. The aim is not to meet all six criteria perfectly, but any weaknesses exposed by this analysis can be addressed to strengthen the decision-making process in future.

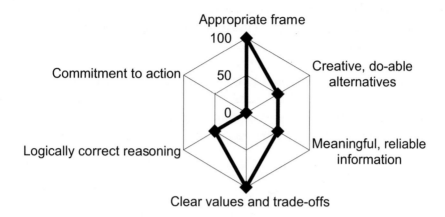

Figure 5.1   Example radar plot of decision quality attributes

Use of such a decision quality model provides a focus on what is needed to present decision-ready information to stakeholders. Influencing stakeholders, particularly senior individuals and groups, relies in large measure on the quality of information presented to them, and the ease with which this information can be processed, interpreted and used. Advising upwards can never assure good decision outcomes, but it can make good outcomes more likely by ensuring that decisions are made using good information and a quality process.

Groupthink and its Effect on Information and Decisions

Groupthink is a term used by Irving L. Janis (1971), a social psychologist, following his extensive studies into decisions made by senior policy-making groups in the USA. Groupthink is most often associated with Janis's work with the John F. Kennedy government decision to invade Cuba (the Bay of Pigs), however Janis also researched other major US government policy decisions including the escalation of the war in Vietnam and preparations for a potential attack on Pearl Harbour.

In organisational life, the term groupthink is used widely, almost as part of our everyday understanding of the potential for group dynamics to influence decision-making. It tends to be used loosely to describe situations when decision-makers feel there is safety in numbers and where groups end up making a decision that none of the individual members of the group would have made alone. Is this what Janis meant by groupthink?

Janis was clear when approaching his work that groups of people working together are subject to powerful social pressures to conform to the norms of the particular group. But is social conformity and group morale more important than critical thinking when key decisions are to be made? Unfortunately, Janis found that it can be.

Writing in 1971, Janis summed up the main principle of groupthink:

> The more amiability and esprit de corps there is among the members of a policy-making in-group, the greater the danger that independent critical thinking will be replaced by groupthink, which is likely to result in irrational and dehumanizing actions directed against out-groups.

Since Janis's original work focused on country-level decisions about national security, many other scholars have gone on to research and write about groupthink in other decision-making situations, how it works as a powerful biasing influence on groups, and how it can be managed. What makes groupthink as a phenomenon so important to organisational life at a practical level is that all the evidence from research supports that the groupthink effect is everywhere – an endemic part of organisational life. As a result, a keen awareness of groupthink when advising upwards has to be of critical importance.

The following list provides a summary of the main symptoms of groupthink, adapted from Janis and Mann's book that analysed conflict, choice and commitment in decision-making (1977).

- *Illusion of invulnerability*: members ignore obvious danger, take extreme risks and are overly optimistic.

- *Collective rationalisation*: members discredit and explain away warnings that are contrary to the current thinking of the group.

- *Illusion of morality*: members believe their decisions are morally correct, ignoring the ethical consequences of their decisions.

- *Excessive stereotyping*: the group constructs negative stereotypes of people with opposing views from outside the group, seeing them as 'rivals'.

- *Pressure for conformity*: there is pressure put on group members who express arguments against the group's stereotypes, illusions or commitments, viewing such opposition as disloyalty.

- *Self-censorship*: group members withhold their dissenting views and counter-arguments.

- *Illusion of unanimity*: members perceive falsely that everyone agrees with the group's decision; silence is seen as consent.

- *Mindguards*: some members appoint themselves to the role of protecting the group from adverse information that might threaten group complacency.

Everyone reading this, can be (and probably is) a member of a group that is advising upwards, and is influenced by some or all of the above symptoms of groupthink. Everyone reading this, can be (and probably is) a member of a group that is being advised, and is rejecting the information because it contradicts current norms, or is accepting the information because it supports current norms. How can organisations have 'good' information and 'good' decision-making processes if we human beings are so susceptible to the need to socially align and conform rather than challenge? What can be done about it?

In our work looking at the influence of groupthink and other influential effects on choices made by human beings in risky and important situations, David Hillson and I drew heavily on the work of psychologists such as Salovey and Mayer (1990) and Goleman (1995) and their work on emotional intelligence and emotional literacy. If the primary causes of groupthink are emotional, representing our need to connect with and stay aligned with other human beings with whom we share key responsibilities; we need to understand how to manage those emotional influences. Without describing emotional literacy in detail here, the starting point is always awareness – self-awareness and the awareness of others.

This is the first point offered by Janis and Mann as the steps to avoiding groupthink, also from their 1977 book; summarised in the list below.

- The group must be aware of the causes and consequences of groupthink.

- The leaders should be neutral when assigning a decision-making task to a group, initially withholding all preferences and expectations and supporting open inquiry.

- The leader must give high priority to airing objections and doubts and be accepting of criticism.

- Groups must always consider unpopular alternatives, explicitly assigning the role of 'devil's advocate' to several strong members of the group.

- Groups should consider dividing into two separate deliberative bodies as feasibilities are evaluated.

- Groups must spend time surveying all warning signals from other relevant groups and organisations.

- After reaching a preliminary consensus on a decision, the leader must encourage and support the expression of all residual doubts so the matter can be reconsidered.

- Groups must engage outside experts in vital decision-making.

- Tentative decisions must be discussed with trusted colleagues not in the decision-making group.

- The organisation must establish several independent decision-making groups to work on critical issues or policy.

It's clear that some decisions made by groups and teams are so important and so risky that all the steps above would be relevant. But for decisions that may be less important and risky, the steps are equally useful as an agenda item for the group. Awareness of groupthink and its influence on information and decisions is important at the individual level of course, but it is the explicit awareness and discussion of groupthink *by the group* that gives license to expose those specific factors that, unchallenged, might lead to poor judgements and inappropriate advice to decision-makers.

Evidence would suggest that all human beings and decision-making groups are silently influenced by groupthink unless they take steps to address this head on. Of course, there will be times when it is in some people's interest to leave groupthink unchallenged, as it suits their individual agenda or purpose. Sometimes that person will be you, or me.

Groups certainly do shape information and decisions – but maybe not always appropriately. The challenge for organisations is how to provide the context where groups provide challenge and think critically, whilst supporting the basic human need to connect and collaborate.

There are many books and other forms of literature that discuss how organisations, and leaders in particular, can provide this context. The author recommends the following further reading as being directly relevant to the challenge of enabling an effective context so that advising upwards attempts can be successful:

- *The Difference* by Scott E. Page (2007). An interesting and scientifically grounded discussion of how diversity (of thought and perception) consistently trumps ability.

- *Primal Leadership: Learning to Lead with Emotional Intelligence* by Daniel Goleman, Richard Boyatzis and Annie McKee (2002). A practical guide to creating the leadership skills that will enable you to counter the invidious connotations of groupthink.

Beyond Groupthink, Other Influences

As already discussed, groupthink has been demonstrated to be pervasive in organisational life, and, at least at a summary level, the risk posed by groupthink is understood in contemporary organisations. But are there other influences that shape a group's ability to provide good quality information and decisions when advising upwards?

To answer this question, it's important to unpick not just the influences of group dynamics, of which there are several in addition to groupthink, but also influences on individual group members. A study by Murray-Webster and Hillson (2008) showed the directly influential impact of the perspectives of the group leader on the decisions made the group. In that study, real situations were exposed where powerful stakeholders who cared about the decision to be made, 'carried' the decision irrespective of the views of other stakeholders. In those situations, it wasn't groupthink at play, but a tendency to 'follow the leader' irrespective of whether the leader's perspectives matched those of the rest of the group, or whether that perspective made sense in terms of decision quality.

Murray-Webster and Hillson's work (2008) is designed to help individuals and groups make better decisions in risky and important situations, and their whole argument can't be repeated here. However, key principles for advising upwards can be explored, as follows.

The Triple Strand of Influences on Perception

In response to a vast academic literature spanning risk psychology, behavioural economics and decision theory, Murray-Webster and Hillson (2008, 2007) propose that human perception of risky and important situations is fundamentally shaped by three categories of influences.

These can be grouped under three headings:

1. Conscious assessments which are largely rational;

2. Subconscious factors including heuristics or mental short-cuts and other sources of cognitive bias; and

3. Gut-level affective factors, including feelings and emotions.

Table 5.1 provides a composite list of the factors covered by each heading, drawing on the work of various authors, some of whom use different terms to describe the same factor.

Table 5.1   Summary of potential influences on perception of risk and risk attitude (from Murray-Webster and Hillson 2008)

Conscious factors (situational and rational)	Subconscious factors — Heuristics	Subconscious factors — Cognitive bias	Affective factors (emotions and feelings)
Familiarity 'I've/we've done something like this before' (or) 'I've/we've never done something like this before'	**Intuition** 'Feels right, I won't look for any more data'	**Prospect theory** 'A bird in the hand is worth two in the bush', 'Double or quits'	**Fear (dread, worry, concern...)** 'Of consequences of something happening'
Manageability 'I/we know what to do to manage this' (or) 'I/we don't know what to do to manage this'	**Representativeness** 'This must be like this other one I've seen before'	**Repetition bias** 'Undue importance given to repeated data – must be true!'	**Desire (excitement, wonder...)** 'Of consequences of something happening'
Proximity 'If it happens it will happen soon so need to sort it now' (or) 'It wouldn't happen for ages, we've got time'	**Availability** 'Most recent data is most memorable.' Closely linked to reality traps where too much value is attributed to existing situations, blinded by what is, cannot see what might be if could disengage from reality	**Illusion of control** 'Exaggerate personal influence, discount luck'	**Love (lust, adoration, attraction...)** 'I want it/more of it'
Propinquity 'If it happens it would really matter to me/us personally' (or) 'If it happens it would affect objectives, but it wouldn't really matter to me/us personally'	**Confirmation trap** 'Undue confidence – selective perception, trust me, I'm a ...?'	**Illusion of knowledge** 'Some knowledge or relevant experience masks what isn't known, particularly if the person feels they "should" know'	**Hate (dislike, disgust...)** 'I don't want it/less of it'
Severity of impact 'It it happens the effect would be huge (or insignificant)'	**Lure of choice** 'Biased by options that include future alternative judgements – keeping options open'	**Intelligence trap** 'Ability to mentally construct and verbally reason (IQ) means that the conclusions must be correct'	**Joy (happy, carefree...)** 'Life is good, more good things are possible'
Group dynamics and organisational culture 'The norms of how this particular group behaves'	**Affect heuristic** 'Seeking pleasure, avoiding pain'	**Optimism bias** 'Delusional optimism driven by cognitive biases and/or perceived organisational pressures and norms'	
	Anchoring 'Attach illogical significance to available data, first impressions last'	**Fatalism bias** 'Ignore probabilities, focus on impact of outcomes – always optimistically, that is the best case will happen'	
	Group effects, e.g. groupthink 'We all think this way'	**Precautionary principle** 'Ignore probabilities, focus on impact of outcomes – always pessimistically, that is the worst case will happen'	
		Hindsight bias 'Fail to learn – I knew it all along'	

Although the various factors affecting perception of risk can be detailed separately under the three headings of conscious, subconscious and affective factors, they do not exist or operate in isolation. They form a triple strand of influence, combining to affect how an individual or a group responds in any given situation, as illustrated in Figure 5.2.

Figure 5.2   Triple strand of influences on perception of risk and risk attitude

Source: The triple strand of influences on perception of risk and risk attitude is copyright 2008 © Ruth Murray-Webster and David Hillson.

The following paragraphs describe each of three strands in turn. While each strand can be teased out separately to aid understanding and explanation, in reality the three are intertwined and each affects the others. There are many cross-links between the different influences on perception, forming a complex web, the effect of which can be hard to predict.

CONSCIOUS FACTORS

These factors are based on the visible and measurable characteristics of the situation within which the decision is being made. Typical conscious factors are listed in Table 5.1. Such factors are known to bias perceptions of risky and important situations for individuals and within groups. They operate in a systematic way, allowing corrections to be made where their influences are exposed. Situational assessments are the most rational part of the triple strand of influences as they tend to be explicit and based on conscious thought.

SUBCONSCIOUS FACTORS

These factors include mental short-cuts made to facilitate decision-making (heuristics) and other sources of cognitive bias. Heuristics operate at both individual and group levels, and provide mechanisms for making sense of complex or uncertain situations. Based on previous experience, many of these heuristics are useful because they allow rapid filtering of data to determine the most important elements, easing the decision-making task. Unfortunately the fact that heuristics operate subconsciously means that their influence is often hidden and they can introduce significant bias into decisions. Whereas heuristics can have a positive influence, cognitive biases do not. The effect is to skew perception and decision-making in a way that is not real or beneficial. Table 5.1 contains common heuristics and sources of cognitive bias that effect both individuals and groups. Groupthink is just one of these potentially biasing mechanisms.

AFFECTIVE FACTORS

These visceral gut-level responses are based on instinctive emotion or deep underlying feelings rather than rational assessments. All human beings store emotion-charged memories in the limbic system within the brain, and these emotions are automatically triggered in situations perceived to be similar to the stored memory. A wide range of emotions or affective states could influence decision-making (as listed in Table 5.1), although some researchers suggest that the primary influence for any human being is to seek pleasure or to avoid pain.

THE TRIPLE STRAND

The three sets of influences which form the triple strand are each important in the context of decision-making, because they each influence perception, and perception drives choices which in turn affects the quality of decisions made under conditions of uncertainty. It is possible to adopt a reductionist approach when considering these factors, examining the influence of each one in turn. However, the triple-strand model has a more important message. The strands do not exist or operate in isolation, but are interwoven to form a complex set of influences. An individual in a decision-making group may have made an apparently rational assessment of the situation and decided on a particular approach, but this assessment will have been shaped by the operation of subconscious heuristics, and coloured by the person's underlying emotions.

An example might be as follows:

CASE STUDY 5.1

A group leader is presented with the challenge of advising the senior management group whether to invest in an expensive upgrade to facilities. The business case for the upgrade has been prepared and this is marginally acceptable in terms of its rate of return assuming that the productivity of the group will increase as a direct result of the new kit, and that productivity gains could not be achieved by other means. The group leader knows deep down that productivity gains could be achieved by other means, but that would involve making some unpopular decisions to change working practices. Previous attempts to implement new ways of working have been unpopular and a decision that would take a renewed attempt in this direction is one that the group leader is fearful of making, but would never disclose. The group leader also perceives that it would be exciting and a key career opportunity to lead the project to purchase and install the new kit. New equipment would provide the 'excuse' for tackling some of the underlying group issues and feels altogether more comfortable and manageable. The group leader is aware of other companies that have upgraded their facilities in the way they are suggesting – in fact they have a close friend who has experience that can be drawn upon. The numbers in the business case are based on this experience from another location. As far as the group leader is concerned, the upgrade should go ahead. But would the advice 'upwards' be appropriate if the effects of the triple strand of influences on perception were left unchallenged?

This assessment is complex enough at an individual level, but would be even more so had the perspectives of the group leader's immediate working group, or the senior management group who must make the decision, have been brought into focus.

The reality is that human judgement is shaped by a complex tangle of influences. The message of the *triple strand* is twofold:

1.   Unchallenged, the tightly intertwined strands appear as one and cannot be distinguished.

2.   With intent, awareness and confidence, the triple-strand can be unpicked when the situation is important enough to warrant 'good' information and a 'quality' decision.

So how can this be done? Not without being willing to tap into the underlying human drivers of the situation. A simple (at first glance) model, the Six As shown in Figure 5.3, is used to explain each of the steps and the complications therein.

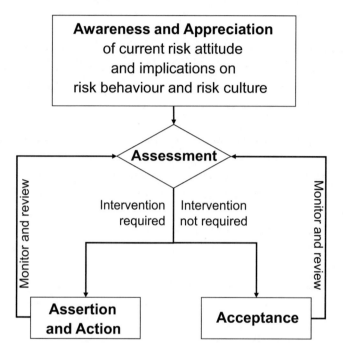

Figure 5.3   The six As model
Source: The six As model is copyright © 2008 Ruth Murray-Webster and David Hillson.

The thinking behind the Six As model is grounded in the management theories that we collectively label *emotional literacy*. The principles underlying emotional literacy suggest that life is largely what we make it; that human beings can be more in control of their destiny than they often realise or accept.

The starting point is not just *awareness*, but awareness with *appreciation*, because these are both essential in any situation that is risky and important, either for individuals working alone, individuals who are part of a group, or for the group itself.

Without awareness, there is no insight or understanding of the behaviours displayed by ourselves or by others. This failure to understand inevitably leads to skewed perceptions and judgements. Lacking awareness leads to a high chance that the situation will manage individuals and the group, rather than them managing it proactively. This is an immature position, and can be potentially dangerous.

If awareness is present but without appreciation, then diversity is squashed, prejudices are reinforced, talent is unappreciated and biases become entrenched. Any or all of these impacts will bias perceptions and judgements, leading to poor-quality decisions.

Awareness and appreciation help individuals and groups move from immature and unmanaged management of risky choices to a more mature approach. In particular it is critical to be aware of and appreciate three distinct aspects of risky and important group decision-making, namely:

1. The risk attitude of self and others, particularly those stakeholders who are powerful and are close to the impact of the decision;

2. The decision context and organisational norms that may bias the decision-making group, consciously or unconsciously; and

3. The group dynamics and how they may help or hinder an effective decision-making process.

Murray-Webster and Hillson's study (2008) also suggested that awareness and appreciation of the secondary factors (that is, less powerful stakeholders, national culture and societal norms) may be important, but found that in most cases these factors do not play a primary role in determining a good decision process and outcome.

Armed with awareness and appreciation of the situation, decision-makers and those advising stakeholders need to make a judgement. Is the current situation going to lead towards an appropriate end if left unmanaged – or not?

This is the assessment step in the Six As model.

Not all situations will warrant any intervention at all. Where a proactive response is not appropriate, affordable or actionable, the situation can be *accepted*.

Acceptance in this regard can be seen as parallel to the accept response strategy in a standard risk-management process – it does not mean ignore! Just as accepted risks have a nominated risk owner who is responsible for monitoring the situation and implementing a contingency or fallback plan if predefined trigger conditions occur, so must groups take responsibility for watching accepted situations to ensure their conditions of acceptability don't change.

It is also important to recognise that accepting the existing group position does not mean it will never be challenged. Using the analogy of a risk-management process again, accepted risks are actively monitored, and contingency or fallback plans may be implemented if necessary. They are also reassessed and different response strategies may be selected if the risk becomes unacceptable. In the same way, some group attitudes may be accepted in the short term but may need to be managed more actively at some later point. A particular group attitude may be accepted over a short period of time (for example within the bounds of a single decision-meeting where a stakeholder has decided in advance not to intervene unless a particular situation arises). However, the same group attitude may be challenged later or in the longer term; (for example if the same group is making a series of risky and important decisions), with use of assertion and action as appropriate.

Management often requires someone in the decision-making group to make a conscious choice to challenge the prevalent mode of thinking and the natural course of the decision-making process in such a way that builds confidence in the final decision, rather than destroying it. To achieve this type of challenge effectively, assertion and action are required.

Such challenging interventions are easier to describe than to carry out. They require highly polished leadership skills to discover and use human discontent or conflict for constructive, positive purpose. They are also difficult because they need to break into the norms adopted by the group as a result of the influence of powerful stakeholders, and/or the context and norms of the situation.

It may not be so hard for the acknowledged leader of a decision-making group to intervene in the natural flow in order to change direction. However, for others in the group, making such an intervention may carry personal risk as the status quo is unsettled. Our research has demonstrated that in practice individuals tend first to decide whether to align with the behaviour of the leader, or with the norms of the situation. Having made the choice to do so, they can then find it very difficult to influence group processes.

This observation is consistent with other views in organisational behaviour that emphasise that alignment and sensemaking are natural human processes (for example Weick 1995). To change group thinking it is necessary to find common ground around which group members can align. If this is to lead to a more successful decision process and outcome, the common ground must not be skewed by perceptual biases. An essential skill in achieving this is the ability to frame context, objectives and questions in a non-biased, inclusive way. Framing the whole on behalf of the group requires an individual to exercise emotional literacy. In particular those parts of emotional literacy called 'intentionality' (alternatively called impulse control or delayed gratification), emotional control and restraint are needed. This requires a motivation to clarify and open up rather than to justify and close down.

In addition to the ability to frame and present situations so they can be discussed and debated with minimal bias, leaders must also have the ability to harness discontent for a constructive purpose. The importance of 'constructive discontent' was recognised by US industrialist William Wrigley Jnr who said, 'When two people agree in business, one is unnecessary.' Wrigley knew that constructive discontent is a prerequisite to effective decision-making in groups, in order to harness the power of attitudes that may be ineffective if left unexplored, and to ensure all perspectives are considered in striving for a quality decision to be made.

Group dynamics can easily become destructive. If this is to be prevented, interventions are required that are assertive, rather than passive or aggressive. It is important to adopt an approach to conflict resolution that is creative, using optimism and appropriate humour to 'oil the wheels', and exercising uplifting human behaviours and an attitude of abundance.

So in summary, it is not always necessary to move from the first two As of awareness and appreciation to the final two As of assertion and action. This is only required if there is a significant risk that the dominant attitude of the 'lead influence' (i.e. the leader or culture, whichever is prevailing) will lead the group towards a poor quality decision. If assessment of the situation leads to the conclusion that the unmanaged position is OK, acceptance is the best approach. However, where there is a significant risk of a poor decision-making process or outcome arising from the unmanaged perceptions and attitudes of the group, then intervention is required through assertion and action.

Barriers to Managing Group Attitudes

The simplicity of the Six As model should not lead us to think that the process is simple to manage. There are a number of barriers that need to be overcome to prevent group dynamics negatively influencing the quality of information and decisions created and communicated to senior stakeholders.

Barriers include the following:

1. Inappropriate alignment;

2. Wrongly-perceived assertion;

3. The lone voice;

4. Contributing vs facilitating;

5. Unsuccessful interventions;

6. Cross-cultural implications; and

7. Corporate habits.

Each of these barriers is discussed below, illustrated with an example from the original Murray-Webster and Hillson (2008) study.

ALIGNING IS NATURAL, BUT ALIGNING WITH THE WRONG THING IS INEFFECTIVE

Organisational behavioural theories emphasise the natural human tendency to seek alignment in order to reduce conflict and maximise sensemaking. Sometimes however groups align around the wrong thing and it becomes necessary to break into this in order to reach a more effective solution. The following factors are important in supporting such realignment:

*   Framing and the use of language to present alternatives in a non-biased and non-threatening way;

- Understanding and using the power bases in the meeting effectively;

- Intentionality, delaying gratification in exchange for a better longer-term outcome;

- Emotional honesty and restraint, managing your own anger, fear, delight, enthusiasm appropriately; and

- An ability to be assertive and use constructive discontent to channel energies into a positive outcome.

CASE STUDY 5.2

The group were almost completely aligned on the decision-outcome. The decision was supported by the most senior person (Chief Executive), and also by the programme manager who had led the work and most other people in the decision-making meeting. A few were more sceptical and cautioned restraint, but their power base was not strong enough to re-direct or halt the momentum on the direction of the ensuing decision. The decision was made to launch a new product on time, even though it had not been completed to specification. The result was a financial disaster for the company. This indicates that alignment in itself is not sufficient to ensure a good decision outcome.

THERE'S A FINE LINE BETWEEN ASSERTION AND (PERCEIVED) AGGRESSION OR MANIPULATION

An intervention that is intended to be assertive can easily be perceived as aggressive or manipulative, if the appreciation step in the Six As model has not been completed effectively. Assertive interventions are coloured by a whole range of aspects of communication, including tone of voice, the words used, non-verbal gestures and facial expressions. If humour is used this can easily be misinterpreted if there is not a common platform of awareness and appreciation on which to build. From foundations of awareness and appreciation, a creative conflict resolution approach, focused on win–win and built upon a belief of 'I'm OK, You're OK' can be adopted.

CASE STUDY 5.3

In this case honourable assertive intentions were interpreted as manipulation, because some of the group members were not aware of themselves or others, and/or did not appreciate the perspectives of others. This was a clear case of conflict arising when a decision needed to be made, when the situation may have been avoided through more open and honest communication earlier in the decision-making process.

Although assertion is good and sometimes necessary, without awareness and appreciation it can be misunderstood by others in the decision-making group. It is also possible for the assertive person to go 'over the edge' into aggression or manipulation if they do not maintain a sufficient degree of self-awareness.

IT'S HARD TO BE A LONE VOICE

If an individual is in the position of holding a counter view to the rest of the decision-making group, it is very difficult to break into the consensus, even if the person has great influencing skills and a persuasive argument.

CASE STUDY 5.4

One powerful stakeholder who cared a lot about the decision outcome wanted a different outcome from the rest of the powerful stakeholders. Interestingly, this person was representing a large number of others not present at the meeting. In this particular example, the decision outcome has turned out to be successful, although this was only predicted rather than known at the time the decision was made. For the person with a differing perspective to have had more of an influence at the meeting, they needed to find ways of being heard among the majority view, perhaps by lobbying or other influencing prior to the meeting. Sometimes such lobbying is unsuccessful, in which case it may be best for the lone voice to make their contribution clearly during the decision meeting, and then allow the process to take its course.

BOTH CONTRIBUTING TO AND MANAGING THE DECISION PROCESS CAN BE TOO DIFFICULT

If a decision is risky and important, a neutral facilitator can be very useful to frame the situation, uncover and challenge positions and perceptions, allow creative alternative positions to be explored and help the process along with suitable optimism, humour and activities to unfreeze entrenched positions.

CASE STUDY 5.5

The process to make an important and very risky decision for the business was managed by an internal neutral facilitator. This person organised the process, brought the players together in advance to gain a deeper awareness and appreciation of each other's views, and ensured that the conflicting stakeholder positions were reconciled and a way forward was agreed that was optimal for the business. The role of a neutral facilitator is generally valuable in many ways, including the fact that it releases key stakeholders to play a full part in contributing to the decision-making process.

TAKING A CHANCE DOESN'T ALWAYS PAY OFF

As with all risks, individuals and groups in decision-making situations win some and lose some. Despite our best endeavours, there are some situations that just don't return the expected result. This is particularly true when individuals in decision-making groups decide to intervene against the prevailing group perspective. Such interventions involve personal risk, and inevitably some decisions to intervene and attempt to manage situations will be unsuccessful. Dealing with this requires resilience and relative regard, which are key elements of applied emotional literacy.

Resilience allows a person to bounce back and be able to manage any stressful side effects of having taken a personal risk but being unsuccessful. Relative regard is important to maintain confidence in oneself whilst at the same time appreciating the positions of the other parties. It would be perfectly natural in such a situation to resort to blaming yourself, or blaming others for the situation, but this is an immature position to take.

CASE STUDY 5.6

The most senior person resisted all attempts to consider alternative solutions. One stakeholder decided to intervene and assert another position using all the leadership and influencing skills he could muster. he failed to influence the position of the most senior person, and therefore the group followed the most senior person into a decision that was more costly for the organisation than it needed to be. This decision eroded value for the organisation, although it met the needs of the senior person and most of the decision-making group. The person who intervened lost significant credibility within the group.

CROSS-CULTURAL GROUPS HAVE ADDED COMPLICATIONS

Although the influence of national cultural differences were relatively less important than other factors in the Murray-Webster and Hillson study (2008), despite a number of the decisions analysed involving people from multiple national backgrounds, these influences cannot be ignored. It is particularly important to appreciate the influence of national cultural norms on the expectations of individuals. For example, a person from a culture where hierarchy is highly respected and there is large 'power distance' between bosses and subordinates (for example France or India) is much more likely to 'follow the leader' than a person from a culture which values each individual's contribution equally (for example the Netherlands or Sweden). The study of national culture is vast in its own right and cannot be dealt with in depth here, other than by acknowledging the importance of being aware of and appreciating cultural influences on perception and behaviour.

CORPORATE HABITS CAN BLIND US

In contrast to national culture, organisational culture was seen to be a significant influence on group behaviour in risky and important situations.

The natural tendency for individuals to align with organisational norms is a double-edged sword. Organisational cultural similarity is highly desirable in order to sustain purpose, meaning and cohesion. It becomes dangerous however when it leads to automatic habitual decision-making processes that are never challenged.

Our research did not explicitly examine the effect of systematic organisational biases that skew decisions. However, our wider experience indicates that these exist and that it is important to understand them if we are to appreciate group behaviour in risky and important situations. One of our client organisations wants all decisions to be backed up by data rather than to be based on intuition and feelings. As a result they routinely delay decisions until they have 'enough' information (though it is not clear how much is enough). This organisation has evidence from the wider market that they are losing strategic advantage by being too cautious and slow when making investment decisions. Another organisation is systematically biased by the desire for people to reach challenging 'stretch' targets. The external competition in the marketplace is matched by an internal competition between managers to achieve more and more challenging targets. This culture drives risk-seeking behaviour and decision-making that is more macho than meticulous. As a result, managers in this organisation are increasingly becoming burned-out and unable to make realistic assessments of what constitutes appropriate risk-taking.

Implications for Advising Upwards

So far in this chapter the notion of good information and quality decision-making has been explored. The role of groupthink and other influences on attitude, judgement and choice in risky and important situations has been discussed, in particular using the triple strand as a way of understanding the many influences that can become intertwined to shape the behaviour of individuals and decision-making groups.

The Six As model has been outlined; building on the field of emotional literacy and applying this directly to understanding and managing group attitudes in risky and important situations. Some common barriers to be aware of when deciding whether to intervene to improve group decision-making processes have briefly been outlined.

So do we now have enough to be able to improve the quality of information when advising upwards? Some final points are relevant.

PERSPECTIVE OF THE GROUP AS ADVISOR

Where the group is in the role of advisor, three further points are relevant.

Firstly, the group needs to be satisfied that their group processes have resulted in a challenged and valid decision-ready set of information. Whether or not the group has not reached consensus, the assumptions underpinning any advice or recommendation must be outlined. The practice of documenting and discussing assumptions has great power in ensuring that there is common understanding between stakeholders and a commitment to agreed action.

Secondly, the group must have considered the stakeholders they are advising – not to second-guess their perspectives but to have gained as much understanding as possible of the context for the decision and therefore the best way to present the information. Techniques for doing this are beyond the scope of this chapter but are covered elsewhere in this book.

Thirdly, it is likely there are many situations where the 'right' advice is not accepted only because the message was not explained well, or could not be 'heard' for another reason. Structuring recommendations so they are logical and 'tell the story' in such a way that senior stakeholders can engage with them is a key skill that is not covered in this chapter, other than to recommend the approach promoted by Barbara Minto (2002) for those who are interesting in improving their skills in this area. There is much that individuals and groups of individuals who are advising upwards can do to ensure that their message is good and it can be heard. However prepared the advising group is, there are influences out of their control regarding the people they are advising.

For good advice to be heard and acted upon, groups of senior stakeholders must be aware of and appreciate the multiple influences on group perception, attitude and choice for their own group – so there is a sufficient internal challenge. They must also be skilled in challenging the advice and recommendations made by advising groups. As a result this chapter contains relevant information for all people working in groups in organisations.

Conclusion

In this chapter I argue two things. First, that advising upwards in organisations is rarely done by an individual advising another individual. Instead, the advising and decision-making, following receipt of the advice, is done by people working in groups. This makes an understanding of groups and group behaviour critical when thinking about how to provide good advice.

Secondly I argue that the purpose of advising upwards is to support effective decision-making by the people receiving the advice, so any advisor needs to provide fit for purpose information that is decision-ready, so it enables quick and effective action.

Accordingly, the chapter brings together ideas about decision-making with ideas about group dynamics to provide insights into the aspects that people need to manage to ensure that they provide high-quality information in an effective way when attempting to influence senior stakeholders. Providing high quality, or fit for purpose information relies on the group, and the people that form part of the group being aware of and appreciating how influences such as groupthink, or other conscious, subconscious or emotion-based factors are affecting their message. Without this lack of awareness, the message could be unknowingly, systematically biased with the potential to provide poor-quality advice.

The chapter provides insights into what individuals and groups of individuals can do to overcome the influence of potentially biasing factors, thus improving their chances of success when advising others to act in the best interests of the organisation. Far from advising upwards being a one-way street when it comes to providing quality information in a way that can be heard and acted upon; the skills required apply to those doing the advising, and those being advised. Effective communication is always a two-way street and the way that groups shape information and decisions is relevant in both directions.

References

Goleman, D. 1995. *Emotional Intelligence: Why it Can Matter More Than IQ*. Bantam Dell, USA.

Goleman, D., Boyatzis, R. and McKee, A. 2002. *Primal Leadership: Learning to Lead with Emotional Intelligence*. Boston, MA: Harvard Business School Press.

Hillson, D.A. and Murray-Webster, R. 2007. *Understanding and Managing Risk Attitude*, 2nd edn. Farnham: Gower.

Janis, I.L. 1971. Groupthink. *Psychology Today*. November, 43.

Janis, I.L. 1982. *Groupthink*, 2nd edn. Chicago, IL: Houghton Mifflin.

Janis, I.L. and Mann, J. 1977. *Decision-making – A Psychological Analysis of Conflict, Choice and Commitment*. Chicago, IL: Free Press.

Minto, B. 2002. *The Pyramid Principle: Logic in Thinking and Writing*, 3rd edn. Harlow: Pearson Education.

Murray-Webster, R. and Hillson, D.A. 2008. *Managing Group Risk Attitude.* Farnham: Gower.

Page, S. 2007. *The Difference: How the Power of Diversity Creates Better Groups, Firms, Schools and Societies.* Princeton, NJ: Princeton University Press.

Salovey, P. and Mayer, J.D. 1990. Emotional intelligence. *Imagination, Cognition and Personality,* 9, 185.

Weick, K. 1995. *Sensemaking in Organizations.* Thousand Oaks, CA: Sage Publications.

6

East Meets West:
Working with a Chinese Boss

Soon Kheng Khor

There is an old saying in China: *your crisis can be an opportunity for someone else*. The impact of globalisation has created a 'flat world' (Friedman 2007) impacting whole countries, companies, communities and individuals: governments and societies can, and must, adapt. Asia-Pacific is the world's fastest-growing region: China and India in particular are making significant impact on the workforce and lifestyle of the rest of the world. The impressive economic growth in China over the last decade has created a phenomenon that multinational companies can no longer ignore. Most of them had made significant investment decisions in China via direct investment, joint ventures or the acquisition of Chinese companies. The 2008–2009 financial crisis might have brought significant negative impacts to many individuals, companies or countries, but some cash-rich Chinese companies have managed to seize golden opportunities in international markets via direct investment and mergers and acquisitions.

These Chinese-originated conglomerates have been operating from mainland China, Hong Kong, Taiwan, Macau and from South East Asian countries such as Malaysia and Singapore in activities such as:

- Australian mining industries;

- The world telecommunication industries, squeezing out European players; and

- Construction projects in the Middle East.

Within a very short time, China has emerged as a leader and major player in the global economy, overtaking many other nations in assets and market presence. The world has been infected by 'China fever'. Worldwide, about 40 million people are learning Mandarin, China's official spoken language and its most common dialect. Nearly 100,000 foreigners went to China to study Mandarin in 2006, more than twice the number five years earlier (Trini Tran 2008). Today, in 2010, while many other countries are still working through the consequences of the global financial crisis of 2009, China appears to have recovered from recession.[1]

This chapter is intended to be a general guide. It is still important to be aware of our tendency to stereotype, and to recognise that national cultural characteristics are only one aspect of an individual's way of viewing the world. Personality, previous experience and professional experience and training will also influence each person's expectations and perceptions: all these influences must be considered in any approach to advising upwards. Remember also that Chinese bosses are incorporating Western culture and Western management styles into their corporations, especially when operating outside of China. They may also have received part of their education and experience outside of China.[2] The structure of this chapter will be as follows: first, a discussion of the management philosophies that characterise the Western and Chinese business environments, and identification of some gaps, issues and challenges for those managers operating in the 'other environment' – that is for Western-trained managers working in Chinese businesses and for Chinese-trained managers working in Western businesses; this will be followed by advice on how to understand the expectations and management style of your Chinese boss, discussion of tools and techniques to improve your relationship and enable you to work closely and effectively together, concluding with a discussion of some practical ways to bridge the cultural divide.

---

1   Chinese influence will continue to strengthen around the world: some of the author's European friends are sending their children to Chinese language weekend classes to broaden their future job opportunities.
2   This has been the experience of the author.

Working with Your Chinese Boss

WE ARE DIFFERENT

It is common to hear an employee ask their boss *'Do you think I will get a bonus this year?'* The response will vary depending on the language and cultural background of the boss. Table 6.1 shows the range of possible answers.

Table 6.1   Range of uncertainty about receiving a bonus according to boss's answer

Answer = no	Answer = maybe	Answer = yes
	Maybe not	
	Perhaps	
	Let's see	
	Let's play it by ear	
	Depends	
	Let me check first	
	Can't decide	
	Can't tell now	
	Let's talk about it later	
Probability of bonus = 0%	Range of probability = between 1–99%	Probability of bonus = 100%

A direct *yes* or *no* is common if your boss is American or European; *maybe* is more common from Chinese bosses. 'Let's see' and 'Let's play it by ear' from a Chinese boss can be a polite way to say *no* without offending the employee. *Yes* would mean 'yes', but every other answer should not treated as *no*.

The Working Environment of a Chinese Company

Theory X and *Theory Y* (McGregor 1960) are theories of human motivation that have application in human resource management, organisational behaviour, organisational communication and organisational development. Theory X management style is often practiced in Chinese companies: it supposes that employees are inherently lazy and will avoid work if they can. Therefore, workers need to be closely supervised and comprehensive systems of controls developed. The resultant structure will be hierarchical with narrow span of control at every level. Employees will show little ambition without an incentive programme and will avoid responsibility whenever they can.[3]

Table 6.2 illustrates some (but not all) of the gaps and challenges a Western-trained professional may face when reporting to an Eastern-trained Chinese boss. It will focus on the differences between the direct process-oriented style of the Western-trained manager and the ambiguous and flexible people-centric style of the Chinese-trained boss, addressing the following aspects of management:

MANAGEMENT PHILOSOPHY

- organisational policy;

- leadership;

- winning the business;

- task planning;

- task execution; and

- reward and promotion.

COMMUNICATION AND DECISION-MAKING

- communication;

- meetings and discussions;

- decision-making; and

- conflict resolution.

---

3   Theory Y supposes that employees may be ambitious, self-motivated and exercise self-control: employees who enjoy their work and achieving work–life balance are not commonly seen in Chinese companies.

Table 6.2   Differences between Western and Chinese management styles

	Western style: direct	Chinese style: ambiguity, flexibility
Management philosophy		
Organisation policy	Results-oriented	Ambiguities, flexibility
Leadership	Leadership is part of a career in management and at all levels	Organisation owner decides scope and responsibilities
Winning the business	Win the business through capability	Win the business via trust and *guanxi*
Task planning	Process-oriented	People-centric
Task execution	Standard Operating Procedure (SOP) or job description	Depends on what the Chinese boss says at that particular time
Reward and promotion	Pre-agreed key performance indicator at individual and group level	'Perceived' value of the contribution. Promotion based on relationship with Chinese boss
Communication and decision-making		
Communication	Able to differentiate work and non-work communication	Not easy to separate work and non-work communication
Meetings and discussions	Scope of meeting is usually constrained to the agenda	There may not be an agenda, or 'etc.' or 'others' may be included: 'etc.' and 'others' are often the main topic of discussion
Decision-making	Follows procedures with consideration of facts, impacts consequences, roles and responsibilities, authorities	No standard decision-making process. Depends on the situation and who has the interest to influence the decision
Conflict resolution	'The facts' and problem-solving techniques used to resolve the conflict	A combination of compromise and face-saving techniques through 'give and take'

Management Philosophy

ORGANISATIONAL POLICY

Results-oriented, with clear objectives. Chinese policies are ambiguous, with the highest flexibility – grey areas.

LEADERSHIP

For the Western-trained manager, leadership is an essential element of a career in management at all levels: in Chinese management environments the 'Leader' is different from the 'Manager'. Leadership is considered the highest quality, reserved for the highest-ranked individual in an organisation. Many Chinese leaders rule by charisma.

WINNING THE BUSINESS

When responding to a Request for Proposal (RFP), Western-trained management will demonstrate capability through documents with information such as:

- current company financial reports;

- technical capabilities;

- past achievements;

- creative ideas;

- competitive pricing; and

- application of contemporary technologies.

They will make commitments and promises to convince the potential customer that the company is the best candidate. In Chinese companies personal trust is the precondition of any deeper discussion. This may explain why a Chinese boss usually has a budget for out-of-office activities with the potential customer before any formal commercial relationship can begin. The Chinese boss needs such interactions to help develop the relationship and build trust before the official tender process begin. Most Chinese bosses will leverage on existing Quanxi[4] direct or indirectly established with the potential customer (Khor 2005).

In a Western-managed bidding environment, it is very common to ask external parties to sign a non-disclosure agreement (NDA) before starting any commercially sensitive discussion. Subsequently, a contract will be signed to reinforce the agreement and the contract will act as legal instrument to protect company interest. In Chinese companies personal levels of trust reinforce

---

4   *Quanxi* describes a personal connection between two people in which one is able to prevail upon another to perform a favour or service, or be prevailed upon. The two people need not be of equal social status. *Guanxi* can also be used to describe a network of contacts which an individual can call upon when something needs to be done, and through which they can exert influence on behalf of another. In addition, *guanxi* can describe a state of general understanding between two people.

agreement. Asking a Chinese boss to sign a NDA before he receives information is unusual and may be perceived as an insult by the Chinese boss. He may believe that he is not trusted and that if this is the case the information should not be shared with him.

The same rules apply when the Chinese boss needs to disclose information. If he doesn't trust the receiving party, then he will not share the information. It is common for the Chinese boss to observe an individual, forming opinions over time about his personality and work capability. If the Chinese boss is not convinced the individual is trustworthy, no sensitive or personal information will be shared. It is usual in a Chinese company for the information-disclosing party to declare the sensitivity of the information at the beginning of the conversation and expect the information to be protected and regarded as confidential by the trusted party.

TASK PLANNING

The Western-trained manager will put procedure first. Before beginning a new task, they will ask: *do we have the right procedure to follow?* The Chinese-trained boss will ask: *do we have the right people to do the job?*

TASK EXECUTION

In Western companies, only tasks documented in SOPs, job descriptions or contracts are done. In Chinese companies, task execution depends on what the Chinese boss decides at that particular point. New instructions which may then impact how the task is carried out or prioritised may come later.

REWARD AND PROMOTION

In Western companies are usually based on pre-agreed key performance indicators (KPI) at individual and group level. In Chinese companies, the reward can depend on the perceived value of the contribution on the completed task. Promotion is not necessarily based on performance: it could depend on the relationship with the Chinese boss.

Communication and Decision-making

COMMUNICATION

It is easier to differentiate work- and non-work-related communication in Western companies. Formal environment and language is used to discuss business issues and challenges faced, and resolutions negotiated openly, whereas informal coffee or dinner networking is for the purposes of socialisation with very little or no discussion about business-related activities. Separating work and non-work communication in a business environment managed by a Chinese boss is not straightforward. The Chinese boss sees the environment as unimportant. It is more important to be able to reach agreement through a series of discussions inside or outside of the office, over dinner and drinks or golf. Once agreement has been reached, announcements will be made through formal channels such as steering committees. Formal discussions will usually tend towards face-saving or 'political' solutions and not necessary reflect reality.

MEETINGS AND DISCUSSIONS

When the Western manager calls a meeting the scope of discussion is usually follows a strict agenda. When the Western-trained boss calls an impromptu meeting, employees can ask about the topic and often ask for time to prepare. It is also understood topics not on the agenda will rarely be discussed at that meeting. When a Chinese boss calls a meeting, he may or may not have an agenda. Even if he has, he will still put *etc.* or *others* as an item on the agenda: the etc. and others are often the main topic of discussion. The main agenda may just be an excuse for him to call for the meeting.

When the Chinese boss calls an impromptu meeting, it is usually in a very informal way and without a pre-agreed agenda. Usually the employee won't ask about the agenda and knows that he or she must be fully prepared for all possible topics the Chinese boss may want to discuss. If the Chinese boss invites an employee out for dinner or a cup of tea outside the office, it is very likely he has something personal to discuss – Chinese bosses like to discuss personal issues in private. These private discussions should never be disclosed to others.

DECISION-MAKING

Western-trained managers follow well-documented procedures which include but are not limited to:

- roles and responsibilities;

- authority levels;

- decision time frames;

- escalation procedures; and

- expectations.

Once the decision is made it will be documented. The Western-trained manager will escalate to higher-ranked managers for decision if necessary, following the appropriate escalation procedures. Team-based decisions are common.

There is no standard decision-making process for Chinese managers; it will usually be a top-down approach that is highly sophisticated, subjective and complex, but depending on the situation and who has the interest to influence the decision. Individual interests may be considered before organisation interests, but equally the opposite may be true – organisational interests before personal interests. Decisions may not be fully documented or if documented, may not reflect the full story. It is common for decisions to be delayed if certain leaders are not available, or if the manager believes that the result will not be in his favour. Some leaders or managers may even avoid involvement in sensitive procurement decisions to avoid being blamed for poor commercial decisions or corruption charges later.

CONFLICT RESOLUTION

When conflict arises between individuals or teams, the Western-trained boss will usually ask the conflicting parties provide 'the facts'. He may then urge all parties to resolve the conflict. The Chinese boss prefers to use a combination of compromise and face-saving techniques through a series of 'give and take' negotiations.

As described in Table 6.2, the Western manager will usually respond in a more direct manner and provide straightforward answers: the Chinese boss will favour ambiguities, flexibility and 'grey areas' but may provide a definite answer or resolution to conflict situations. Case study 6.1 below provides further analysis and descriptions of these assertions.

CASE STUDY 6.1   WHAT WOULD YOU LIKE TO DRINK?

This is an example from the experience of the author (SK) and illustrates the differences between the direct style and ambiguity and flexibility.

The author (SK), in his role as project manager believes that a relaxed and informal environment can promote better communication and productivity. Before an official project kick-off meeting, SK will seek the sponsor's views and privately obtain his support. SK often invites his sponsors to join him for coffee. SK lived in San Francisco and Shanghai for two-and-a-half years each: this case study describes two interesting conversations in these two very different cities.

The question to the sponsor was: 'What would you like to drink?'

In Starbucks San Francisco:

SK: *Mr Western Boss, what would you like to drink?*

Mr Western Boss: Coffee please.

SK: *Milk and sugar?*

Mr Western Boss: Milk but no sugar please.

A few minutes later

SK: *Here is your coffee.*

Mr Western Boss: Let's discuss the project changes.

And by the time we have finished our coffee we have almost finished our work.

In Starbucks Shanghai:

SK: *Mr Chinese Boss, what would you like to drink?*

Mr Chinese Boss: *Anything.*

SK: *Would you like me to get you a cup of coffee or tea?*

Mr Chinese Boss: *Both would be …*

SK: *Can you be specific, please.*

Mr Chinese Boss: *In that case, please get me something not too much of a hassle to you.*

A few minutes later

SK: *I got two cups of espresso. Here is yours. I am not sure that may suit your taste or not. If not, I am more than happy to change it for you.*

Mr Chinese Boss: *Thank you very much. Don't worry. It should be OK.*

They proceed to talk about housing market, stock tips, news, social issues, and also about work in no specific order and just before leaving the café...

SK: *Mr Chinese Boss, as we have already known each other for some time, can you please tell me honestly if you liked the espresso?*

Mr Chinese Boss: *Since you ask, I think I'd better tell you my honest opinion. I felt it was a bit bitter; perhaps I am not so used to it.*

SK: *Me too. The espresso from this specific Starbucks' outlet is no longer that good any more. Perhaps, I should let you suggest a better café or Chinese tea house next time?*

Observations and Analysis

THE DIRECT AND PERSONAL PREFERENCE

In Starbucks San Francisco, Mr Western Boss responded directly to the question and his answer is very specific: he preferred a white coffee without sugar. This definitely helped SK. If for some reason there was no white coffee, most likely SK would return to Mr Western Boss and ask for an alternative. It would be perceived as discourteous if SK proceeded to purchase an alternative without checking. If Mr Western Boss didn't like espresso, he would tell SK directly and not drink it. His personal preference is more important than an opportunity to avoid a situation which may embarrass SK because he chose the wrong drink.

THE ART OF FLEXIBILITY

In Starbucks Shanghai, the 'anything' response of the Chinese boss could be interpreted in the following ways:

- he is a very humble person and will accept whatever the host offers;

- he has no allergies to food nor has any preferences; or

- he is very flexible.

When SK heard the Chinese boss was not happy with the espresso, he responded with the necessary flexibility to allow the Chinese boss to choose another café next time or even go a Chinese tea house.

THE ART OF SAVING FACE

The Chinese boss may have very limited knowledge about the food and drinks available at Starbucks. To avoid losing face by asking for something not available, such as Chinese tea, he decided to allow SK to make the decision. However, he didn't ask SK to make a recommendation despite his limited knowledge and exposure because that is a 'losing face' act. This is an indirect way of asking SK to make a recommendation. The second response: *both also can* and third response *something not too much hassle to you* hint to SK that he shouldn't embarrass the boss any more and that he shouldn't assume the boss is a coffee drinker and knows Starbucks well. The boss said that the espresso did not suit his taste rather than blaming SK for ordering it. SK was trying to save his own face by saying that the espresso from this specific Starbucks outlet is no longer that good, implying he had bought great espresso here in the past. He was justifying his decision to purchase the espresso without obtaining consent earlier.

Saving face is the responsibility of all parties. Sometime you save your own face, sometimes others. When SK heard the Chinese boss complain that the espresso was not suited to his taste, SK responded that he himself was not happy with the taste either and suggested that the boss propose a better café or Chinese tea house next time. SK was able to save his own face because it was SK's decision to purchase the espresso. SK saved face by acknowledging the boss's opinion that the espresso was not that good and giving him the option of choosing the next meeting place.

THE ART OF SAVING SOMEONE ELSE'S FACE

When SK asked the Chinese boss for his honest opinion about the espresso, the boss did not give a definite answer. He did not say it was a wrong choice within Starbucks or a specific problem with the cup of espresso. He is saving his host's (SK) face by stating it could be his own problem for not being accustomed to the taste of espresso. However, this could be a very indirect way of sending a message to SK: *I don't like espresso.*

THE ART OF AMBIGUITY

SK's plan was to order two drinks quickly and proceed with the discussion. But he didn't know exactly what the Chinese boss wanted. The Chinese boss wouldn't simply pick one item from the menu because if his choice was the most expensive drink available at Starbucks, he might send the wrong message to SK (that he is greedy). These are signs that the boss may not know SK well and that he was trying to evaluate SK's personality and capabilities: most importantly, whether SK can be trusted. In this situation an ambiguous response seemed to be best.

THE CHALLENGES OF ASSUMPTIONS

SK assumed that his boss would suggest a change of venue if he/she doesn't drink coffee. Because the boss had agreed to meet at Starbucks, SK assumed his boss liked to drink coffee or was familiar with Starbucks and its products.

The wrong assumptions on acceptable behaviour during a simple coffee meeting might lead to embarrassment and future conflict.

Knowing the Western boss's preference for a direct communication style versus the Chinese boss's preference to communicate through ambiguity and flexibility may help. However, managing the boss's expectations is never easy, and the first challenge may come during the job interview.

In Case study 6.2, SK was asked to respond to the following story modified from ancient Chinese History, during the last round of interviews for a Programme Director position for a mega-programme in China. It illustrates concepts of the differences between *responsibility* and *authority*.

CASE STUDY 6.2   THE JOB INTERVIEW

Once upon a time, there was an Emperor in China. He was drunk and fell asleep halfway through a party. Servant A, who was responsible for the emperor's clothing, was not present at the time. Servant B, who was responsible for the emperor's food and drinks, was around. Out of his concern that the Emperor might catch a cold if he continued to sleep without sufficient warm clothing, he quickly took off his own jacket to cover the Emperor's body.

The Emperor was very pleased when he awoke and saw the jacket. He was happy that his servants served him with care and love. However, when the Emperor realised it was Servant B instead of Servant A who placed his own jacket onto the Emperor's body, he immediately instructed that Servant B be executed because he performed a task beyond his authorised level. The Emperor also punished Servant A by transferring him to another department because he failed to do his job.

THE INTERVIEW QUESTIONS ANALYSIS

1.   If Servant B didn't provide his jacket to the Emperor, he would be seen as a servant without care and love for the Emperor. Once he provided his jacket, he would be seen as overriding his authority

level as only Servant A has authority to serve the Emperor. What is your comment?

2.   Which one has bigger impact to your career? Your responsibility or your authority? When you failed to execute your duty or when you performed beyond your authority level?

3.   If you are the Emperor, how would you handle the situation differently?

4.   If you are Servant B, how would you handle the situation differently?

5.   How could Servant B handle the situation without overriding his authority level and or failing to execute his responsibility yet still be able to demonstrate his care and loyalty?

OBSERVATIONS AND ANALYSIS

The Chinese interviewer was trying to evaluate SK's management style and his analytical skills in handling responsibilities and authoritys. SK's responses are below, based on assessments of:

- the Emperor's expectations;

- his tolerance levels; and

- the interpretations of responsibility and authority.

EXPECTATIONS

The Emperor was expecting Servant A to do his duty, which was to ensure that the Emperor's clothing met his needs at any time and anywhere. Servant A failed to meet the Emperor's expectations because he was not present at this particular time. The Emperor decided to use this situation as an example to other servants: they must meet his expectations of performance of their particular duty any time and anywhere. He punished Servant A by transferring him to another department.

TOLERANCE LEVELS

The Emperor was not happy that Servant A failed to do his duty. But this failure is still within the Emperor's tolerance levels. The Emperor sentenced Servant B to death because he could not tolerate anyone in his empire performing tasks beyond their given authority level. From the Emperor's perspective, any attempt to override authority may eventually threaten the peace and harmony of the working environment in a centralised management system based on command and control. In this case, the Emperor decided remind all his people: *don't ever attempt to override the authority bestowed upon you*. It is unlikely that such expectations would be documented in an official job description.

RESPONSIBILITY OR AUTHORITY?

When a Western-trained manager assigns a new task to his subordinates, he will usually also communicate clearly defined responsibilities. When a Chinese boss assigns a new task to his subordinates, he usually makes it a top-down non-negotiable order. He will still retain authority to execute the task himself or assign to another person if he decides it is necessary.

LESSONS

Applying this story in today's work environment and replacing the character of the Emperor with a Chinese boss, most employees would respond by saying that they would choose *to do what they were authorised to do rather than what they were not supposed to do, even if it produced greater benefits*.

It is not easy to find an example of a situation in a Chinese-managed organisation where a staff member did what they were not authorised to do, even if this action is for greater organisational benefit. If the Chinese boss discovered such actions, he could interpret them as a challenge to his authority and leadership. He may see this as a sign that the employee is no longer within his span of control, and may fear that he or she may do more damage. The employee will eventually lose the trust of the Chinese boss.

Encouraging Initiative

Some Western-trained bosses encourage their staff to think 'out of the box'; introducing new ideas and innovation to help the organisation deliver better results. These suggestions may be about improving efficiency, productivity and cost saving. To the Chinese boss, going beyond the appropriate power/authority level is serious, as shown in the case study. This may explain why the encouragement of staff suggestions for initiatives, heavily promoted by the Western-trained boss, is difficult to implement in a Chinese organisation. The staff member is afraid his ideas may be interpreted as an attempt to go beyond his current authorised level. The protocol-oriented and hierarchy-based Chinese organisation promotes a working culture that the boss is always *smarter* than the staff. Staff should never underestimate the boss's intelligence and outperform the boss. This may lead to a situation where a smart employee will pretend to be dumb in the Chinese organisation, and may explain why the suggestion box is empty!

Law versus Trust

Western-trained bosses usually emphasise the importance of:

- laws;

- regulatory frameworks;

- organisation structures and policy; and

- checks and balances through adherence to procedures and processes.

The Chinese organisation has the most trusted and capable 'buddies' of the owner or CEO in critical positions such as financial controller, chief operating officer and purchasing manager to reduce any potential for abuse of power and authority. This leads to centralisation of all critical decisions with the Chinese boss. In larger organisations, the highest-ranked Chinese boss is the only one who is able to see the entire picture: such is the application of *divide and conquer* methods enforced by piecemeal and tightly controlled delegation levels and approval procedures.

The Western-trained boss will use advanced management tools such as the Balanced Score Card, or KPIs to measure staff performance. If the staff member does go beyond his authorised level, the Western-trained boss will use counselling, closer supervision or, for major transgression, demotion, transfer or dismissal. The Chinese boss will usually use *show cause* letters as warning, and then perhaps monetary penalties or threats of dismissal as punishment.

SK had the opportunity to experience the following situation in one of his projects in China. The conflict resolution techniques used by the Western-trained were very different from those employed by the Chinese-trained management teams.

CASE STUDY 6.3   THE BIG BANG!

In a Government-funded multimillion dollar mega-infrastructure programme in China, a seller project manager from a multinational US listed company was not happy about how he had been treated by the buyer project manager (PM) who strongly believed that the customer is always right. During one meeting, one of the participants bangs his hand on the table to show disagreement. This action triggered another bang from the other party in the dispute. No-one was really sure who actually started the banging. SK, who was part of the Western seller project team, heard more than 10 bangs. The meeting adjourned with both buyer and seller PMs and their respective team members leaving the meeting room by two separate exits avoiding eye contact! Within a few hours, all the steering committee members (both buyer and seller representatives) had heard the news.

PREPARING TO MANAGE THE CONFLICT

The seller PM quickly informed the project director (PD) and requested that the highest-ranked Singapore-based senior Vice President (SVP) fly in to China as soon as possible to resolve the crisis. The seller PM, PD and the Senior VP agreed over the phone that they must respond with 'facts', excluding personal or emotional elements, and employ a joint problem-solving approach to resolve the conflict. The team started preparing, recording in detail the actions and conversations leading up to the table-banging event. The Western team's strategy was to try to defend the situation by providing evidence the customer was at fault and that the seller PM was defending his company and team; responding to the bang with bang in the belief that there was equality between buyer and seller. The SVP approved the strategy and the report and prepared to meet his equivalent in the buyer team at a meeting the next day.

THE MEETING

Mr Wu, the Chinese buyer's highest-ranked manager, arrived at the meeting room ahead of anyone else; and personally greeted his counterpart the seller organisation's senior VP when they entered the room. As the host, Mr Wu started the meeting with greetings to his counterpart and acknowledged his continuous commitment to the success of the programme. He then announced a change in the project organisation: he had just promoted the buyer PM to another government division and appointed a new PM to begin within the next few days. During the transition period, Mr Wu would take charge of the project. Mr Wu then asked the senior VP the reason for his unplanned visit to China, pretending he was not aware of the current 'crisis' and asking the seller team to explain the reason for their request to see him at such short notice.

The seller VP, not accustomed to the speed with which a Chinese boss can adapt and change the rules of the situation, began to systematically read the script prepared by his team. Mr Wu interpreted this as an insult and responded angrily.

Observation and Analysis

Mr Wu's response was based on Chinese business culture plus his political skill, and is summarised below:

- He never made definite statements.

- He never admitted his PM was wrong.

- He never asked seller's VP to remove his own PM.

- He, as the buyer's highest-ranking boss, must be in control at all times.

If he admitted his people were wrong he may be perceived as losing face internally and externally: this may cause him to lose control in the seller team. If his own boss heard about it, his boss's response may harm his own career.

Table 6.3 summarises a survey conducted at the time of writing of this chapter to understand conflict resolution techniques from the perspective of managers from the West and East.[5]

Table 6.3   Conflict resolution techniques

Survey questions based on Case study 6.3 'The Big Bang'
Q1: If you are the seller project manager, how would you resolve the conflict? Q2: If you are the seller senior management accountable for the success of this project, how would you resolve the conflict? Q3: If you are the buyer PM, how would you resolve the conflict? Q4: If you are the buyer senior management accountable for the success this project, how would you resolve the conflict?
The survey
We conducted an email interview of 20 managers from around the world to learn how they would respond to and resolve the conflict as described in a scenario based on the case study 3. The respondents were from both the East and West, with experience ranging from 5 to 20+ years in management: 12 out of 20 managers had a Chinese background from mainland China, Taiwan, Malaysia, Singapore, the USA and UK.
The results
Western managers In a democratic Western culture, managers argue their points and defend their stand or company by justifying using facts and figures. Our respondents from the West preferred to discuss the issue with senior management and formulate strategies to resolve the conflict. Senior management is expected to act as guidance to PMs, and typically empower the PM to execute agreed strategies in the next meeting or during negotiations. Senior management rarely – if at all – intervene directly. PMs see their counterparts as equals. Four out of twelve Chinese managers who live in the USA and UK held the same view. Despite their Chinese origin, their responses have been influenced by their time working in Western management culture. **Chinese managers** In the Eastern culture where things may not be so direct, eight of the Chinese respondents held the view that the 'customer is always right', and that the customer always has the upper hand in conflict resolutions and negotiations. This is not unique to China. One Malaysian respondent working in Bahrain shared similar views. The seller PM or senior management is expected to call and offer apologies. This action is expected to build goodwill with the buyer in exchange for an opportunity for further discussion with the buyer. The buyer PM and senior management's attitude would be 'I have the money and the upper hand', and they would likely wait for a short period in the expectation of a positive move from the seller PM or senior management. Remember that any delays would only adversely affect the seller side. In the East, when such untoward incidences occur, senior management (on both sides) is likely to take a more direct involvement and intervene together with the PM. The PM is also expected to report/refer to senior management to formulate a plan of action, and not be proactive. Five respondents suggested that the buyer senior management immediately contact his counterpart and demand the removal of the seller PM, and 'get a more agreeable PM' on the seller side.

---

5   A second reason for the survey was to ensure that the author's past experiences, which are the basis for this chapter, were still relevant. The results of the survey have supported the case studies and the analysis and guidelines for advising upwards in a Chinese organisation.

Western managers with experience in Chinese organisations

Five Western respondents who also have experience managing projects in the East had a mixed approach to resolution. While PMs are empowered to take initiative and strategise with senior management, they echo the view that it is essential to 'give face' to adversaries. One respondent even suggested the use of a third party with established good *Quan Xi* at highest level to help to resolve the conflict, rather than just seeing each other as negotiating partners. This further illustrates the importance of *Quan Xi* when doing business in China.

UNDERSTANDING YOUR CHINESE BOSS

Knowing how your Chinese boss attained his current position, through information about his past and any special relationships with others in the organisation, may help you to position yourself more positively with the boss. You may want to analyse your Chinese boss's thinking process, his consideration and behaviours. This is a challenging and sensitive task that must be handled delicately. It is important to note that not all Chinese bosses were promoted based on their past performance or merits. Perhaps it was because he has certain *Quan Xi* relationship with someone high up in the organisation? Or perhaps he is the political appointee of someone with an interest (pecuniary or political) in the organisation.

If he was promoted to the current position because of his knowledge or past performance, you may want to study his background to gather as much information as you can about his strengths and weaknesses, and credibility. How did he achieve the position he is currently working in? If he is close to retirement age, what behaviours or characteristics do you need to display to motivate him to groom you to be his successor? Or is there no chance at all of this happening?

UNWRITTEN PRIVILEGES FOR THE CHINESE BOSS

There are certain unwritten privileges granted to the Chinese boss. Most people won't appreciate these privileges or understand their real power or impact. They include:

- his daily schedule;

- unfair communication;

- special rights;

- discussion;

- the 'right' state of mind; and

- decision-making.

HIS DAILY SCHEDULE

The Chinese boss doesn't need to disclose his daily schedule. His secretary just needs to say, *the boss is not in the office*. The secretary may not even know where he is. But you must disclose your schedule if your Chinese boss asks you. Sometimes you may need to obtain approval from the Chinese boss in advance to attend meetings outside the office.

UNFAIR COMMUNICATION

You cannot ask what the Chinese boss was doing even though you know he was playing social golf with someone. But he has the right to question your activities and your reasons for doing them.

SPECIAL RIGHTS

The Chinese boss can do random checks on your work. He can change his priority, timing, activities, but you have to work within constraints imposed by the Chinese boss. Some of these constraints may be imposed unnecessarily. He can expect you to adapt to the situation, changing your work style to suit his work style, but not the other way around. The Chinese boss doesn't have to tell you when he is going to review your work but he can require all staff to ensure that everything is up-to-date and ready for inspection at any time.

DISCUSSIONS

When the Chinese boss calls you for a 'discussion', he doesn't need to disclose the reason or content of this discussion. He can expect you to be prepared with information about anything within your areas of responsibility. When you request a meeting with the Chinese boss, you must submit the agenda in advance. During the meeting if you raise a topic not mentioned in this agenda, the Chinese boss can decide whether to continue the discussion or ask you to request another meeting. However, the Chinese boss can discuss on any topic beyond the agenda.

THE 'RIGHT' STATE OF MIND

You should ask yourself, is it the right time and/or right place to raise this issue with the Chinese boss? If the boss is not in the fame of mind of environment to listen to you, it would be pointless. Choosing the right time may require a series of observations to understand the Chinese boss's preferences, dislikes and expectations.

DECISION-MAKING

Standard procedures attempt to reduce ambiguity within the Western management organisation. If procedures define a specific decision process as not requiring consultation with others, these decisions can be made without hesitation. Occasionally you may find a standard procedure manual in the Chinese organisation. But the procedures will also state that *the manager shall decide the needs of consultation from senior management as and when the situation arises*. If you see this in your current job scope, it is very difficult to judge when not to consult the Chinese boss. This approach can be time-consuming as most front-line managers will consult the Chinese boss to prevent censure for not consulting.

WHAT'S STOPPING YOUR CHINESE BOSS FROM SLEEPING AT NIGHT?

If you can find out which of the following anxieties stop your Chinese boss from sleeping at night, you may able to take them into account when you are advising upwards.

FEAR OF LOSING CONTROL

If the boss came from a *command and control* culture such as military or government, he would be most comfortable with total control. If he must delegate, he will only delegate to people he trusts absolutely.

POWER DISTRIBUTION THREAT

The Chinese boss has many calls on his time and availability, so he cannot possibly do everything and make every decision. He must delegate some authority to his leadership team to keep the day-to-day activities running smoothly. To ensure that this power distribution doesn't become a future threat, he would not distribute the power to just one individual. He would allocate power to a few trusted individuals. These trusted individuals can also become his 'eyes and ears', supplying critical information.

The Chinese boss will monitor the individuals on whom he has granted authority, looking for any signs of power struggles, power abuse and power manipulation among these trusted individuals.

DISTRIBUTE THE POWER TO A LOW-TRUST MANAGER

When the Chinese boss distributes power in a low-trust environment, he may apply the 'divide and conquer' technique, distributing power to a group of three or more and impose group consensus decision-making on their approval processes. The Chinese boss may have a concern that he might have wrongly chosen an individual who will betray him later; through the consensus decision model he can guarantee his position: it is unlikely that three or more persons could consolidate and betray him. The cost is that consensus decision-making is slow and may encourage more bureaucratic and political behaviour. Interestingly, the Chinese boss argues that this is not so much of an issue because the highest-ranking Chinese boss always has the power to veto bureaucratic processes and make fast decisions.

WHY IS MY STAFF CHALLENGING THE AUTHORITY GIVEN?

Managers or staff working for a Chinese organisation who try to exploit their authority should be fully aware of the consequences if such activities are discovered. For example, the Chinese boss gives a manager the delegation to sign purchase orders to a certain monetary value without group approval. If the Chinese boss discovers that the manager has signed a purchase order of a value even one dollar more than his authorised level, it will be interpreted as a challenge to his boss's span of control, rather than a small mistake. The Chinese boss cannot allow managers to exploit or challenge his authority level.

The Chinese culture of never being too definite makes the situation even more complicated. Sometimes the Chinese boss doesn't like to define in writing the precise level of authority, or puts etc. in your Chinese employment letter. In a dispute, the boss can interpret the meaning of etc. to mean whatever he needs it to mean. This leads to the creation of corporate culture in a Chinese organisation of *unless it is very clear you are authorised to do it, don't do anything.*

PEOPLE: ASSET OR LIABILITY?

People are an asset in China and the size of China's population makes it one of the world's largest economic markets. People are also one of the biggest problems in China. The political system has led to the creation of many state enterprises or government-linked organisations which carry high social responsibilities, such as ensuring that the basic needs of Chinese citizens, such as food and shelter, are being met. The highest-ranked Chinese boss of such a large organisation will give highest priority to incidents which can threaten the organisation's stability or cause the market to perceive that they have failed to carry out their national and social responsibilities.

The Chinese boss will acknowledge staff contribution to the organisation's growth through events such as New Year open houses, or Labour Day celebration parties. Some government-based organisations may even conduct monthly or quarterly government propaganda talks. The Chinese boss can be very sensitive to any new formation of groups within his organisation that might lead to development of a European-style union movement which may eventually threaten the stability of the organisation.

Similar to Western-trained bosses, the Chinese boss is afraid that a single mistake may destroy the creditability built through years of hard work. He will try to avoid being caught in situations where a mistake made by a direct report will reflect poorly on him. This is different from the Western corporate governance framework. The head of department or manager is accountable for the wrongdoing of his staff even if he has delegated the responsibility. The CEO is ultimately responsible for all the actions (good or bad) of the company.

A Chinese boss who does not have strong political or organisational backing may be afraid of making critical decisions which will lead to a witch hunt. He is afraid that the next person in power within or outside his organisation may search for perceived wrong-doers or enemies later. Revenge or blaming of the previous bosses by the new person in power is common.[6]

WHY IS MY STAFF TAKING THE LIMELIGHT?

You are young and you are a rising star in the organisation because your knowledge of new technology and innovative ideas helped the organisation to reduce costs. If your success is not credited to your immediate Chinese boss,

6   This situation also occurs in Western organisations.

then the Chinese boss may lose face, and out of jealousy may do harm to your reputation. He may start to create tougher assignments for you to encourage you to seek his help. He may even put you on the toughest job, with reduced resources and aggressive timelines in the hope that when you fail the task, he has reason to remove you from his organisation.

Cheating or lying behaviour is considered to be unacceptable in both the Western and Chinese organisations. Exploiting authority limits is different: it usually lies in the grey area. If no one questions authority limits they may be ignored or tolerated. For example:

> *A manager from a Chinese company has no monthly limit on dining expenses but is allowed to claim up to rmb200 per dinner with potential customers without pre-approval from his Chinese boss. One day he took two potential customers from the same company out for dinner. When he discovered that the total dinner bill for three people was rmb350, he asked the restaurant to split the bill with amount rmb180 and rmb170 respectively. He submitted two expenses reports with separate customer's names for his boss's approval later.*

The restaurant manager is flexible and will accede to the customer's request to split the bill. This practice is often frowned on in the West where the rules of the restaurant support only one bill per table. This problem is not unique to Asia. Generally speaking, the people-centric Eastern-based business owners are more flexible with special requests from the customer. The procedure-driven supplier is likely to refuse customer requests not listed as part of the approved standard procedures. In a Chinese organisation, the manager is expected to use his experience and knowledge to make judgement calls in situations like this. He has to please the customer to retain the business or because denial may lead to further complications.

Getting Ready to Work with Your Chinese Boss

Your Chinese boss may not have the same priorities and concerns as you. A typical example is when you do not receive a salary increment after years of hard work for the same organisation. You may start to chase your boss, to attempt to speed up your promotion and salary increment by sending him a letter of complaint. Your impatience may backfire and lead the Chinese boss to view you as a threat to his position.

Your chances of getting a promotion and salary increment may be increased if you can understand what your boss's views about giving you a promotion are before you ask officially. If your boss considers this request as a threat to his current position, then it is best to wait a little longer. If your boss can see that you are adding value to his organisation and he will get promotion as a result, then the empty seat after his promotion could be yours.

INTRODUCING NEW IDEAS

Western management heavily promotes the benefits of a corporate culture of innovation and creative thinking. Attempting to create a similar culture in a Chinese organisation would be difficult, if not impossible. Western-trained bosses like staff to provide new ideas and new concepts for organisational success in a competitive market. Communicating a new idea to your Chinese boss is not that straightforward. Whether it is a good or bad idea is not as important as when and how the ideas are presented to the Chinese boss and whether he was receptive at that time.

For example, your suggestion on a change to the organisation's structure to promote better communication among stakeholders may be viewed as an act with negative intent. The Chinese boss may think his approval of the new organisation structure will allow you to communicate directly to the company's highest management and bypass him. He may interpret your suggestion as affirming that he has no value in the communication chain.

To be on the safe side, your intention for any new tasks or ideas must be in line with what your boss is thinking at that moment. Otherwise, you may be at danger of a pre-emptive strike from your boss. A more successful approach may involve providing enough information to your Chinese boss to enable him to present the new idea to his direct boss as his own.[7] If the new idea is adopted, he will get the credit and you will get credit too. You definitely do not want to propose new ideas to your Chinese boss which can lead you to have more power, as all these will increase the suspicion of your Chinese boss as to your intentions.

Table 6.4 may be useful in evaluating your current relationship with your Chinese boss. None of the options:

---

7   This strategy is also often employed in Western organisations.

- do more;

- do less; or

- do nothing

are healthy from a Western-trained boss's perspective: any of these approaches will prevent initiative and limit individual innovation.

Table 6.4   Evaluating your relationship with your Chinese boss

Do more – more mistakes	The more suggestions you bring to him, the more negative perceptions he may have of you. He may suspect your motives.
Do less – less mistakes	The less you suggest, the less mistakes will be perceived.
Do nothing – no mistake	Just focus on your day to day job. If you don't bring in new ideas, then you give him no opportunity to develop a negative perception of you.

Between Earning Trust and Being Suspicious

A high level of trust between leader and followers will usually result in a more productive and happy working relationship, both in Western and Eastern business organisations. Earning trust is another matter entirely: there is no rule or formula to apply to become trustworthy. So, what can you do to earn more trust from your Chinese boss?

You might try the following if you are in the lower ranks of an organisation:

- Develop a reputation as being reliable and productive.

- Add value to the overall organisation.

- Adhere to organisation policies.

- Develop a reputation as a great team player.

All these can help to increase your chances to be seen as trustworthy.

If you are middle management, you may want to seek to understand your boss's version of the unwritten privileges of being a boss and his expectations. He may be expecting you to save his face in any potential embarrassment or conflict. SK observed the following when he lived and worked in China:

- speak to death;

- silence to death; and

- speak right to stay alive.

SPEAK TO DEATH
(Mandarin words and pronunciation: 先说先死 xian shuo xian si)

This can be summarised by the following:

- Speak when you are not invited or granted permission to speak;

- Speak at the wrong time; or

- Believe that if you are the first person to speak, you will provide others more opportunities to evaluate you and allow those others to re-position themselves, either for or against you.

SCENARIO 6.1

The seller's programme director (PD) took the customer's CEO and his team to visit an airport system testing and integration laboratory. As he explained the project's progress and the integrated system capabilities, he proudly presented the latest flight display panel his team designed and built. Someone from the customer's team asked why the display for that particular panel was blinking. The PD responded that according to IATA standard, the display starts blinking 10 minutes before the flight departs. This is world's most intelligent way to inform the passengers to board immediately. The Western-trained engineer then said 'Sir, not exactly. The loose cable connection was actually the cause of this blinking display!' This unsolicited comment embarrassed the PD and caused him to lose credibility.

SILENCE TO DEATH
(Mandarin words and pronunciation: 不说也死 bu shuo ye si)

Not exactly the opposite of 'Speak to Death'. If everybody has voiced their views and opinions except you, you may be perceived as not adding value; or may be identified as the one who should naturally bear any negative consequences. *Die* because everybody has spoken except you.

SCENARIO 6.2

The seller's PD usually had a lunch meeting with the customer's project sponsor without the other team members. For this particular meeting, he decided to bring you, the chief engineer, along. Many project-related topics were discussed but he had forgotten to make a critical request of the customer to delay the server installation due to a contractor's problem. You have noticed but you have decided to keep silent because you have learnt the theory of 'Speak to Death'. Back in the office, the PD realised that he had forgotten to discuss that issue with the customer's project sponsor. He blamed you for not reminding him or raising the request directly yourself, as he would expect that you, a chief engineer, should do. He further argued that the reason he brought you there was to 'remind' him on certain important items that he may have forgotten. Of course, you never knew what and when your Chinese boss might forget or remember!

SPEAK RIGHT TO STAY ALIVE
(Mandarin words and pronunciation: 说到不死 shuo dao bu si)

As soon as you have realised you are caught between *talk also die* and *not talk also die,* to protect your best interests you have to find the right:

- time;

- environment;

- audience;

- words;

- tone/speed; and

- depth of meaning and intent.

SCENARIO 6.3

The seller's PD usually had a lunch meeting with the customer's project sponsor without other team members. For this particular meeting, he decided to bring you, the chief engineer, along. Many project-related topics were discussed but he had forgotten a critical request to delay the server installation due to contractor's problem.

Approach A:

You waited until almost end of lunch meeting and said, *'The PD has forgotten to mention the request of delay of the installation due to contractor's problem.'*

The PD angrily said,

'SK do you think I am that old? I have not forgotten the unreasonable request you asked me to raise to customer's attention. It is our internal problem and customer should not be the one dealing with the delay. That's why I intentionally did not mention this to the customer. Since you have brought this up, let's hope our customer can help us on this.'

This is a typical planned good guy (the PD) and bad guy (you) negotiation technique often seen in the Western-managed business world too.

Approach B:

Before the end of discussion, you quietly write a short note and pass to the PD to remind him to request the customer's approval to delay the installation. If the PD decides to keep silent after your reminder, he cannot blame you because he said nothing. He may increase his trust of you because you privately reminded him. You had previously mentioned the subject of timeline extension to the project sponsor. The decision to raise the issue at the meeting is the PD's, not yours. You are protecting your company and your Chinese boss by reminding him but also protecting yourself from being blamed later.

THE DILEMMA

If you do something you will *die*: if you don't do anything you will also *die*. You are caught in a situation where you can't escape:

- If you do something at that time, your Chinese boss may perceive your action as challenging his knowledge, exposure and authority.

- If you don't do anything, your Chinese boss will accuse you of not doing your duty (remember your job description may have the etc. as your duty) or not being proactive enough.

You must inform your boss as soon as possible. Make a request to meet your Chinese boss in front of another manager or email your Chinese boss and copy it to others so you will have witnesses that you have attempted to inform the Chinese boss. Then if for some reason your Chinese boss doesn't receive your information in time and things go wrong, he can't blame you because you tried bring this to his attention. If the Chinese boss does meet with you, then you can politely ask him for his advice and a decision. This is acceptable to the Chinese boss because you are letting him take control through giving advice and making decisions.

Catch 22

- Your Chinese boss is not happy because you don't make the decision! You are caught: if you don't decide on behalf of the Chinese boss, he may accuse you later for not adding value because all minor issues also have to wait for his decision!

- Your Chinese boss is not happy because you made the decision! When you go ahead and make decisions, your Chinese boss may then accuse you of lack of consultation!

WORKING PRODUCTIVELY WITH A CHINESE BOSS

When you are reporting to a new Chinese boss:

- You may want to show him you are self-motivated.

- You are looking for opportunities to learn from him and invite him to be your lifelong mentor.

- You want to show him that you care about the organisation's growth and success.

You must demonstrate that he is the ultimate decision-maker and he can exercise his veto power when necessary. It is common to see a lower-level manager step back and invite the highest-ranking Chinese boss to become involved in the final negotiation over a dinner. You need to know how to make your Chinese boss feel comfortable when he is present at a meeting or dinner. You won't move up to the next authority level if your Chinese boss is not comfortable with this new arrangement. Respecting your Chinese boss's view will build trust in the long run.

NEGOTIATIONS

In the larger Chinese organisations, involvement of a high-ranking Chinese boss in the negotiation can be interpreted as progress. Usually, the lower-level parties in the negotiation will reach agreement before the customer involves their big boss. High-ranking Chinese bosses do not want to get involved in discussion on issues that can't be agreed at lower level: it implies the loss of face. In some situations, you may need to use the 'good cop, bad cop' technique where your Chinese boss is 'good cop' and you are 'bad cop'.

ACCEPTING A NEW ASSIGNMENT

In the West, when the boss gives you a new assignment, you can openly discuss with him the powers, authorities and support you need from him before accepting that assignment. You can even ask the boss what makes him think you are the best person for this job. In a Chinese organisation, the Chinese boss expects you to feel honoured and that you should appreciate his efforts to give you this opportunity. If you show any sign of hesitation or start to question him about powers and authority, he may think you are challenging his judgement or decision to give you this opportunity. Sometimes, he may 'force' you to accept the new assignment by threatening that he will give the opportunity to someone else. If you ask for more power and authority before you accept the new assignment, the common response from the Chinese boss is to ask you to show him results before he can consider your request. He will say you must demonstrate you can execute your responsibilities successfully. If you were born and educated in the West, you will likely say, *if you don't trust my capability, then you should not ask me to accept more responsibility.*

If you were born and educated in China, you may understand why the Chinese boss doesn't give you more power and authority when assigning you new responsibilities. The Chinese boss may be convinced about your capability to do the job but he may still have some concern or reservation about your loyalty to him. In simple terms, he does not fully trust you yet. You may see this as a positive sign for you to contribute more and get closer to your Chinese boss. At the very minimum, your hard work and capability are being recognised and appreciated by your Chinese boss. But you have to continue to work on earning his trust.

Converting Crisis into Opportunity

This is similar to the Western-based *zero to hero* concept but the execution could be totally different. When a crisis occurs in an organisation managed by a Chinese boss, try to avoid being a hero and volunteering your service or setting wrong expectations in public. You may approach the boss privately and share your concern and volunteer to be part of the team to resolve the situation or do things most people don't like to do. You need to seek his view on how he thinks you can help or add value to the situation. But don't ask for power and authority during a crisis. You should not offer new ideas for his consideration if you are the only person who can execute the ideas. This will be perceived as an attempt to take advantage of the situation. You must not ask for extra power or authority – this may be seen as arising from ulterior motives. If your eagerness to assist can earn the trust of your Chinese boss, it will be reasonable to acknowledge that your Chinese boss will polish or modify your idea and take credit for this idea as his.

If you become part of the crisis management team, build your credibility with your Chinese boss by showing him that you have control of the situation. Keep your Chinese boss informed on news and abnormal situations as and when they arise. You may want to present action plans for resolution and seek his views on improvements. If the plan fails, the Chinese boss can't say you didn't consult with him.

However, seeking the boss's consent may lead you to come back with alternative solutions and a series of discussions. When your boss asks you what else do you need in order to execute your job faster and better, this can be an indicator that:

- He has agreed with your action plan;

- He is satisfied with your performance so far in handling the situation;

- You have earned his trust; and

- He is relying on you to deliver the result.

Dealing with the Indirect Culture

The 'indirect' culture in Chinese society creates difficulties for middle managers who may need to disagree with the ideas of the Chinese boss. This may be perceived as actions that may cause the boss to lose face. Commonly used techniques include suggestions about:

- Advising the top boss to form a special task force for feasibility study;

- Engaging external forces such as foreign consultants, expert group for advice; or

- Visiting other industry standards domestic or internationally.

These suggestions may influence the top boss's thinking process and decision.

Presenting, and acting on, the recommendations of reports funded by top bosses is an art rather than a science: how do you say no to an obviously outdated, failed business model proposed by the top boss?

The Art of Giving a Hint

The indirect Chinese culture makes working with the Chinese boss more complicated.

When the timing and environment is right, you may 'hint' to your Chinese boss that he needs to consider giving you additional power or authority in order for you to be more effective in your current portfolio. However, it would be pointless if the boss fails to understand the reasons behind the hint. You can hint but never ask directly for additional power and authority because of the indirect nature of Chinese business culture. Avoid the possibility the boss may misunderstand your motives and interpret your request as a grab for more power to form your own kingdom. This will be considered as a threat to his position in the organisation.

This requires a very subtle approach and involves recognising the following challenges:

- How do you 'hint'?

- How do you know your boss understands what are you hinting?

- How do you know if your boss understands your hint but pretends he doesn't?

- When should you change your communication technique to incorporate the hint?

- How to say 'no' without saying 'no' to your Chinese boss?

RESPONDING TO AMBIGUOUS INSTRUCTIONS

It's difficult to read the boss's mind. If you report status on tasks you are responsible for, he may say *no need to inform me those things you are responsible, just tell me about exceptions*. If you don't inform him on status, he may think you have something to hide. The boss may pursue this further, insisting you to tell him everything. He may press you for honesty! The top boss always maintains the right to check the status of your work at any time; be prepared all the time. Officially, all the decisions in a Chinese organisation must be made by the authorised personal, but you must also beware of unwritten authorisation or political and undocumented decisions.

Conclusion

This chapter is intended to be a general guide only. It is still important to be aware of stereotypes, and to recognise that national cultural characteristics are only one aspect of an individual's way of viewing their world: personality, previous experience and professional cultures and training will also influence each person's expectations and perceptions and must be considered in any approach to advising upwards. Remember also that Chinese bosses are changing, and incorporating Western culture and Western management into their companies especially when operating outside of China. The purpose of the chapter is to assist Western-trained managers to understand the Chinese boss better and to make available tools and techniques to help with working closely and effectively with your Chinese boss. To achieve those objectives, a series of case studies described situations that the author encountered while working for Chinese bosses. Through comparing responses of Western-trained managers to similar situations the differences and traps that a Western-trained manager might fall into have been described.

References

Friedman, T.L. (2007). *The World is Flat 3.0: A Brief History of the 21st Century*. New York: Picador

Khor, S.K. (2005). Quan Xi project management in China. *Proceedings of PMI Asia Pacific Global Congress*. Bangkok, Thailand, conference paper. Newtown, PA: Project Management Institute. Available at http://marketplace.pmi.org/Pages/ProductDetail.aspx?GMProduct+00100836900&iss=1.

McGregor, D. (1960). *The Human Side of Enterprise*. New York: McGraw-Hill.

Tini Tran. 2008. New York Times, http://www.nytimes.com/2008/03/24/business/worldbusiness/24iht-yuan.1.11360433.html?scp=25&sq=damand%20chinese&st=Search, 24 March.

7

The New New Confucian Communication Game: Communicating with the Nintendo® Generation

Robert N. Higgins V

The Changing Communication Landscape

The way that we communicate is changing. The ability of the boss to control communication is becoming as common as the use of manual typewriters. But there is a problem with management's loss of control of the sources and means of communication. The problem that corporations face is the increasing democratisation of information flow. The issues are these: *how can corporations control reputation, coordinate projects and create wisdom from knowledge?* The answers to these questions are demonstrated every day by their youngest generation of employees – gamers. Gamers use sophisticated communication processes to manage their reputation, achieve their goals and improve their performance. The rules of this new paradigm of *always on* communication can be found in the Ancient Chinese social philosophy of Confucius. The underlying message of this chapter is that these Confucian rules apply in games and in modern organisations. To investigate this assertion the chapter will first examine the skills gamers have acquired playing online games. At the same time we will explore how gamers can apply these skills in the business world to support advancement in their organisations. We will try to provide some advice to gamers so they can recognise the gaps between how they communicate in the gamer culture and how they might communicate in 'real world' culture.[1] Finally, we will analyse how organisations can leverage the skills and attitudes of the gamer generation to improve their communication strategies in line with the generational changes of their markets and other stakeholder communities. The main premise of this chapter is that the secrets of effective communication can be learned from the Chinese philosopher Confucius: these secrets will benefit both current organisations' management teams and the emerging generations who wish to be involved in shaping and participating in future organisations.

Confucius is cool. Confucius teaches us 'how to be superior'. He advises us how to live with and how to communicate with others. His audience is the common man. His teachings from 472BC are recorded in *The Analects*.[2] The common thread that runs through Confucianism is *the way*. If we view today's organisations as a form of government we can apply his concept of the way or the proper course of human conduct in our organisations. Today, we would label Confucius as a 'social media expert'. In China he was called Master Kong.

Confucianism can be interpreted as *good businesses have potent leaders*. The culture of command and control leadership in business is changing. Globalised businesses are becoming more flexible and flat. For example, Google is a good business that has potent leadership in Eric Schmidt but continually grows from grass roots employee innovation. Flat organisations are opportunities for competent people regardless of age to emerge because *'everyone has access to identical amounts of information'* (Bryant 2010, p. 1).

> *Chi K'ang Tzu asked Confucius about government, saying, what do you think of killing the wicked and associating with the good? Confucius replied, 'In your government what is in need of killing if you desire what is good, the people will be good. The character of the ruler is like wind and that of the people is like grass. In whatever direction the wind blows, the grass always bends.'*
>
> Analects *12:19*

In this extract, Confucius is saying:

- Organisations with potent leadership don't need command and control. The leadership sets the direction.

---

1   The real world is the physical world excluding virtual worlds.
2   The *Analects* of Confucius are the written record of the words, acts and discussions of Confucius and his students.

- This direction is agile like the wind.

- The culture of such an organisation is flat and flexible like grass to the rapidly changing environment.

The New New Confucian Communication Game is a metaphor that discovering *the way* to lead in business is very similar to being a superhero in an online game. The superhero or potent leader emerges because of:

- identical access to information;

- competency based on comprehending information; and

- communicating the meaning of the information.

The methods of communication are new, but how we conduct ourselves in games and business parallels ancient Chinese communication strategies.

THE NINTENDO® GENERATION

> *When the Master was in Chi'i he heard the Shao, and for three months did not know the taste of flesh. 'I did not think' he said, 'that music could have been made so excellent as this.'*
>
> Analects 7:14

In a Confucian world view, we evaluate past and present culture to create a contemporary culture (Graham 1989, p. 12). The Shao is a lost Chinese imperial music that combines poetry, music and dance (*People's Daily* Online 2003). Legend has it that when the Emperor Shundi ordered the Shao performed in battle enemies would drop their weapons and dance. The implication is that when Confucius discovered the Shao he lost touch with the real world because he was so involved with this form of ceremonial performance. Gamers can easily identify with his passion. Research by Carnegie Mellon University's Dr Luis von Ahn (Ahn and Dabbish 2008, p. 1) shows that by 21 years of age an average American will have played 10,000 hours of online computer games. Gamers can easily identify with Confucius's passion for ceremonial performances.[3]

---

3   This chapter is focusing on the demographics of people who were born between the late 1970s and early 1990s who especially have a ubiquitous familiarity with digital communication. Gamers may refer to 'Generation Y' or 'The Nintendo® Generation' (Black, Eng and Oispov 2009, p. 1).

Gamers consider online gaming an interactive art. It is a contemporary art form combining storytelling, visualisation, music and most importantly action.

NON-GAMERS HINT

We will be discussing facets of gamer culture from the perspective of gamers who have experienced it. If you are not in the crowd of tens of millions of people who have embraced Massively Multi-Player Online Role Playing Games (MMORPG), it is recommended that you do a quick search on http://wikipedia.org/wiki/MMORPG (2010): 'Massively multiplayer online role-playing game (MMORPG) is a genre of computer role-playing games in which *a very large number of players interact* with one another within a virtual game world.'

Gamers have the ability to immerse themselves in compelling stories. Success in the world of the organisation may be achieved through the same passion in business as in gaming. We can view the Nintendo® generation broadly as the generation that has grown up playing video games, specifically online video games. Online video games are very different from single-player games. Online games require socialisation and multiple layers of communication. If you are part of this generation, then you know or have the feeling that you are creating a new contemporary culture. This community of gamers thinks of online games as beautiful, visual and aural art enhanced by social chat.

The art designed by the developers is secondary to the art created by the community of gamers. The game is a canvas. While the canvas may be a modern Monet, the meta-level art is the people, the contemporary Jack Kerouac or Li Bai who wander the virtual worlds. This is an interactive community that plays roles and practices sophisticated communication.

Competency

NON-GAMERS HINT

The first step in an MMORPG is character creation and a tutorial. Initially, your avatar or computer character has rudimentary skills and assets. The first step is to learn how to walk. After the tutorial you will enter a 'sandboxed' area. The sandboxed area has only low-level avatars. Here you must complete tasks that demonstrate you can control your avatar and this part of the MMORPG is played solo. This chapter follows the path of avatar development from solo, to group, to raid and guilds.

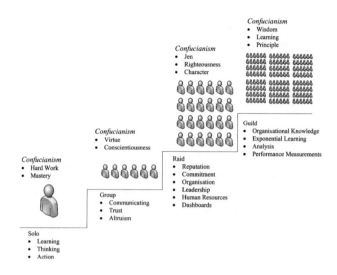

Figure 7.1   Game value map – progressing from solo to guild

Solo

> Confucius said, 'Is it not a pleasure to learn and to repeat or practice from time to time what has been learned? Is it not delightful to have friends come from afar? Is one not a superior man if he does not feel hurt even though he is not recognised?
>
> Analects *1:1*

Let's listen and think more deeply about the meaning of this segment from *The Analects* 1:1. Confucius is using a rhetorical device, asking a question. The question is: 'Does learning motivate us?' Confucius is telling us that hard work and mastery provide purpose in life.

A TEAM OF ONE

The core skills in today's virtual environment can only be developed by diligent hard work. The first time you enter a new virtual environment can be very intimidating. We do not know which way to go or what to do. If you want to progress in this environment you need to know the goal. Secondly, you need to identify activities that will 'level up' your skills. Finally, you must repeat and complete activities over and over. Gamers call it 'rinse and repeat': it means becoming proficient. It is also a learning curve: activities that were once foreign and seemed difficult become easy and second nature. Gamers are willing to work hard all the time if they are given the right work – *'blissful productivity'* (McGonigal 2010, p. 9:54). The equivalent in Confucianism is self-perfection.

NON-GAMERS HINT

Online games are designed to be easy in the beginning, but to master a character is difficult. For example to progress from level 1 to level 2 may involve 100 points. To progress from level 49 to level 50 may involve 10,000,000 points. To earn points in game you can complete quests or do activities. Game developers design games to keep customers paying every month. There is essentially no finish line. Developers design endgame activities that can only be played after you have mastered your character, joined a guild and devoted many hours every week coordinating with 24 other players. The challenge is to do all quests and earn the points to master a character. This involves persistence, hard work, commitment and repetitive activities. Gamers call this grinding.

Why do people grind? The developers are exploiting human nature; they structure the game so it is hard to progress.

> *In a famous passage of Mark Twain's novel* Tom Sawyer, *Tom is faced with the unenviable job of whitewashing his aunt's fence in full view of his friends who will pass by shortly and whose snickering promises to add insult to injury. When his friends do show up, Tom applies himself to the paintbrush with gusto, presenting the tedious chore as a rare opportunity. Tom's friends wind up not only paying for the privilege of taking their turn at the fence, but deriving real pleasure from the task – a win–win outcome if there ever was one. In Twain's words, Tom 'had discovered a great law of human action, without knowing it – namely, that in order to make a man or a boy covet a thing, it is only necessary to make the thing difficult to attain'.*
>
> Ariely, Loewenstein and Prelec (2006, p. 1)

Figure 7.2   Sisyphus 'grinding' every day

How to Grind

In Confucianism, what is known as 'the middle path' is the preferred path and requires that you have a sense of the ground rules of your society or organisation. In games, risk attitude must match environment. A risk-seeking individual may attack high-level Mobile Object Blocks (MOBs) to rapidly earn experience per hour (XP). A risk-averse individual may attack lower-level MOBs: the expectation is that they will have more success and will consistently earn XP. Confucianism identifies a middle path that can be applied socially and financially. Financially, the middle path is to have a risk attitude that is not risk-seeking or risk-averse. Socially, the middle path is to balance introverted and extroverted behavior.

NON-GAMERS HINT

A soloist gamer who is hunting in a virtual environment will understand the strengths and weakness of each MOB or Non-player Controlled (NPC) enemy character, and whether or not a MOB is social and will AGGRO – when aggravated will attack – nearby enemies. If you hunt a MOB that is too weak, the result is that you will get no credit or experience for your kills. If you hunt a MOB that is too strong you will be incapacitated. The goal is to maximise XP. This metric is difficult to judge, because it may involve performing seemingly unrelated tasks such as non-XP activities. The result of the non-XP-related activities may improve the performance of the avatar which will directly impact XP per hour.

Soloing in business and games is the art of knowing exactly how much you can take on. We are walking the middle path, the preferred path that Confucius spoke of 479BC.

Once you are good enough, age is not important. You are old enough! Strive for competency! There is no point in attempting to move upwards until you are competent in your domain. If you are a healer, it is imperative that you understand your roles and responsibilities. In business, be careful, but at the same time do not be afraid of failure. If you are always successful than perhaps you are not trying hard enough, or you are not taking enough chances.

Online games have different classes of avatars. Picking one class limits you to only the skills that are available to that class. For example, the role of the 'healer class' is to be in the background more than on the front line. A healer will nurture and may attack, but often their damage is much lower than a 'damage-dealer class'. Damage-dealers in games have one role: give it everything they have in the beginning and be the last one standing. A healer, on the other hand, is slow and steady: their strategy is to be able to outlast everyone by being careful.

There is no point in discussing which approach is better; the point is just to recognise that there are different approaches that are equally important. 'Noobs' are people that play their avatar in the wrong way. 'Learn to play you noob!' is one of the first things said to a healing avatar that incorrectly advances too fast in combat and does not understand that the strength of the avatar is to endure. When you first enter an online game you are a 'noob'. Noobs, newbs or newbies are players that have no clue how to control their avatars.

Novel Activities

Frequently, business environments do not have repeatable products or deliverables that can be replicated. The activities to produce these novel deliverables are critical skills to master. The reason is that activities that can be replicated can be outsourced or automated. It is good advice to actively seek out these complex activities that cannot be replicated. If you master a novel activity you are making yourself irreplaceable.

Gamers know the art of soloing. This is a core skill that applies directly in a dynamic work environment. Soloing is an attitude that requires commitment.

You must master the fundamentals: in addition, you have to have the analytical ability to plan ahead and reflect strategically. Ambiguity, chaos and conflicting information in business are the heavy vegetation and rocky paths in games. Pits and marshes that will slow down progress are found in virtual environments. Is this not like business? Business MOB's or enemies that may outflank you are global competitors, political situations, shifting economic or technological conditions. If you rush headlong into these enemies you may find yourself trapped without an exit plan. In business and in games being a noob means you will succumb: on the other hand, when we master activities we become superheroes who can 'slay dragons'. Cultivation of the character by effort and learning is the main theme in Confucianism.

Multiple Roles and Responsibilities

Confucius said:

> *He who learns but does not think is lost; he who thinks but does not learn is in danger.*
>
> Analects 2:15

Picking only one role or position at a company may limit your ability to be competent. In virtual environments the best players are often the ones who commit enough time and effort to play multiple roles. The same is true in business. It is more effective to be competent in different roles in an organisation and to be able to understand how those roles interact. Being competent in different roles in organisations provides you with 'opportunity flexibility'.

Confucius said:

> *It is man that can make the way great, and not the way that can make man great.*
>
> Analects 15:28

You have to commit in the beginning. Study everything very hard. Learn the technical details. 'Play that feels like work must be good' (Rettberg 2008, p. 25). Spend your own time grinding out how to do things. Once you have mastered a task, learn another task. This must be repeated over and over. Often in games these tedious small details become so effortless that at some point in the learning curve it actually becomes relaxing.

NON-GAMERS HINT

Games will include bonus attributes for a character. These bonuses may increase the amount of health you have, or you can get a good reputation and get a discount on resource cost. The soloist in a game does not hesitate to grind out some reputation for some virtual tool or skill. Sometimes people will spend a month's gaming just to get a different colour horse, for example. In games some players prefer grinding over questing. Some players prefer grouping up and questing over grinding.

In the business environment, use the same focus to grind out challenging or even boring work. Competency equals learning plus thinking plus action plus communication. The skills acquired through gaming can successfully be applied in your organisation.

Group

NON-GAMERS HINT

Group work is the next step in avatar development. In virtual reality environments, soloing will initially level up your character, but there will come a time when you can no longer be autonomous. After you have acquired the fundamental skills that enable you to manoeuvre and utilise tools you must socialise. Games provide players with tools to find groups. For example you can put a tag on your character – LFG, which means 'looking for group'. You can list your objectives in a live in game list that other players can browse. Good game design facilitates communication between people.

Having earned control of your avatar, teaming up, taking care of business and playing with others is fun. Why is it fun to drop everything you are doing and help a total stranger with a quest for 30 minutes or an hour? Think about it. Why is it fun to solve a problem as a team? The answer is the fellowship. We can all identify with the characters in Tolkein's classic *Lord of the Rings*. The dwarf, the elf, the hobbits and the men all had different skills and weaknesses: the important thing is that even though they were from different races and backgrounds they came together as a team. This is the key to problem-solving: the composition of the group, the trust of the members and understanding each other's roles and responsibilities. This is an ancient theme that runs through Confucianism.

Confucius said:

> *A superior man in dealing with the world is not for anything or against anything. He follows righteousness as the standard.*
>
>   Analects 4:10

> *The superior man thinks of virtue; the inferior man thinks of possessions. The superior man thinks of sanctions; the inferior man thinks of personal favors.*
>
>   Analects 4:11

> *If one's acts are motivated by profit, he will have many enemies.*
>
>   Analects 4:12

> *Confucius said, 'Shan there is one thread that runs through my doctrines.' Tseng Tzu said, 'Yes.' After Confucius had left the disciples asked him, what did he mean? Tsen Tzu replied, 'The way of our master is none other than conscientiousness and altruism.'*
>
>   Analects 4:15

Confucius is advising us to create a better environment we need to establish the character of others. This is the same in good games that force you to group. They force you to socialise.

'*Gamers are virtuosos at weaving a tight social fabric. Committing to playing games creates trust. They trust (other people) will play by the same rules, value the same goals, stay with the game until it is over*' (McGoningal 2010, p. 9:42). When Confucius is talking about righteousness, virtue and sanctions we can directly apply his philosophy in our organisations:

- know yourself;

- do the right thing;

- join teams that have similar beliefs; and

- trust your teammates.

And by sanctions what Confucius means is:

- support your teammates;

- embrace new ideas; and

- give your consent.

Confucius is telling us to work on things that matter. This is the heart of Confucianism. Work on things that are interesting because they are part of something important. Results from a survey by MIT and The Federal Reserve of the United States indicate that what motivates knowledge workers are autonomy, mastery and purpose (Pink 2009, p. 12:43). To find purpose at work, think of yourself as a player. Players seek out projects at work that are meaningful business problems. Players group up and master the challenges and solve the problems as a team. These are the same ancient values that Confucius espouses: *hard work and mastery creates purpose*. Improve your social environment by establishing or helping your team members. Game developers exploit this universal need for help, and the generosity of gamers to lend a hand and help out virtual strangers they just met.

Virtual Socialising

Some problems are easy to solve in a pair. Some problems are trivial in a team of five or six. Socialising is related to the Confucian concept of *Jen* (仁) or humanity. Jen is an etymological combination of the character for 人 a noble person and 二 two. The implied meaning is the virtuous relationship between two people, ideally based on humanity and benevolence. The translation is 'Humanity, benevolence, perfect, virtue, goodness, human-heartedness, love, altruism' (Chan 1963, p. 788). A noble person may be considered civilised and cultured (Graham 1989, p. 19); an avatar who is fully developed might be considered noble or elite. Gamers while chatting may spell it in 'Leet speak' as '31337' or '1337'. This is a playful numerical puzzle on elite or ELEET or LEET.

How do we socialise? We make eye contact, we smile, we speak and we have to have good body language. For Confucius transforming social relationships by propriety is important and deeper than the Western concept of good manners (Graham 1989).

The path of socialising is old and universal. Consider the relationships of a master and a student. The Japanese traditional mentoring system 'Shu Ha Ri' is a social relationship (Nagaya 2010). The master agrees to spend time with a student. The student desires knowledge that the master has. This kind of knowledge is in a form that cannot be written down. The student must learn from the master by observation, by sense, by feeling. Once the student has spent time with the master, they can begin the process of learning the deeper answers. A sushi master does not email his student instructions for how to make sushi. The proper way to prepare a sushi is not explained in words but by sense, feeling and observation. The goal of the student and the master is for the student to eventually surpass the master. To outstrip the master, the student will have to combine their own experiences with those of the master. This type of transformative relationship frequently forms in games.

Style a Gamer's Weakness

While gamers may understand altruism and a sense of purpose in games, they often fail in real world socialising, with a lack of understanding of body language. What are the things we have to do, to team up and meet people? *We have to communicate.* Gamers often lack the skills to survive in the real world. As a gamer, how much time do you spend at the auction house looking for the right equipment or mount because it looks good? As gamers we need to devote even more time to developing awareness of the culture and behaviours of our real-life organisations. Consider: how do the people that surround you view you? How do you relate to their impression of you? It is good advice to open people up by listening and asking good questions, find out their goals, attitudes and interests. Use style as a way to break the ice, meet people, align interests and team up to solve problems.

> *Chung-Kung asked about humanity. Confucius said, 'When you go abroad, behave to everyone as if you were receiving a great guest. Employ the people as if you were assisting at a great sacrifice. Do not do to others what you do not want them to do to you. Then there'll be no complaint against you in the state or in the family.' Chung-Kung said, 'Although I am not intelligent, may I put your saying into practice.'*
>
> Analects 12:2

Respect for humanity and the rules of socialisation are universal in business or a game: the *golden rule* (Chan 1968).

> *Wishing to establish its own character, he also establishes the character of others, and wishing to be prominent himself, he also helps others to be prominent.*
>
> Analects 6:28

This is the balance that gamers know very well: the balance between an individual and a group. In business this is called stakeholder management, balancing a competing group's interests and communicating within the group to balance stakeholder goals. Wing-Tsit Chan refers to the balance and harmonised individual with their society as 'the Golden Mean' (1968, p. 17). In games, groups break up because of lack of agreement or failure to balance competing interests. This is the same in business when projects fail because of lack of agreement. The journey to becoming a superhero in the business world is very similar to the path learned in games:

- become competent;

- understand deeply the needs of your peer group; and

- help them 'level up'.

Building a good reputation is very familiar to gamers. Don't be a selfish employee whose only intention is to advance your own career and manipulate others. Helping others provides satisfaction. The Confucian concept of *Jen*, the quest for balancing perfection of the self and perfection of society, is intrinsic in good games and business.

Raiding

While many gamers enjoy wandering beautiful virtual scenery at their own pace, the hardcore get into 'raiding'. Raiding is another class of meta-gaming. It is a social game that exists within the game content. While many non-gamers may laugh or become puzzled at the idea of raiding, to gamers it is serious business. Raiding builds on everything previously mastered in groups and quadruples it. Have you ever thought about it? Take a football team and multiply it by two. That is how many people are in a raid.

NON-GAMERS HINT

Raids are a lot of fun. The basics are four groups of six. The raid leader is a kind of super administrator who controls all of the members in the raid and rearranges the groups to balance the raid. Raids may involve exploring dungeons or participating in 'player versus player' (PVP) content.

Raiding is serious business. To be eligible to play in raids you have to have a good reputation. If you are great soloist you may not necessarily be a good raider. To be good at raiding you need to have trust, commitment and competence. Raiding is a social activity, a kind of end game content that never ends.

Raids are groups of 24 people. Game developers design content with objectives so difficult that only a highly organised team of around 24 people can solve problems. Raiding requires group problem-solving. Raids are like projects. They are temporary organisations. Raiding is remarkably similar to the ideas of the Behavior School of project management. The Behavior School (Bredillet 2008) focuses on organisational behavior, team building, leadership, communication and human resource management.

Raid leaders are master of social systems: they are organised and communicate and publish the goals and objectives of the raid, frequently out of game in forums. Gamers browse the forums and find raids that match their time schedule and objectives. Raid leaders select candidates based on their reputation, class and team balance.

We cannot master raiding unless we have mastered reputation. Twenty-three other people must trust you to commit and play. It is the same in business. Wiping out the raid or losing a key client because of your error may result in rejection. Clear and open communication is key to effective raiding. The point is communicating. Communicating lessons learned to all raid members is critical for eventual success. There are 276 different communication channels among raid members, which creates huge communication challenges. Gamers that have mastered raiding are virtuoso at reputation management, behavioural project coordination and communication.

Confucius said:

If a ruler sets himself right, he will be followed without his command.
If he does not set himself right, even his commands will not be obeyed.

Analects 13:6

Gamers know that raiding involves superior human resource management. Regardless of a raid leader's age, the key factors for success are skills in

- integrity;

- communication;

- organisation;

- leadership; and

- human resource management.

Frequently raids are temporary organisations that only last as long as it takes for the objective to be completed or the raid leader can manage the conflicts. Players that understand how to lead successful raids have valuable business skills. Raiding is a great place to practice leading teams of diverse stakeholders. The great news for us is that today's agile organisations value people that can plan, adapt, communicate and lead.

Guild

In online games if you want to achieve anything you have to join a guild (Brown 2010). Guilds are the organisations in online games. The game dynamics of communal discovery in guilds is a powerful motivator for individual performance. Organisations should study and leverage this game dynamic. If you have only played video games by yourself as a single player, you will have a lot of difficulty understanding why, or what is the point. Gamers know the joy of collaborating with people. Good guilds create quality connections and relationships. Players in a guild get to display their 'guild tag' in the game, usually below their avatar's name. Being a member of a great guild provides people with purpose, community and wisdom on how to improve.

NON-GAMERS HINT

The guild or kin is a permanent organisation. Avatars that join guilds are committing to join an organisation. They are committing to donating time and resources. Guilds involve fellowship, politics and reputation. To form a guild you may need a minimum of 10 other players' avatars, in-game money or other requirements.

After you have met the requirements or you join an existing guild, you will get to create a name for your guild that will be associated with your avatar. Guilds will also have community resources, perhaps a guild bank account or a guild storage area for items. The guild will also gain a guild chat tab. This chat tab is an instant messenger that can broadcast to all the guild members.

Frequently, guilds will also create out-of-game 'guild portals' or websites so people can check in and stay up to date on guild activities. Most serious guilds will also have their own voice servers. Team speak® and Ventrillo® are the popular voice servers. A voice server is a kind of Skype™ for the whole guild. Other tools frequently employed are YouTube channels, Twitter announcements and Facebook fan pages.

Guild management is a complex job. The elections of leaders and the management closely resemble a well-managed company with a CEO and a board of directors. Guilds are complex permanent social organisations.

Exponential Learning in a Knowledge Economy

The guild is a repository for knowledge. Popular online games are very dynamic and have frequently changing content and adjustments to class skills. Developers publish content to exploit people's desire to want the next great thing. In *World of Warcraft* Brown (2010, p. 1:40) states that 'on a good night 20,000 new ideas are created'. The high-end performing guilds are processing centres. These guilds extract wisdom or best practices from this barrage of information overload every day. In a virtual environment, all the data may be captured. Great guilds function as meta-level virtual organisms that create meaning from this constantly changing data.

> *The hundred artisans work in their works to perfect their craft. The superior man studies to reach the utmost of the way.*
>
> Analects *19:7*

Guild members research, study, analyse and create strategies to constantly improve performance. Brown is arguing that these are the exact skills that business needs today.

TACIT TO EXPLICIT

In education there should be no class distinction.

Analects *15:35*

Guild performance and character performance is sometime difficult to quantify. 'Tacit knowledge is highly personal and hard to formalise, making it difficult to communicate or share with others' (Nonaka 1995, p. 8).

Some players just seem to know what to do. Converting their techniques and teaching others how to improve their performance is difficult. Guilds do this by analysing key performances.

NON-GAMERS HINT

Games have complex metrics. The basics are health bars which measure health. If you get to zero you are incapacitated. There are many other indicators, such as 'cool downs' which limit the time that action can be performed. Some games have other ratios: DPS (damage per second) or HOT (heal over time).

Good games will even allow for the player to parse the raw data and build their own metrics. For example the 'recharge rate for health'. Different combinations of avatar attributes, equipment and techniques will affect the rates and metrics. Hard-core gamers will simulate, measure, adjust and modify their avatars based on these real-time metrics. Guilds will record video of actions and the detailed logs of the data are combined to provide 360° feedback for all guild members. The tacit knowledge is converted to explicit knowledge to improve collective performance.

Interestingly, it does not matter if you a guild leader or a new guild member, there is no class distinction in this quest for performance (Brown 2010). In this meritocratic environment 'lessons learned' are rapidly applied by players using custom player-designed dashboards that display the key performance values in real time.

A ruler who governs his state by virtue is like the North Polar Star, which remains in its place while all the other stars revolve around it.

Analects *2:1*

Players will adjust their character attributes to deliver the optimum performance. John Seely Brown (2010, p. 4:50) describes this as proof of 'exponential learning'. Competitive raiding guilds are obsessed with organisational knowledge dissemination superiority. The superhero or guild leader emerges by:

- demonstrating competency of tacit knowledge;

- communicating proficiency by converting tacit knowledge to explicit knowledge;

- dissemination of wisdom;

- good reputation earned by mentoring others;

- leading;

- 360° degree analysis; and

- study.

The reward that players get for performing, communicating, studying and innovating is reputational power.

Tzu-hsia said, 'A man who has energy to spare after studying should serve his state. A man who has energy to spare after serving his state should study.'

Analects *19:13*

LEVERAGING GAMERS

Organisations that can understand the motivating factors of their members can activate gamers as a resource for their benefit. It is a win–win for both gamers and organisations to perform at maximum potential. Gamers are virtuosos at analysing complex real-time environments, collaborating, reputation management, creating trust and communicating. We will analyse communication rules, sophisticated communication practices, simulation and strategy. We are shifting to the perspective of how organisations can exploit this resource.

Communication Rules

The Nintendo® generation are masters of electronic communication. The game environment is extremely demanding in terms of multi-tasking. It is common for people to have two active voice channels with multiple members in each channel. Text chat is layered and complex with multiple channels. There is:

- global chat in which a player can chat with a particular region;

- local text chat that broadcasts players' chat in a local area;

- guild text chat that is communication between guild members that can span regions;

- raid text chat which is between members of a large group of 24 people;

- team text chat which is between a team of about six; and

- player-to-player chat.

Out of game there are forums, blogs, videos and all the other types of modern communication. Skilled teenagers adroitly manage these complex levels of chat seamlessly, with the occasional 'mt' or miss-tell.

How electronic communication is used in the game is based on the role of the people we are communicating with. The success or failure of an in-game quest relies on similar business skills of choosing which communication method to use.

> The superior man seeks [room for improvement or occasion to blame] in
> himself; the inferior man seeks it in others.
>
> Analects 15:20

Manners or game ethos parallels the Confucian worldview, games and business.

Players learn and invent the moral order of the game, coming to understandings about the right way to play. The moral order cannot be reduced to simple acquisition of knowledge. It is in flux, under negotiation, emergent in conversation, and only temporarily stable.

Nardi, Ly and Harris (2007, p. 6)

Many aspects of games are learned through persistent conversations among distributed peers. Leaders emerge from articulated discussions and consensus-building among peers.

Online gamers have to master 'in-game' communication. Gamers may spend a lot of time in-game acquiring clothes, armoir or mounts that offer no technical advantage, simply because it communicates the gamer has earned something in-game that is difficult to acquire. The main problem that the Nintendo® generation has is 'silent communication'. Silent communication is the silent body language embedded in culture and applied (often unconsciously by) people and organisations. Non-verbal communication is powerful. If two people can look each other in the eye and get that spark of simultaneous understanding and realisation it creates powerful connections.

GAMER HINT

Gamers need to use the same passion to master 'the game' in business. Smile when you enter a room, pay careful attention to your grooming and your dressing. A bright white smile, a fresh suit of clothes communicates rapidly that you are social and ready. In meetings, use 'airplane mode' and turn off all your electronic devices. Pausing to check your smartphone sends a quick message to an older generation. That 'silent message' is that what they are saying is not important. Observe how your leaders use their body to communicate subtly. For example, the Japanese have a silent form of communication known as *a-un*. From the author's personal experiences this form of paralingual understanding of the context of a situation and 'reading the air' or glancing at a person's face to 'simultaneously realise the truth' involves a kind of give and take, in which deep meaning is conveyed because of the context. This kind of silent communication may be cultural, not only nationally but organisationally. This type of communication is silent and effortless and happens with a team that is working together: they can 'read each other's thoughts'. We can all get this feeling being with our family or close friends. Understanding how to use body language and voice to communicate is a skill we can all improve. Mastering these skills will create more opportunity for us to rapidly understand situations in real time and choose the correct path. The same techniques we use in game are applied on the job.

Sophisticated Communicative Practices

TOOL FOR REPUTATION MANAGEMENT

> *The superior man does not seek fulfillment of his appetite nor comfort*
> *in his lodging. He is diligent in his duties and careful in his speech. He*
> *associates with men of moral principles and thereby realises himself.*
> *Such a person may be said to love learning.*
>
> Analects *1:1*

Confucius is telling us to be mindful of our reputation. He is speaking to the individual. His advice is to surround ourselves with reputable people. If we can associate with good people we can realise our full potential.

Success in massive multi-player online games depends on personal reputation. Gamers know they must use the communication tools appropriately. The role play component of games means that in local chat players must send text messages in character. Avatars that only communicate in local chat in character gain a favorable reputation as a role player. Frequently, players align to complete activities based on future promises. For example, 'If I help you now will you help me later?' If a player drops out of the group and breaks a promise they may lose reputation. In groups, a leader will need to spend time coordinating members. How the leader engages and communicates with the group is critical: conflicts between group members must be managed and communication is critical to success.

Reputation takes a long time to build in a game environment. Many of the 'high end' raids are elitist. To gain admittance to an elite raid may involve personal commitments that can impact relations in the real world. Reputation may be lost in an instant. When 24 people are in the middle of critical raid activity, it may be impossible to complete if just one person leaves. Trust and commitment are paramount in these situations.

Corporations that have respected guild leaders or guild masters as their employees have a precious resource. Success in the virtual world translates into success in the real world.

To run a large guild, a guild master must be adept at many skills: attracting, evaluating and recruiting new members; creating apprenticeship programmes; orchestrating group strategy; and adjudicating disputes. Guilds routinely splinter over petty squabbles and other basic failures of management; the master must resolve them without losing valuable members, who can easily quit and join a rival guild. Never mind the virtual surroundings; these conditions provide real-world training a manager can apply directly in the workplace (Brown 2006, p. 2).

Tools for Corporate Management

Corporations are experimenting with social media, mass collaboration, wikis, crowd sourcing and virtual worlds. Although the goals of corporations and online games are different they share the same goals for communication. *That goal is sustained collaboration.*

GAMER HINT

Collaboration projects have been instituted by senior management: participation is association. Earning a solid reputation in these virtual corporate communities is a valuable commodity. This is a very old Confucian concept of *Jen*, meaning that a superior person is in harmony with their community. Balance your communication strategy. Conscientiously pursue your goals, while altruistically engaging in your corporate community.

Organisations can simulate having fun at work and encourage gamification or the use of game mechanics. For example an emerging tool to facilitate understanding and commitment is a game called 'planning poker'.

Planning poker is played with co-located or virtually with distributed teams. Novel activities are discussed in terms of requirements, duration and dependencies. Because an activity is novel, its actual duration may be hard to quantify. Planning poker is a communication game that both qualifies the requirements for a novel activity and provides quantitative data.

You play planning poker with activity cards and a deck of 'time cards'. Each member receives a set of the time cards which estimate the duration – for example 15, 30, 45 or 60 minutes. First the team discusses the activity card, the requirements of the activity, the mandatory dependencies, risks, and so on. After this discussion each person picks and plays their time cards face down. After that the cards are turned over. The results are recorded on the activity card and analysed. A team of three or more can determine the maximum time, minimum time, mode and standard deviation. This will also uncover invalid assumptions and provide realistic metrics for task completion. The best part is the laughter and play that planning poker creates. Planning poker players are adamant that they can complete a novel challenging task in a realistic time. This game creates passionate engagement, a type of Tom Sawyer communication of shared values and commitment.

Organisations should encourage collaboration and play among diverse employees. They need to create positive places that encourage creativity and communication. These places are fertile environments for people who are engaged and have a reputation for having fun and getting things done.

Simulation

Game play involves gaining experience by doing. Confucius says: 'I hear and I forget. I see and I remember. I do and I understand.' Games have action. Correct actions are the way. What games can do, part of their value, lies in showing us the consequences of our actions and strategies. 'The game can also show us how choosing the right path or preferred path of decisions can lead to success while other paths can, ultimately, lead to failure' Black, Eng and Oispov (2009, p. 1). Simulation may involve issue resolution. This is done by testing out various scenarios to optimise the chance of a favorable event, for example switching avatars or trying a different combination of team members.

But accidental learning transcends intentional training. When role-playing gamers team up to undertake a quest, they often need to attempt particularly difficult challenges repeatedly until they find a blend of skills, talents and actions that allows them to succeed. This process brings about a profound shift in how they perceive and react to the world around them. They become more flexible in their thinking and more sensitive to social cues (Brown and Thomas 2006, p. 1).

Why would people spend 7.5 per cent of their waking hours playing a game? 'World of Warcraft serves as a tool to educate its players and their range of behaviors and skills specific to the situation of conducting business in an economy controlled by corporations' (Rettberg 2008, p. 3). Online games simulate the monotony of repetitive actions as a path to progression. Questing may involve repeated trips 'commuting' to resource areas. These repeated monotonous actions force gamers to consider the most efficient way to gather resources.

Exploiting a resource in-game means to use the game mechanics to gain an unfair advantage that was not intended by the developers. There is a constant adversarial relationship between developers/designers in-game and players. There is a fine line between learning from simulation, strategising the optimum rate of return and exploiting a game mechanic. Generally, many gamers frown on explicit exploits, but in practice will strive to optimise their experience. These skills are directly applicable in a competitive global business environment. Today, companies must continually optimise their strategies using all the legal methods possible in a complex global regulatory environment.

Players have to calculate the probability of success or failure in real time. Failures are often the result of communication issues. When playing as a team, people must communicate the causes of failure for longer-term sustainable success. Simulations in-game are multi-learning opportunities. People may learn from personal experience, conversation and researching walk-throughs. The main goals of problem-solving in-game are to discover the way forward, obtain resources, improve their character and acquire better equipment. In addition to explicit knowledge, people must create relationships. Progression in games or the way forward is complex and players need to collaborate and discover their own proper course of conduct.

McGoningal (2010, p. 2:24) has identified the 'epic win' as a major motivator in games. She defines an epic win as something that is so challenging that it is beyond expectations. Simulations in games create 'urgent optimism' – the sense that everything is possible – and the feedback on simulation is real time. For example players can adjust their avatars' attributes or items and redo an activity. The real-time dashboard provides metrics that can help fine-tune an avatar's performance.

Dashboard Models for Organisations

Organisations need to learn from this new generation. In online environments gamers are implementing tools that are mashing up intangible values, analysing performance and radically accelerating their real-time exponential learning.

Dashboards display these synthetic key performance indicators (KPI). In the future corporate dashboard displays may merge and report metrics in real time.

- *Earned value management:* which measures the progress of producing deliverables on time and on budget.

- *Technical performance measures:* 'attributes that determine how well a system or system element is satisfying or expected to satisfy a technical requirement or goal' (Alleman 2010, p. 21).

- *Sustainability indexes:* which might measure, for example, CO_2 emitted.

- *Happiness indexes:* which might measure the smiles of team members.

- *Communication indexes:* which might measure the frequency and types of communication between people.

- *Twitter velocity:* which might measure the frequency of tweets on a topic over time.

Organisations must creatively analyse the data they have and use technology to empower their employees. Dashboard visualisations of real-time events provide instant feedback. This will allow organisations to extract wisdom from knowledge using the same type of exponential learning skills that millions of gamers are now using

Organisations have to create environments that allow the flat communication of facts, data and contextual information. To create wisdom the processes and procedures should be streamlined based on the principle of joint value creation between the individual and the organisation. Users can utilise their invisible intuitions to convert and combine this messy information and change it into knowledge. This synthesised internalised knowledge can be distributed using the sophisticated gamer communication methods. This is the connected information model of action based on wisdom.

Strategy

> *Confucianism roots all its general ideas is in the minute study of existing custom, arts and historical precedent, it alone held the promise of the full integration of the individual into his culture, community, and customs which must be part of the secret of China's social immortality.*
>
> *Graham (1989, p. 372)*

Organisations should exploit MMORPG game dynamics to create free individuals and social harmony.

Online games can be an indirect way to discover the risk attitude of people. Instead of assuming that we know what type of people we are working with – risk-seeking or risk-averse – we can utilise the simulation environment of games for free. Awareness of an individual's or a group's risk attitude is the critical first step of proactive risk management (Hillson 2009, p. 5). Games can provide organisations with a fun way of solving the issue of how to become aware of an individual's risk attitude. An organisation with a new global project may not have the budget or time to fly personnel for team building activities. Organisations can exploit free MMORPG to assemble a team in a virtual environment. Furthermore these environments already have numerous activities that teams can complete for building the team culture.

Managers and members can learn tacitly about each other's risk attitude. If team members as 'players' can *appreciate⁴ individuals' attitudes then we can perform an assessment* of the spectrum of attitude for this newly-formed global project team (Hillson 2009, p. 5). If we can accurately assess current risk attitude then we can manage future performance proactively. A person's reputation can be qualified as risk-seeking, risk-averse or risk-neutral. This is a strategy the United States Department of Defense employs with their online virtual game *America's Army 3*®. The goal of utilising simulation to understand risk attitude is one example of how simulation can improve productivity by harmonising or integrating individuals into high performing global teams.

---

4   The Six As model is described in more detail in Chapter 5 of this book.

Old Game

The practical advice that Confucius provides us is 'Doing one's best'. *The way* is not linear, it is layered and ambiguous. We all need to discover the proper course of conduct. Good advice for gamers includes:

- be passionate;

- if there are things you can do, do them;

- perfect yourself;

- if there are things you cannot do make sure you communicate with others;

- communicate the barriers you have that prevent you from solving them;

- know the social environment of your organisation;

- follow the golden rule of 'do unto others as you would have them do to you';

- understand your impact on your social environment;

- help your peers;

- work for the perfection of society;

- engage your superiors in a master/student relationship; and

- learn by doing.

It is also important to practice personal reputation/risk management – be aware of your office environment and of abuse of authority from superiors. Do not be naive and allow others to use you to get what they want. In online gaming, people will be banned from games if they 'gank', 'camp' or harass lower level players by overpowering them repeatedly. Society also has rules about discrimination and abuse of authority. Know your organisation and the rights that all people have as employees in a fair working environment.

Protect yourself from power harassment. Sometimes doing one's best involves defending yourself. Be proactive and document situations that might involve the abuse of authority or power harassment.

> *By nature men are alike. Through practice they have become far apart.*
>
> Analects 17:2

Take responsibility: we all make mistakes. How we handle mistakes establishes our reputation.

New Rules

Today, tools, techniques and methods of communication are rapidly changing. Society's values and customs and our social behaviour are also changing. As recently as 10 to 15 years ago, our ability to find and form communities was limited to our local social groups. Now, in cyberspace we can connect and exchange ideas with anyone, anywhere, and at any time. As Confucius says: 'Is it not delightful when friends come from afar?' Global projects and business are increasing because of technology, and real-time exchange of images, video and text are commonplace.

We will all be under more pressure to open up our private social lives to the public. More than ever before, choices we make when we are young will impact us not only now but throughout our lives and in ways we can't know or predict. The new rules of reputation management are now defined: being an honest player, who works well in groups and is fun to play with. Reputation is earned by mastering the complex communication methods and channels available in modern online games. The new rules that gamers need to learn are the old Confucian rules of:

- Understanding situational context;

- Paying close attention to the silent details of the organisational culture and atmosphere; and

- Discovering *the way*.

Multi-learning

Only the most intelligent and the most stupid do not change.

Analects *17:13*

We all need to create and find our own path. When will we accept mobile video phone calls in an always on 24/7 connected global society? The old rules of defined time for work no longer apply. Concepts of privacy and the sharing of personal information are also undergoing a tectonic shift. How we respond to this pressure of becoming fans of online communities, commenting on topics that are important to us and managing our reputation will involve forming new rules. Personal reputation management skills are a microcosm of the organisations privacy policies. These are the new problems that organisations need to simulate to formulate simple robust policies.

Because members of the project team stay in close touch with outside sources of information, they can respond quickly to changing market conditions. Team members engage in a continual process of trial and error to narrow down the number of alternatives that they must consider. They also acquire broad knowledge and diverse skills, which help them create a versatile team capable of solving an array of problems fast (Nonaka and Takeuchi 1985, p. 7).

The Confucian ideal is to take the middle path. Passionately learn everything you can about a subject. Confucius said: 'By three methods we may learn wisdom. First, by reflection, which is noblest; second, by imitation, which is easiest, and third by experience, which is the bitterest.'

Engage in communities that create meaning in your life. Observe others and realise that there are multiple perspectives and ways to view things. Harness the superpowers we all have in virtual communities (McGonigal 2010). These superpowers are:

- the power of optimism;

- the power of blissful productivity by mastering something and doing it very well;

- the power to lend a hand and help someone; and

- the dream of achieving something greater as a group, than what we can achieve as individuals.

Leading

Lead by doing. Take actions. Engage your community and your organisations. Do not worry about getting recognition. 'Is one not a superior man if he does not feel hurt even though he is not recognised?' Experience is a great teacher and earning reputation is something that is hard to get and easy to lose. Observe your colleagues silent communication methods. Knowing when someone needs help and lending a hand creates synergy and is a positive reinforcement of teamwork. At the same time open up and communicate with others, when you have questions or barriers to solving a problem. Although it may be difficult to express the problems, if you can identify the problems and communicate them to others you are on target to solve them.

While not all work replicates the environment of games, be conscious that choices in work impact happiness in personal life. Align your beliefs with communities and organisations that share your dreams and ambitions. '*Choose a job you love, and you will never have to work a day in your life.*' Follow the age-old path of proper course of conduct:

- Master all the tasks you can.

- Understand your role in an organisation, sometimes we must all submit to accepting damage at work.

- Be professional and communicate: if some problems are too large to handle for you as an individual, seek out your organisations professional help. Many groups and companies offer counselling as a form of healing, and utilising health services if you need to is not a bad thing.

Humanity and society are best when everyone can achieve the peak of their potential. We all have roles to play in organisations and in our society. How we perform those roles creates our reputation.

Conclusion

In this chapter we talked about the powerful game dynamics that have shaped the Nintendo® generation. This generation of gamers consists of individuals who are virtuosos at analysing complex real-time environments, collaborating, creating trust and communicating. Potent leaders will emerge from this generation. In order for organisations to leverage this strategic asset, management has a vital role to play in creating a game overlay. Managers can also use the universal human values of self-improvement, mastery, optimism, generosity and propriety. The humanism of Confucianism frees the individual by creating fertile environments for personal growth. These are the same in business or a virtual environment – the novelty is the overlay of game dynamics. This synthesis of contemporary culture is a new direction for organisations. Managers need to trust the younger generation and give them leeway to discover the proper course of conduct.

We found that the skills and practices of winning in games are reflected in the rapidly changing communication landscape that business needs to adopt. There are many lessons for both the Nintendo® generation and the management generation:

- Management must set the vision and create epic challenges;

- Work on meaningful problems;

- Employees must take initiative to master tasks;

- Altruism, righteousness, generosity are important values for organisations;

- Broad access to raw data and detailed information;

- Utilise modern sophisticated flat communication practices;

- Institute a mentoring system;

- Master the silent real world communication;

- Facilitate sustained collaboration or 'fellowships' with an open mind that help and respect others;

- Create environments for simulation;

- Leverage guild dynamics for extracting wisdom from knowledge;

- Recognise that failures are opportunities for improvement;

- Utilise real time dashboards and metrics;

- Take decisive actions based on wisdom;

- Three hundred and sixty degree feedback focused on performance; and

- Recognition of emerging superheroes by rewarding excellence with power .

If today's managers can give the younger generation the leeway to find the best path utilising the younger generation's mastery of sophisticated communication, massive collaboration, exponential learning and information dissemination then organisations will not only incrementally improve but increased communal discovery will create new combinations that will result in breakthrough innovation. The New New Confucian Communication Game Strategy is *to play the old game with new rules*. The old game is to follow humanity's universal path of Confucian social harmony.

References

Ahn, L.V. and Dabbish, L. 2008. Designing games with a purpose. *Communications of the ACM*, 51(8): 58–67.

Alleman, G. 2010. *CPM-500-B/C/F: Integrating Systems Engineering with Earned Value Management. CPM-500-B/C/F*. Naples, FL: PMI – College of Performance Management.

Ariely, D., Loewenstein, G. and Prelec, D. 2006. Tom Sawyer and the construction of value. *Journal of Economic Behavior & Organization*, 60: 1–10.

Black, R.LT., Eng, P. and Oispov, I.A. 2009. Gaming in the education of project managers. *Proceedings of 2009 PMI Global Congress*, Orlando, Florida, conference paper.

Brown, J.S. 2010. *The knowledge economy of World of Warcraft*. Stanford University's Entrepreneurship Corner, accessed 14 April 2010, http://ecorner.stanford.edu/authorMaterialInfo.html?mid=2432.

Brown, J.S. and Thomas, D. 2006. You play World of Warcraft? You're hired. *Wired Magazine*, 14(4): 1–3.

Bryant, A. 2001. Structure? The flatter the better. *The New York Times*, accessed 16 January, http://www.nytimes.com/2010/01/17/business/17corner.html.

Chan, Wing-Tsit. 1963. *A Source Book in Chinese Philosophy*. Princeton, NJ: Princeton University Press.

Confucius. 2001. *The Analects*. The Classic Library. http://www.classicallibrary.org/confucius/analects/index.htm.

Graham, A.C. 1989. *Disputers of the TAO Philosophical Argument in Ancient China*. La Salle, IL: Open Court.

Hillson, D. 2009. How groups make risky decisions. *Proceedings of 2009 PMI Global Congress*, Orlando, Florida, pp. 1–7.

McGonigal, J. *Gaming can make a better world*. TED, transcript, accessed February 2010, http://www.ted.com/talks/jane_mcgonigal_gaming_can_make_a_better_world.html.

Nagaya, H. 2010. *Shu Ha Ri, Japanese Mentoring Systems*, Interview.

Nardi, B.A., Ly, S. and Harris, J. 2007. *Learning Conversations in World of Warcraft*. Irvine, CA: University of California.

Nonaka, I. and Takeuchi, H. 1986. The new new product development game. *Harvard Business Review*, January–February: 137–146.

Nonaka, I. and Takeuchi, H. 1995. *The Knowledge-Creating Company*. New York: Oxford University Press.

People's Daily Online. 2003. *In pursuit of Lost Ancient Imperial Chinese Music*, accessed 6 May 2011, http://english.peopledaily.com.cn/200301/03/eng20030103_109475.shtml.

Pink, D. 2009. *The Surprising Science of Motivation*. TED, accessed 6 May 2011, http://www.ted.com/talks/lang/eng/dan_pink_on_motivation.html.

Rettberg, S. 2008. *Corporate ideology in World of Warcraft*, accessed 6 May 2011, http://retts.net/documents/rettberg_corp_ideology.pdf.

Wikipedia. 2010. *Massively multiplayer online role-playing game*, accessed 6 May 2011, http://en.wikipedia.org/wiki.

8

How to Train Your Manager: A Darwinian Perspective

S. Jonathan Whitty

Introduction

ADVISING UPWARDS? HELPING MANAGEMENT TO HELP YOU?
HELPING MANAGEMENT TO HELP YOU DO WHAT?

Perhaps it is to help you do your job better or help you keep your job, even help you to get promoted! Whatever it is, surviving as the 'meat in the sandwich' between slices of senior management and front-line workers is not easy. In the corporate environment where the modern manager lives, the ability to plan, organise and deal with unexpected events is highly valued, admired, even celebrated. These traits act as cues or signals to senior management that the manager with these abilities is productive and able to generate profit, both of which are paramount for corporate survival. In this corporate environment a selection process takes place. Certain behaviours are condemned whilst others are rewarded through cultural inclusion, acceptance through employment, promotion and membership of a community. Surviving this selection enables these managers to live and reproduce, passing their behavioural characteristics, tendencies and ideals on to further generations of managers who will again undergo further selection. This struggle for survival as a manager sounds a lot like the evolutionary process, doesn't it? Well it is, and the evolutionary process impacts on every manager, from how they are selected and retained, to the tools and techniques they use to report, influence and get help from senior management.

Anything that we do that gives us a better chance at surviving in the corporate environment has the possibility of being passed on to future generations of managers, not by biological genetic means, but by cultural *memetic* means. A meme can be considered to be a behaviour, concept, idea, or technique that gets copied from person to person. *Memetics* is the study of why and how they get copied from an evolutionary point of view. Just as dairy cattle and domestic dogs have been selectively bred (copied) by humans for various reason, so behaviours, ideas and techniques get selected and passed on from person to person, from manager to manager, from manager to senior manager.

In this chapter I want to look at advising upwards through a completely different lens. I want to change the whole point of view about what is going on during the advising upwards process and present what I consider to be the beginnings of a Darwinian explanation for what goes on. More particularly I want to explore an evolutionary basis for the advising behaviours and tools managers use. One might reason that the act of advising upwards is one of the social mechanisms that underpin our cooperative behaviour. For example, if we are to divide labour to make our organisations work, then information and advice needs to be passed from the front lines to the managers and from the managers to senior managers. However, if we take an evolutionary perception on advising upwards then we find that some of the techniques involved also provide survival advantages to managers because they enable them to influence the behaviours and choices of those they report to. For example, just as an octopus receives survival advantages in the natural world from its ability to change its camouflage colouring, so a manager can use various reporting tools in the social corporate world to obscure from senior management the uncertainty of various aspects of the work they are managing. This behaviour might have the effect of placating senior management, which therefore buys some time for the manager to get matters back on track and under control. Furthermore, just as the Viceroy butterfly receives survival advantages in nature for looking like a real poisonous butterfly, so a manager in the social corporate world can receive favourable attention from senior management because they appear to be organised and in control when at that particular moment they are not.

As the optical lens of the microscope has enabled us to understand the previously obscured bacterial world, so the Darwinian lens of evolutionary science can help us to understand why managers do what they do. In short, I am going to use the Darwinian lens to point out some of the convoluted, intricate and occasionally devious activities managers engage in, and explain that it is not their fault – they have been bred that way. And senior managers are the way they are because they have been bred that way too. Not only did the microscope enable us to observe the bacterial and molecular world, it enabled us to manipulate it in beneficial ways. I suggest the same is true for the Darwinian lens. Not only do evolutionary principles expose the biological foundations of our behaviours, they show us how we can use this information in constructive behaviour-changing ways.

I begin with a play on the words 'evolution at work' and attempt to explain how evolution works whilst at the same time explain how it manifests at work. In the section 'Peacocks, chocolates and managers' I focus on the process of selection and how it sculpts both the natural and social world we inhabit, most particularly the corporate world where we adopt the role of manager and where senior management take part in the selection process. Next, in the 'Domestication of managers' I take the selection process further and illustrate how the traits of the modern manager have been selected for in a form of domestication, and how managers have had to take on new behaviours in order to survive the pressures of the corporate environment. In 'Management camouflage and mimicry' I reference a small study, and further show how practising managers have adopted various tools and techniques for the purposes of influencing senior management, and I attempt to reconcile these behaviours in terms of camouflage and mimicry. In the last half of the chapter I attempt to strike a more positive note with the section on 'management whispering'. Here I point out how the traits and behaviours of managers and senior managers are intertwined and interdependent as they continue to evolve together in a symbiotic relationship. From a very practical point of view, advantages can be taken of this situation, and managers can learn when and how best to influence senior management.

Evolution at Work

> *Evolutionary theory argues that species change over time. In the struggle to survive the competition for finite resources, only those species that are optimally adapted to their environments survive while others perish. Individuals tend to produce offspring that have characteristics that are more like their parents than they are like the competitors of their parent's. Over time improvements are preserved and accumulated as characteristics will be a gradual refined and improved.*
>
> *Darwin (1890)*

When Charles Darwin published this in his *Origin of Species* the Church of England were not much disturbed about the concept of evolution: churchmen had for many years encouraged people to believe that much of the bible was metaphorical rather than the literal truth. After all, a linear evolution might have been part of God's plan. What did disturb them was that Darwin showed them that nature does not care, and that the beauty that one perceives in a harmonious woodland meadow is actually a façade that conceals a natural world that is locked into a vicious and brutal struggle for survival, where all life is hungry, and where animals are afraid and are largely destined to die a horrific death.

Of course this façade of the harmonious woodland meadow is conjured up by the human brain, which also conjures up a façade of how our social environment works, including that of our corporate and work environment. Beneath the façade of reporting to senior management, teamworking and aligning our actions to the vision and mission of the company, there is a brutal struggle for human survival. After all, none of the managers I know have to hunt and kill their own food, make their own clothing, or build their own houses in order to survive. Nevertheless they still acquire adequate food and shelter to survive and a mate to reproduce. But the acquisition of a suitable mate is far removed from the topic of this discussion. The modern manager acquires food and shelter in a complex manner that involves the intermediary stage of acquiring money which is used in exchange for food and shelter. For most managers the only way to legally acquire money in modern society is to receive it in exchange for productive work. Work leads to money, and money leads to the acquisition of survival resources. This is how we have constructed the corporate West, and each of us born into this environment has very little choice but to comply with this work = money = survival equation. Unlike other animals, food is not the scarce resource we humans in the West all compete for. Neither are clothes, houses, or money. What we all compete for is a job that pays good money. Of course, getting the job is only half the battle. The other is holding on to it and using it as leverage to get a better one that pays more money. But as we shall see, there are some simple tools and techniques that modern managers use to get the help from senior management that increases their chances of success in this battle.

What is it that drives us to battle or compete for a job and hold onto it? At a very fundamental level our human emotions and behaviours have a biological foundation. For example, receptors in the brain detect the levels of salt in the bloodstream. If they are too high, this means we (or another animal) are at risk of dehydration and the resulting behaviour or physical gesture is the reflexive response of moving to find water. The emotion we humans feel under these conditions might be described as that of being 'thirsty'. Reflex responses such as thirst enable a primitive animal to rectify a chemical deficiency and therefore maintain a chemical balance (that is a healthy body). However, as primitive animals evolved, those with brain-like functions became selected (by the environment, that is, they stayed alive) because it is advantageous for an animal to use its capacity to assess different courses of action, such as referring to past experience (memory function), as well as using available sensory information. In an environment where water is scarce, the animals that can remember or create a system for remembering where the nearest waterhole is will over time do better than those who search randomly. As the environment becomes more and more complex, successful behavioural strategies become more and more elaborate. Today we humans exist in a biological environment, a complex social/cultural environment, an ever-increasing virtual environment, and our behaviour to satisfy various physical and physiological 'thirsts' is extraordinarily complex too. Holding a job down or getting selected for more interesting work or promotion, as I've mentioned previously, is just one of them.

One great aspect of the evolutionary process is that it does not demand perfection, and the modern manager can use this feature to their advantage. To survive one needs to find a niche, and then be better than others in the niche at acquiring scarce recourses essential for survival. There is an old joke about the hunter who threw away his gun, his backpack and his jacket and started to run away from the enraged tiger. 'Why did you do that?' shouted the second running hunter, 'you can't run faster than a tiger.' 'No I can't' said the first hunter, 'but I can run faster than you.' To survive in the corporate environment, a manager doesn't need to be the best; they just need to be better than the others in their niche area. But this statement is not quite complete, as in our human social environment, at least in the short term; creating the *impression* that you are better can also give you a competitive advantage over others.

Next I am going to put forward the case that the modern manager competes to secure their job or attain promotion in a way likened to that of how a peacock competes to secure a mate. The latter has evolved a feathered tail that has become complex in structure and has the effect of securing a mate; the former has evolved a set of advising and reporting tools and techniques (amongst other things) which also have elaborate structures and has the effect of attracting and reassuring senior management. What I'm suggesting is that the selection of managers is somewhat akin to the sexual selection process amongst peacocks. Some management artefacts like carefully crafted emails, reports or charts can be considered to be a form of expressivity where the manager can demonstrate or advertise through their displays that they possess the attributes of being well organised, able to plan and can be trusted to deal with unexpected events. And these attributes can get them preferential treatment; they can help senior management select them.

Peacocks, Chocolates and Managers

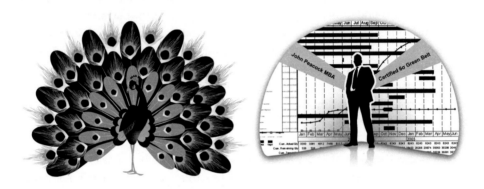

Figure 8.1   The peacock and the manager

To restate Darwin earlier, the evolutionary process requires species to change both their physical and behavioural characteristics in order to become better adapted to their environment. However, not all adaptations can be clearly associated with creating survival advantages. For example, natural selection *should* have eliminated what appears to be the opulent and ornamental tail of the peacock, as it is hard to consider a peacock's tail as something other than an impediment to its survival. Their tails are large, heavy, difficult to carry, require a lot of energy to grow and they make the animal conspicuous and slow it down as it runs away from a predator. In spite of this, the tail does win sexual partners, as there is something about its extravagance that attracts peahens. Peacock evolution has not only been shaped by its environment during the competition for survival; it has also been shaped by the choices of peahens. The peacock's tail appears to be a cue for, or perhaps a costly advertisement for, its health and fitness, as only fit and healthy peacocks can afford to grow spectacular tails. Another way to think of this is that peahens are selectively breeding peacocks in the same way as dog breeders breed dogs or farmers breed cattle.

Before I discuss managers and how they display or advertise their attributes to senior management, it is worth trying to be clear about what selection behaviour is, as it is tempting to think in the peacock example that the peahen is somehow consciously considering her options in the same way that one might deliberate over which chocolate to choose from the chocolate box. There are similarities, and they are more hard-wired than one might think. In the case of the peacock's tail, the peacock does not grow its splendid tail *because* it attracts a mate. The tail is a consequence of the selection process: an elegant tail is a product of a healthy and reproductive bird. Evolution is very much a numbers game played over large amounts of time as it speculates by randomly varying offspring ever so slightly. In the early stages of the evolution of peacocks, all hatchlings will be slightly different to their parents. Some will be fitter and more biologically stable (because of genetic mutation caused randomly or by the environment that the embryo develops in) than others. Some fit and healthy peacocks channel energy into growing plumage and survive long enough to reproduce with the peahens who are attracted to them, and this 'plumage growing and being attractive to peahens' trait gets passed on to offspring. Others barely survive to sexual maturity or give birth to even weaker offspring. And so the direction of evolution (whether they have tails or not) of peacocks and peahen is set in place. The trait of growing tails (the peacock) and the trait of being attracted to tails (the peahen) becomes biologically wired, so to speak, into the species. This selection process is the non-random feature of the evolution of peacocks because it is always the peahen that makes the selection.

Surprisingly, this directional process happens with the evolution of boxes of chocolates too. In the early days of chocolates, manufacturers would experiment by creating boxes of chocolates with varying selections and test them out on the market. Some people don't like chocolates so they don't contribute to the selection process because they never consume the product, but perhaps they may purchase for those who do. However, those who like having a variety of chocolates steer the types of chocolates in the boxes manufactured via their signalling to those who buy them, and after a period of time the various types or 'species' of boxes of chocolates in the market become relatively stable. In a similar way that peacock tails and peahen preferences evolve in a wired-together manner, so do the types of chocolates in chocolate boxes and the chocolate-lover's tastes. The contents of chocolate boxes have been sculpted by human selection and modified in the direction of the consumer's taste. Having said all this about how selection takes place with peacock's tails and boxes of chocolates, how does selection take place with managers, and what does this have to do with advising upwards? The short answer is that managers are selected, and perhaps even domesticated, and their senior managers (those they are advising) play a part in the selection process.

In the next section I discuss how managers are being selected and domesticated, and how their domesticated traits aren't helpful to leading a quality life in the corporate environment. However, there is an upside, and it is brought about by an awareness of what is going on – but more of this later.

The Domestication of Managers

Whilst it might be obvious that we humans have domesticated or tamed a variety of animal species for various purposes, it might not be so obvious that we have domesticated ourselves too. One way of understanding domestication (there are others) is that it is a process whereby a species has been selectively bred (or allowed to breed in a managed way) for its ability to be controlled by humans. We can also recognise a domesticated species because it is dependent to a significant extent on humans for food, shelter and safety.

Broadly speaking, pets are animals bred for their companionship, amusement and looks, whereas livestock are bred for food or resources such as wool and milk. Taking the latter as an example, the modern dairy cow was first domesticated by humans some 10,000 years ago. Its ancestor the Auroch was designed over billions of years by its natural environment. Breeders (artificial selectors) have been working, first unconsciously, then consciously, for thousands of years anatomically redesigning and optimising the dairy cow to be a better producer of milk/meat/dairy produce for humans. Like the modern dairy cow and other domesticated animals we humans have deliberately domesticated and redesigned, through selective breeding, pollinating and planting, various species of plants such as corn, carrots, rice, wheat and fruit trees, to name but a few. It has taken us only 15,000 years of selecting traits to go from the wolf to all varieties or breeds of domesticated dogs. Dog traits have been selected for their ability to perform various roles for humans, such as pulling, herding, hunting and protecting. Perhaps more recently for companionships, and later still for aiding those with a disability, though the purpose for the chihuahua remains a mystery to me. Nevertheless, its trait of small stature has been selected by some.

Whilst dogs, cows, carrots and corn are today selected directly by humans for certain traits, other species can prosper because traits have been indirectly selected. One way this indirect selection is brought about is by the increase of human settlements such as villages, towns and cities. The rubbish dump is a classic feature of such human sedentary communities, and they act as a selection mechanism, and more than likely took part in the early evolutionary stages of wolf to the modern domestic dog (Coppinger and Coppinger 2001). Some wolves would scavenge around human dump sites and those with a relatively low flight distance (scare factor of humans) would stay longer to feed. Therefore, over time, the rubbish dump (with humans around) selects for wolves (proto-dogs) that are relatively comfortable to eat around humans. And so begins (indirectly) the first stages of the selection and anatomical reshaping process of the animals we today call domestic dogs. This last point about anatomical reshaping of an animal is important to our discussion because it highlights the fact that dogs are not wolves and dog training should not be structured around appealing to their wolf-like instincts because they don't have any. I am stressing this point, because when training or taming techniques are to be derived for animals, one needs to appeal to their present instincts, not those of their ancestors. As I discuss later in the section on management whispering, the techniques for training senior management needs to be developed in the same manner, by appealing to their instincts and preferences.

Other features of human settlements behave as selection mechanisms by creating niches for various species to exploit and thrive. Roof spaces become safe nesting spaces for birds and bats; seabirds substitute high-rise buildings for coastal cliffs; abandoned areas create niches for plant and wildlife; even concrete paved and walled areas create microhabitats to be exploited. So adaptation and exploitation for survival purposes takes place constantly. As new niches (environments) appear, so certain traits will offer better survival advantages over others. This is the case with the fairly recent emergence of the corporate or organisational environment, which like the physical world of human settlements has its own physical and social structures that take part directly and indirectly selecting for certain traits.

ADAPTATION TO CORPORATE LIFE

So whilst we directly or consciously select for some traits, as a by-product of our actions we also indirectly or unconsciously select for other traits. Next I explore how we directly select for some traits in managers that benefit the organisation and the individuals, and also indirectly select for traits that are detrimental to the organisation and working relationships.

A form of domestication or taming goes on in our human cultures too. I'm not suggesting that we are selecting mangers based on their anatomical characteristics, but I am suggesting that the corporate environment puts pressure on behavioural changes: there could be said to be managers that pull, herd and hunt! The selection process for the modern manager begins with the job advertisement as applicants are culled from the pool of potential managers based on their ability to be able to address the selection criteria for the vacancy. The interview is the next opportunity to select for particular traits. Those who *perform* well at interview get through to the offer and following up references stage. I emphasise the word perform because success at interview can come about by presenting the desired traits even if you don't have them. One could argue that the significant traits that have been selected for in this process are those of performativity – the ability to portray or create a particular identity, on paper and in person. But this notion could prompt the question 'what are the traits of this particular identity, and why particularly those?'

To answer this we need to acknowledge that 'the manager' is a relatively recent creature, or breed of employee, that began to be shaped as owners of businesses in the late nineteenth century pushed the responsibility for managing labour onto their foreman. The current direction of evolution of the types or breeds of manager begins in America at the beginning of the twentieth century as business evolved into complex corporations with ever-expanding ranks of middle management. There were possibly three ways to rise to the level of upper management: come up through the ranks; transfer from engineering to management; or have some undergraduate business knowledge. Most managers lived out their careers in the same company or at least within the same industry.

However, businesses today are run by professional managers who are largely shaped by business schools that have since the late 1950s reshaped their curricula to be focused on the pseudo-sciences of accounting, finance, economics and marketing. I say pseudo-science not in a disparaging way, but rather to highlight that these topics (and I'm sure I've left out others) have the appearance of some sort of scientific foundation to their body of knowledge because they can draw on the tools of mathematics and statistical analysis, but they are largely based on heuristics.

Modern university business school programmes such as the MBA (Masters of Business Administration) produce professional managers who are generalists rather than specialists. What variations there were between management styles has been swamped out by the normalised 'little bit of everything' MBA curricula. And as the global and technologically connected marketplace puts pressure on corporations to continually improve their share price in the short term, the corporations have responded by selecting their senior managers from finance rather than other disciplines.

Consequentially, businesses have been reconceptualised in financial terms, and a new breed of senior managers who understand financial markets has become prevalent. At a fundamental level, these senior managers survive in their jobs by improving the share price of their corporation. They in turn will select from the pool of aspiring managers those who can enable them to meet their goals. Therefore, to be selected and retained, managers need to advertise those attributes that get them selected, such as being organised, in control and productive, whether they actually possess them or not. It is this last point which is most concerning, because it points to the fact that the modern manager is being selected on their ability to create an identity, for a period of time, that placates senior management and buys them time to be productive with the messy business environment they find themselves emersed in. After all, this performativity is just an adaptation managers have made in order to survive in today's corporate environment.

Looking the part can have survival advantages in the natural world as well as the corporate world. Butterflies have an endless list of predators, and they have evolved various methods to protect themselves. Some taste good; some taste bad. Predators quickly learn which is which, and avoid the bad-tasting ones. The good-tasting butterflies that survive long enough to breed have therefore developed in such a way that they are rather plain, dull-coloured and hard to see, and they have survived because they blend into the background and camouflage themselves. Bad-tasting butterflies like the poisonous Monarch butterfly have been able to evolve bright colours because their toxins make predators sick and their colours serve as a cue to those previously poisoned to stay clear.

Therefore they have less pressure from predators, which enables them to breed and pass on their bright colour traits. Even more interesting, this reduction of predator pressure and breeding advantage is also given to those who don't taste bad but just happen to develop bright colours, like the orange and black-coloured Viceroy butterfly that looks very similar to the poisonous Monarch. Just looking as if you taste bad in an environment where those sorts of visual cues are acknowledged or biologically wired is enough to provide a survival advantage.

One breed of modern manager is the project manager. My research findings have shown that those who survive well in the project environment have certain characteristics (Whitty 2010). For example, they forage for project work, and they use various tools to placate their senior managers. I will return to the foraging behaviour and how an awareness of this might be useful later. Next I want to expand on the use of tools and techniques for placating senior management, and how this has been inadvertently or indirectly selected for in the process of domesticating the modern manager. Broadly speaking, the set of tools and techniques amount to camouflaging the messiness of the real work environment, and the mimicry of being organised and in control.

Management Camouflage and Mimicry

Much has been written in academic literature and popular books about how those in a subordinate position use many strategic methods to influence the decisions of their managers. The social psychology literature uses the phrase strategic impression management which is designed to advance the self-interests of the individual, to gain approval and therefore achieve valuable interpersonal goals (Jones 1964; Goffman 1973; Arkin and Baumgardner 1986; Baumeister and Tice 1986; Leary and Kowalski 1990). Perhaps more informally this behaviour is characterised as 'gamesmanship' and focuses on how people strategically package (conceal and use) information to accomplish their objectives (Kiechel 1982). Dale Carnegie's (1999) book *How to Win Friends and Influence People* is probably the most popular book sold on the topic, with over 16 million copies to date and translations in all languages, and it has generated a whole network of training courses and centres that are patronised by many Fortune 500 companies. Corporations such as KPMG, Coopers & Lybrand, Ernst & Young and Price Waterhouse employ image consultants to instruct their employees in the art of looking, acting and sounding professional (Wellington and Bryson 2001). The key trait here is the ability to construct and maintain an appearance.

More broadly speaking these methods of influencing manager's decisions might range under the banner of playing office politics and include such tactics as befriending important people (forming coalitions and networks), managing your outward appearance and style (impression management), managing how information is shared with others (information management), or by giving compliments or doing favours (ingratiation). There are no doubt other methods not mentioned which could be deemed to be devious, dishonest and even immoral. But evolution cares nothing for the human distinction of whether something is right or wrong, and when considering what follows in the rest of this chapter we must also try not to be too judgemental about the behaviours discussed. Behaviour is simply behaviour, and as we shall see, even if it appears to be devious or dishonest, that is largely not its intent.

For this chapter, in order to investigate the evolutionary basis of how managers successfully advise or influence upwards in their organisation, I conducted a short survey which I emailed to an international cohort of present University of Southern Queensland postgraduate project management and MBA students. I was careful not to ask managers directly 'how do you successfully advise your senior manager?' because from my experience the answers are likely to be subjective, opinion-based and align very much with the cultural norm of today of being politically correct. In an attempt to find out how managers successfully advise or influence upwards I asked some direct questions which they would have less experience in answering about how they gained the favourable attentions of their senior managers. In short, how do they advertise themselves to senior management such that benefits, whatever they may be, would come their way?

Forty-one people who would classify themselves as either practising managers or project managers (from hereon I will refer to them as 'the respondents') answered my five questions, which are summarised here:

1.   To what extent do you adopt management tools, processes and practices to gain the favourable attentions of people you report to such as your manager?

2.   What are these tools, processes and practices?

3.   How do these actions benefit you in the short and long term?

4.   How do you know you've gained any favourable attention?

5.   How much of your time do you devote to these activities?

The number of respondents to this study is of course small, and they all self-selected to complete the survey. But this sample was never meant to be a representative sample of the whole pool of possible managers and project managers. What it does demonstrate is that these behaviours do take place, and that those who participate in them are to some extent aware of their own behaviour. The responses can be placed under the strategic themes of camouflage and mimicry. Camouflage was not as prevalent as mimicry, but nevertheless camouflaging does take place. It is worth mentioning that camouflage and mimicry are human distinction and that mimicry can be considered a form of camouflage, just as a stick insect camouflages itself by beautifully mimicking a stick. However, for the purposes of this discussion I have made the following distinction so the strategies are more easily recognisable and demonstrable. By camouflage I mean the strategy of concealing from senior management the often chaotic and sometimes uncertain nature of one's work. By mimicry I mean the strategy of presenting oneself to senior management as one who is confident, in control and organised when that is not the case.

Generally speaking, the responses are interesting because primarily the methods of attracting favourable attention centres on tools and techniques traditionally associated with advising and reporting upwards, such as emails, status briefings and report documentation, as well as preparing and presenting planning documents. In the discussion that follows I highlight how these various tools and techniques can be associated with the strategies of camouflage and mimicry, and I punctuate the discussion with actual responses which best represent this association. It is worth mentioning that although I am talking about how managers misdirect or camouflage what is going on in a way that deliberately conceals some information from senior management, these actions do not appear to have any ill intent associated with them. The purpose of this behaviour can perhaps best be characterised by the remarks of one manager who quite bluntly said

> I might sell my Director some bullshit along the way to conceal the mess I have to manage, but in the end, if I don't deliver the project satisfactorily I'll fail in my role and eventually lose my job. I only conceal the mess because he's got enough on his plate without worrying about my troubles. And I don't want to be seen a whinger. I want him to see me as capable and someone who can get the job done – which is what I do in the end.

It is also worth mentioning that an analysis of the responses from the study show that the tools and techniques used by the respondents to influence senior management also have the effect of increasing their self-esteem and improving their self-image, which in their opinion leads to some short-term and long-term benefits. The respondents consider the long-term benefits to be job security and promotion, and the short-term benefits to be satisfying the needs and even placating senior management and stacking the odds of success in their favour.

CAMOUFLAGE

Respondents felt that because their working environment was to some extent unpredictable it was important not to display this to senior management:

> My manager doesn't really understand the job I have to do. If he knew how much of it was flying by the seat of my pants he'd be micro-managing me just to keep his stress level down.

Charts and graphs are seen as useful reporting tools with a camouflaging effect. In one way they offer a method of conciseness, but in another way they are considered to be a method of placating or sheltering senior management from the day-to-day messiness of managing. 'For me the Gantt chart is more of a security blanket for upper management than a good management tool.'

It was also important to them to stack the odds of success in their favour. They use a number of reporting tools and techniques to do this. Amongst them are using the risk analysis process to their advantage by adding in some time and cost padding on risky tasks; being selective about what information is shared; and spending time with clients and senior management to ensure an alignment of expectations.

I've learnt that telling everybody everything all the time is not helpful to me. I find it more beneficial to keep some information back and release it when the time is right. I also find it much easier to sell favourable chance happenings as intended results when I haven't been updating everybody about everything all the time.

Some of the jobs we have to do are impossible to estimate properly. So if I want to stay in the good books I need to be a little creative in how I estimate, what I show and what I don't.

Being seen to be using company processes appears to be important, even when the processes are not that effective. I suggest that there is a little of the mimicry as camouflage effect taking place here. The camouflage strategy is to pretend or play along with a particular behaviour whilst covering up the fact that they are actually performing another that appears to be more effective with regard to productivity. The mimicry strategy is that not using them reflects poorly on a professional image. This obviously leads to a level of redundancy in what the manager has to do, but nevertheless this is seen as necessary in order to display a credible professional image which in itself has benefits. The cost of this redundancy appears to be less than the cost of not playing along with the company process.

Yes, there is a degree that project managers who do not use this system, even when it's not that effective, are seen to not have their project under control as the project sponsor is expecting to see reports etc. in a certain format.

I do not think my managers know the PM [project management] process we use, however in the past I have noticed managers being impressed by the structure implied.

MIMICRY

The respondents felt that in order to satisfy the needs of senior management, and therefore keep them on their side, it was important to understand and speak the language of senior management's key performance indicators (KPIs).

They [senior management] only seem to be interested in two things – time and cost, most likely related to their employment key KPIs and resourcing planning in reducing overhead costs. And that's how I communicate with them.

They just want 'on time, on budget' and no issues. All the issues I keep to myself.

Communication to senior management is focused on matters of cost and time and even time is also considered in terms of cost. One respondent felt that it was not only important to report on this information as concisely as possible to senior management, but also that this information is packaged in a way for senior management to use in their reporting.

Of great personal benefit has been the deliberate use of more efficient and precise verbal and written communication which saves time, moves quickly to address the issues and provides a clear expectation of beneficial outcomes.

Appearing to be professional, organised and in control is seen as important, and there appear to be some simple advising and reporting tools and techniques for doing this. Amongst them are using 'business-like terminology' in correspondence such as emails and reports; presenting charts of graphs using Microsoft Excel® or Microsoft Project® and simplifying them for executives; spending time preparing and structuring meetings and briefings; spending time thinking about the content of communication, keeping emails short, only when necessary, and to the point. 'I use the classic charts and graphs, but I find that he [senior manager] responds best to short emails. I get short answers back.'

Respondents felt that retaining their job and succeeding in future promotions requires the display of a credible and professional image. 'They [senior management] need to be confident that I am confident and in control.'

So what? So what if we camouflage our behaviours from senior management and mimic those who are well organised and able to cope with uncertainty? Even though the sample for the study I've mentioned was small, I suspect that there is a good likelihood that these behaviours are more common than not. We [managers] just need to admit that we engage in these behaviours, not because we choose to, but rather because we have little choice if we wish to compete for the attentions of our senior managers and survive in the corporate environment. This whole situation strikes me as a rather sad state of affairs, as respondents claim the amount of time they devote to the camouflage and mimicry activities is not trivial. But as I've already mentioned, investing or accepting the cost of camouflage and mimicry is more preferable to the alternative of baring to senior management our human condition of being higgledy-piggledy in our approach to work, somewhat disorganised and not always in control. Perhaps part of the problem stems from how senior management are trained and recruited from a strong finance background. If their skill set was not so generic then perhaps they would understand and appreciate why some aspects of a manager's work are necessarily messy and uncertain at times. This is not a problem that this chapter or book can resolve, but a Darwinian perspective of advising upwards can help reveal some of the issues and ethical dilemmas a manager has to face when helping management to help them. A Darwinian perspective can also provide a rationale for attempting to influence senior management when they are at their best.

Figure 8.2   In the zone

Management Whispering

Where are you most likely to find a new species of flora or fauna? You might think it would be in an unexplored jungle or perhaps on a remote island. But you are just as likely to find a new or extraordinary species in your back garden as the evolutionary process is taking place all around us. Plant and wildlife are constantly producing an abundance of offspring, far more than will ever live to reproduce offspring of their own. Each offspring has a slight variation of the traits inherited from the parent because the replication (reproduction) process is not completely error free. The offspring then take their chance with the environment, and those who survive long enough to reproduce, perhaps because of the survival advantages they received from their tweaked inherited traits, get to repeat the cycle again. Similarly, but not exactly, we are constantly varying our behavioural traits, tweaking what we have done previously in similar situations in the hope that this outcome will be more beneficial than the last. As managers we should be mindful of this process and constantly tune or hone our behaviours towards outcomes that were better than previous ones.

At the beginning of the chapter I pointed out how all plants and wildlife are locked into a vicious and brutal struggle for survival – and it is a struggle. The idea of harmony or mutual cooperation to overcome the hardship in the natural world is an idea or mental construct we humans have fashioned about the natural world. For example, the cleaner fish and the shark do not live 'in harmony' in any contrived or agreed way. When one observes the cleaner fish darting in and out of a shark's mouth removing dead skin and food from around its otherwise predatory teeth, one might think that the shark (or any other predatory fish that takes part in this practice) *decides* to let the cleaner fish clean their teeth. But what has happened, over an enormous amount of evolutionary time, is that the cleaner fish and the shark have been selecting for these *'don't eat me while I'm in your mouth'* and *'clean all the dead bits out of my teeth'* traits. Those predators that come and eat the cleaners don't get cleaned and increase the chance that they might die from complications that ensue from not being cleaned. On the other hand, those cleaner fish that don't venture into the predator's mouth will have to find food elsewhere and risk their lives by going outside the cleaning zone.

In a way, the cleaner fish have tamed the predators to bring their food to them, and the predators have tamed the fish to clean potentially harmful debris from their teeth. What we learn from this example is that even though there is no contrived harmony or an agreed cooperation between the two species, there is a relationship between them that can be described as non-zero sum and this has been selected for. Like the peacock and the peahen, the shark and the cleaner fish are hard-wired into this mutually beneficial relationship. Managers and senior managers are similarly locked into a non-zero sum relationship, but more often than not they don't realise it, and a Darwinian lens can help bring it into focus.

Before discussing how this concept of a non-zero sum relationship relates to managers and senior managers, it is important that we unpack the non-zero sum terminology a little. For example, we could say we observe a zero sum relationship between competing teams in a football match, or any other sporting competition for that matter. If the final score of the match is Team A = 3 points, and Team B = 0 points, then one could say that not only has Team A won 3 points, but that Team B has lost 3 points, and in this sense the wins of Team A are balanced by the losses of Team B. Hence summing the wins of Team A and the losses of Team B results in a zero sum. In short, a zero-sum relationship means that we are in a relationship where my win comes from your loss. So the more chocolates I eat from the chocolate box, the less there is for you!

However, relationships in the natural and human social world are more complex than our sporting metaphors for work and life portray. To explore this further we need to talk about the non-zero sum relationship. If Team A and Team B play a great match and keep the fans on the edge of their seat, then even though one group of fans will have their hopes dashed, they will still return another day to support their team in another match. In this sense, Team A and B are in a non-zero sum relationship because there is a net gain (a win) for both of them. There is no scoreboard for attributing points in this non-zero relationship, but for the players in both teams to do what they enjoy doing, there needs to be a recognised sporting code called football, with fee-paying patrons. Therefore, it is in the interest of all players from all teams to uphold the rules and play a great game so that they have the opportunity to play more games in the future. Of course all football teams are also in a non-zero sum relationship with their fans too. Non-zero sum relationships are everywhere, all you need is an eye (perhaps a Darwinian one) for seeing them.

Unfortunately, we often see the social world of our organisations in a zero sum manner where some make gains at the expense of others. We can glimpse these zero sum mindsets through the sporting analogies in our management speak and how some people have signs on their office saying Senior Manager and others don't. We often talk about competition and independence rather than mutual cooperation and interdependence. But a Darwinian perspective can justify and rationalises the bold behaviour of practicing natural managementship, where managers tame, train, or perhaps condition their senior managers to support their decisions in the interest of creating mutual benefits.

Natural Managementship

I propose that natural managementship is a little like natural horsemanship in that the latter is a philosophy of working with horses by appealing to their natural instinct, and the former is the same but working with managers; particularly, senior managers. So how does one appeal to the natural instincts of senior management in a way that captures their attention and brings about a strong and conspicuous non-zero sum relationship?

I am going to focus on two principles that I suggest need to be adhered to, both of which can be derived from our brief Darwinian look at what it means to advise upwards. The first is the principle of flow. At a biological level we all experience the emotional moments of psychological flow, and communication can be enhanced when one understands what they are for you and for your senior manager. The second is the principle of intelligent disobedience. In the spirit of domesticating and training, managers need to train senior management to become conditioned to the messiness and uncertainty of front line management work so that they become accustomed to managers including them in the resolution of problems in a manner that their support for these solutions brings about mutually beneficial results.

In short, the two principles work nicely together because the former enables the manager to harness the benefits of communicating during or following flow experiences when learning and positive emotion is high. The latter is a strategy to rationalise management decisions and bring senior management onside with their support.

The Principle of Psychological Flow

It is common to think that we select the task and jobs we engage with, but the lessons we learn from the natural world invert this way of thinking (Anderson and McMillan 2003). It is not we who select the task, or that the task selects us: rather it is a bit of both. The structure of the task aligns with our preference for it. Earlier I promised to discuss the matter of how project managers forage for project work, and this is the moment for it.

Flow is a term used as a metaphor for an engaging or absorbing activity that is exhilarating, stimulating, challenging and overall brings about a feeling of enjoyment (Csikszentmihalyi 1990). Flow is an emotional experience, and we all know when we have been in this flow state because time passes incredibly quickly and we feel extremely satisfied after it. My research has found that project managers experience flow states in their project work. However, not all experience it from the same type or structure of tasks. Some get immersed in planning and scheduling activities, whilst others get a buzz from preparing and delivering status presentations to stakeholders. Natural managementship requires you to understand what pushes your psychological 'flow' buttons and how to recognise flow states in your senior manager.

Flow states are achieved when the challenge of the task corresponds to the skill level of the individual. If the task is too difficult then anxiety sets in, and if the task is too easy then this results in boredom. During flow states individuals are very alert, aware and sensitive to detail (decision-making and information-processing is high), they are extremely focused, and experience a positive emotional state. As I mentioned at the beginning of the chapter, our emotions have a biological foundation, and flow states appear to correlate with higher levels of the neurotransmitter dopamine which also acts as a marker for when the brain is in learn and reward-seek mode (Donahoe and Palmer 1993). So during or immediately after the flow state might be a good time for introducing new ideas that lead to mutually beneficial results.

Before learning to recognise flow states for your senior manager you need to learn to recognise when you enter flow states. If a researcher were to try and elicit this information from you they might ask; 'what are some of the tasks you do throughout the day that you find really enjoyable?' As a strategy to find your senior manager's flow states you might watch out for themes of tasks that your senior manager finds really enjoyable and make a note of these, and carefully listen to the language and terms they use. To generalise on what these task and terms might be for a moment (whilst being aware of the problems with generalising) it is worth considering the traits or preferences inherent in the definitive modern senior manager discussed earlier, which are financial performance in nature and short-term based because of their requirement to be part of the chain of command that responds to the changing economic demands of the market. Generally speaking, senior management need to be communicated to in these terms. Ideas or solutions to problems should be brief and presented in terms of cost–benefit, with some form of financial analysis or business case of how these ideas tie into larger business matters.

Knowing about flow states might help us better capture the attention of senior management. The next section deals with the matter of what to do or what conditioning to perform once you've captured their attention.

The Principle of Intelligent Disobedience

Intelligent disobedience is a term derived from the concept whereby a trained animal, such as a seeing-eye or guide dog, is trained or conditioned to go against the commands of its owner, because those commands could or would place the owner in harm's way (Sanders 1999). An example of this could be a blind person attempting to cross a road or negotiate a train platform with the aid of a trained guide dog. The dog is trained to refuse the command to move forward if moving forward puts the owner (and the dog) at risk. Intelligent disobedience can be reframed into the corporate environment and could manifest is such a way that the manager respectfully refuses (being sensitive not to damage their career or professional relationship) to follow instructions from a senior manager because following those instructions would have a negative impact on the organisation, the project, and/or the manager and senior manager (Carkenord 2009).

As discussed previously, both managers and senior managers are in a non-zero sum relationship, but most of both ranks are not aware of this, nor do they know how to take advantage of the situation. At a practical level, intelligent disobedience can be about bringing critical issues (with proposals for solutions) to the attention of senior management. This is of course an inversion of the trait of camouflaging and concealing issues for a time in order to appear organised and in control.

Senior management will probably need to be broken in gently with this principle. Not by highlighting small problems first as this might be regarded as being trivial, but by bringing issues that are already or almost solved to their attention. This way senior management become conditioned to the messiness and uncertainty of day-to-day management, and see that the manager has the skills and abilities to resolve problems rather than conceal then. The next stage of senior management training involves presenting them with critical issues not quite solved, with the intention of seeking their input on solutions. Here the principle of intelligent disobedience can be realistically and tactfully practiced by means of an open discussion where the manager can rationalise the actions to be taken in terms of benefits to the company and the senior manager, and the gains or wins for all as a result.

Concluding Remarks

I began by drawing back the veil on our corporate social world to show that evolutionary principles apply just as much in the office environment as they do in the grassy meadow or a grassland savannah. All living creatures are struggling to survive, and those of us animals and plants alive today have successfully survived because we have, over an enormous amount of time, been built to survive. Survival is literally in our biological wiring which has been sculpted by the living creatures around us (today other humans and their ideas play a significant role in this) and our physical environment (today technology impacts on us in a significant way). One of our survival strategies is to find a niche and exploit it for our own benefit.

I explored two mechanisms that take part in the selection process; the preferences of others, and the environment. When discussing the preferences of others my intension was to demonstrate how inextricable and entangled our world is. For example, one cannot speak about the magnificent peacock's tail without speaking about the preferences of the peahen. Similarly, in the way that the design of a modern box of chocolates is entangled with a chocolate lover's preferences, so the design of the modern manager is entangled with preferences of modern senior management, and their traits are in turn shaped by the modern ideals of capitalism.

Following on from the 'all entangled together' idea I introduced the concept of domestication and how entanglement leads to a sense of mutual reliance and non-zero sum relationships. I used the modern cow and dog to illustrate how our preferences have the enormous power to anatomically sculpt another species over relatively short periods of time. However, we typically see the domestication process from our human point of view, and rarely do we consider that it is us who have been enslaved by our livestock and pets who have trained us to bring them food, to provide them with shelter and safety.

We even nurture their offspring which enables their species to flourish. The point I hoped to make here is that species shapes species. As we shape our livestock so our livestock shape us. To extend this further, as our cultural values shape our senior managers who select our managers, so our managers are (but perhaps not knowingly) shaping senior management. We are all locked in various mutually reliant relationships, and when managers are aware of this they can capitalise on it.

But there is a problem! Whilst we consciously and directly select for certain traits based on our preferences, we change the environment which can out of our awareness and indirectly select for traits that may not be mutually beneficial or align with our cultural values. I highlight this in the case of modern project managers who are being directly selected for their ability to bring order and stability to the possible messiness of project work. But indirectly, because of the environment they are immersed in, the traits of camouflage and mimicry are being selected too. This situation is not conducive to constructing mutually beneficial relationships between manager and senior management.

Finally, in an effort to modify the selection of traits in the direction of mutually beneficial relationships I introduced the idea of management whispering or natural managementship, which is basically the idea of communicating to senior management by appealing to their natural instincts or preferences. In short this involves identifying when might be a better moment than others to raise issues, and how to present them (in their term) so that a solution may be found that is mutually beneficial and zero-sum in nature.

References

Anderson, C. and McMillan, E. 2003. Of ants and men: self-organized teams in human and insect organisations. *Emergence*, 5(2), 29–41.

Arkin, R.M. and Baumgardner, A.H. 1986. Self-presentation and self-evaluation: processes of self-control and social control. In R.F. Baumeister, ed., *Public Self and Private Self*. New York: Springer-Verlag, pp. 75–97.

Baumeister, R.F. and Tice, D.M. 1986. Four selves, two motives, and a substitute process self-regulation model. In R. F. Baumeister, ed., *Public Self and Private Self*. New York: Springer-Verlag, pp. 63–97.

Carkenord, B.A. 2009. *Seven Steps to Mastering Business Analysis*. Fort Lauderdale, FL: J. Ross Publishing.

Carnegie, D. 1999. *How to Win Friends and Influence People*. Pymble, NSW: HarperCollins.

Coppinger, R. and Coppinger, L. 2001. *Dogs: A Startling New Understanding of Canine Origin, Behavior and Evolution*. New York: Scribner.

Csikszentmihalyi, M. 1990. *Flow: The Psychology of Optimal Experience*. New York: Harper Perennial.

Darwin, C. 1890. *The Origin of Species by Means of Natural Selection*. London: Murray.

Donahoe, J.W. and Palmer, D.C. 1993. *Learning and Complex Behavior*. Boston, MA: Allyn & Bacon.

Goffman, E. 1973. *The Presentation of Self in Everyday Life*. New York: Overlook Press.

Jones, E.E. 1964. *Ingratiation: A Social Psychological Analysis*. New York: Appleton-Century-Crofts.

Kiechel, W. 1982. Lies on the resume. *Fortune*, 106, 221–224.

Leary, M.R. and Kowalsk, R.M. 1990. Impression management: a literature review and two-component model. *Psychological Bulletin*, 107(1), 34–47.

Sanders, C. 1999. *Understanding Dogs (Animals Culture And Society)*. Philadelphia, PA: Temple University Press.

Wellington, C.A. and Bryson, J.R. 2001. At face value? Image consultancy, emotional labour and professional work. *Sociology*, 35(4), 933–946.

Whitty, S.J. 2010. Project management artefacts and the emotions they evoke. *International Journal of Managing Projects in Business*, 3(1), 22–45.

PART III

Being Extraordinary

9

Creative Metaphor as a Tool for Stakeholder Influence

Arthur Shelley

This chapter highlights the interdependence between influence, relationships, behaviour and leadership and describes how the use of metaphor can enhance outcomes from these interactions. The first half, 'Understanding metaphor as a tool', describes how and why metaphor works as a medium of influence and learning. The second half, 'Applying metaphor to build and maintain relationships', provides examples of how to apply metaphor in your organisation to engage stakeholders and communicate more effectively. This will ultimately enhance your own performance as well as the performance of those around you and the organisation as a whole.

Traditional leadership and management styles tend to underestimate the importance of emotions and behaviour on the outcomes of decisions. It was generally accepted that logic based decision-making was cleaner, fairer and more easily measured in an objective manner. However, behavioural, subjective and emotions-based aspects have always been involved in decision-making and delivery of outcomes (such as personal networks and social relationships), although their influence was often hidden. These subtle influencing factors have only relatively recently been more publicly acknowledged or openly discussed as a key tool for success. More recently, there has been a wider acceptance of the important influences 'soft aspects' of management and leadership, such as principles of emotional intelligence (Goleman 2006), relationship, behavioural and social aspects (Hofstede 2001, Gannon 2004, Chia 2005), storytelling (Denning 2005) and narrative (Snowden 2002). Acceptance and more deliberate application of these concepts have changed many perspectives of how we consciously influence others. Goleman (2006) popularised the concepts that humans are fundamentally social beings who make decisions with the emotional parts of the brain based on patterns of prior experience and then logically justify their choice afterwards. Snowden and Boone (2007) highlighted that in a complex world, decision-making needs to be more experimental than absolute and allowing for emergence of opportunities is important to success.

This research highlights that the ability to influence upwards depends heavily on the strength of the relationships with one's stakeholders and that this is extremely dependent on emotional synergies and behavioural interactions. Our behavioural preferences and those of our stakeholders need to be understood as a fundamental foundation of our ability to lead others as well as interact constructively with peers and other members of the teams in which we work. This chapter investigates the pragmatic power of metaphor to simplify the complexity of behavioural interactions such that we can not only understand behaviours, but use them productively to develop strong relationships with those around us. This enables us to positively influence in all directions, including those above us, in a way that is mutually beneficial.

Understanding Metaphor as a Tool

Dictionary.com (2010) summarises the sense of a number of definitions of metaphor found in traditional hard copy dictionaries:

> *a figure of speech in which a term or phrase is applied to something to which it is not literally applicable in order to suggest a resemblance, as in 'A mighty fortress is our God'.*

Or

> *something used, or regarded as being used, to represent something else; emblem; symbol.*

Illustrative examples from Lakoff and Johnston (1980) include 'time is money' or 'argument is war'. In addition to words, images and symbols can also be used as a metaphorical representation – this is seen in the use of caricatures and metaphoric cartoons.

In this sense, a metaphor transfers a meaning between one party and another by highlighting a similarity with something more familiar or more easily understood. This aspect of metaphor, understanding and experiencing one kind of thing in terms of another, makes it a powerful mechanism for transferring new meanings. For example, Ivie (2003) adjusted the thinking of students by describing life as a waltz rather than using the predominant competitive games-based metaphors. This mind shift provided a vastly different perspective and influenced their behaviours and approach, enabling the students to consider interactions with each other as learning new steps with partners instead of constantly striving to win.

Despite the recent interest in metaphor, its use is not new – not even to business. Metaphor has been embedded into our customs, religions and language for centuries. Metaphor has also historically been used to simplify learning and knowledge transfer in scientific fields. The military metaphor is still in wide use in business despite confrontational methods of leadership being less well accepted (Windsor 1996). Metaphor is widely used across cultures in a range of ways and is embedded into how we interact with each other.

Metaphor has a wide variety of application across a range of fields including social research, problem-solving and policy making (Schön 1993) and understanding organisational culture. Machine and organism metaphors were used by Morgan (2006) to highlight the differences in organisational cultures and as a way to understand how to act within these (mainly business-related) different environments.

Metaphors can be effective for understanding, even when they do not directly apply to the situation. Vinten (2000) discussed how religious metaphors are common in the business environment to convey meaning, highlighting Charles Handy's (1978) *Gods of Management* as one example. Haley, Low and Toh (1996) described how the Singapore government successfully developed Singapore Incorporated as a metaphor for their sophisticated marketing plan to focus their strategic efforts and attract outside investment.

It is the common understanding of the metaphor, rather than the literal context, that make it useful. Inns (2002) created six categories of metaphor aligned with how they are applied:

1. to examine the root meaning of a subject;

2. for research;

3. for teaching;

4.   as a generative tool for creative thinking;

5.   to help deconstruct or question embedded assumptions; and

6.   as a means to influence perception and interpretation.

These categories help to understand the specific ways metaphor can be applied as a tool. One example of a creative metaphor that addresses several of these applications is the 'Tango Metaphor' proposed for the understanding of cultural norms devised by Nielsen and Mariotto (2006). They analysed how the iconic tango can represent recognisable aspects of Argentine behaviour and values and can help others to learn more about that culture.

Using a range of metaphors provides a different set of ways to interpret or make sense of the subject we are seeking to understand. Each metaphor provides a different perspective and each also has limitations. Looking through a metaphor provides a specific context to find similarities between the topic and the metaphor as well as differences. These in turn provide perspectives to discuss amongst those involved in the sense-making exercise. Dialogue around these metaphors enables rich conversations and a creative exchange of ideas that would not happen as well without the influence of the metaphor.

Two useful examples of this are:

1.   The 'diagnostic reading' of Multicom by Morgan (2006, p. 350) in which he uses seven different metaphors to gain a comprehensive understanding of the corporate culture.

2.   The comparison of a park ranger and a 'leading lion' to contrast collaborative and control and command leadership styles (Shelley 2010).

ANIMAL METAPHOR AND IMAGERY IN CULTURE AND BUSINESS

Animal metaphor and imagery is very common in most cultures and has been so for a long time: so much so that they seem to fit naturally and we hardly even notice they are there. Ancient cultures such as the Australian Aboriginals incorporated animals into the way they believed their world was created and how they should interact. Aesop incorporated animal metaphors and images into fables to educate and reinforce cultural expectations and George

Orwell's (1946) *Animal Farm* was written as a political satire to expose political shortcomings in society. Animals have been used as a source of inspiration and derision since early civilisation. We can be 'busy as a bee', 'quiet as a mouse', 'cunning as a fox', 'stubborn as a mule', 'quick as a hare', and 'wise as an owl'. All forms of literature and online resources present examples of animal metaphor or identities which are accepted across cultures. However, some care needs to be exercised as the significance of some animals can carry different meaning in different cultures. What is viewed as a positive metaphor applicable to people in one society could be considered culturally sensitive or derogatory in another.

Most people can intuitively relate to the use of animal metaphor and readily identify themselves and others with animals. Both positive and negative metaphors are in common use, which are bestowed upon lovers, family, friends and enemies. There seems to be no boundaries to how they can be applied. Our behaviours can be described as 'catty', 'bitchy', 'snaky', 'ratty', 'off with the birds' or any number of endless possibilities borrowed from our animal cousins. We may be 'like a bear with a sore head' or a 'cuddly bear'. Perhaps we may be 'sheepish' about 'ferreting out' whether our partner is engaged in some 'monkey business'. Or becoming more colloquial in Western language, when someone 'ratted on a friend, their goose would be cooked'.

In many cultures, exposure to animal metaphor happens very early in life through traditional children's stories such as Beatrix Potter's stories of Peter Rabbit and farmyard friends. These stories use animal characters to represent certain personality types that children can relate to. They come to understand which are acceptable and which are less desirable. Peter Rabbit is a typical disobedient young boy who was always getting into trouble, which was a real contrast to Benjamin Bunny and Jemima Puddle-Duck who represented more conservative behavioural styles. Animal characters can be built from a common interpretation that spans cultures. Almost generically, owls represent wisdom, eagles represent leadership and snakes represent political behaviours. Some animals have specific meanings or significance in their home countries such as elephants in Thailand, pandas in China or koalas in Australia. Mickey and Minnie Mouse, Goofy, Pluto, Pooh Bear and Tigger (Disney 2010) as well as Daffy Duck, Tweety, Wile E. Coyote and Bugs Bunny (Warner Brothers 2010) are examples from broadcast media forming part of the behavioural stereotypes we begin to recognise and identify with from a young age. They are meant to influence and engage through representing a certain set of behaviours that are more effective and creative than using a human character.

Commercial enterprises have long known of the power of using people's warmth and affection for animal tokens – Rosella (Australian foods), Kiwi (international shoe polish), Eagle (USA Insurance), Camel (Global cigarettes) are just a few. Because of this constant exposure, animal metaphors have infiltrated languages around the world in subtle ways and as a result are quickly understood. This is exactly why they have so much power for engagement and are a great place to start a conversation about meaning.

Applying Metaphor to Build and Maintain Relationships

Understanding how and why metaphor works in theory does not mean that we know how to apply it in an effective way in the real world. To achieve our desired outcomes – that is, to positively engage and influence others, especially those above us in an organisation – we need to design and implement interactions that work in practice. This section explores how metaphor can be applied in practice to achieve desired outcomes such as developing trust, enhancing relationships, understanding behavioural dynamics (especially in teams) and targeting behaviours of stakeholders to influence them.

Presenting theories to business leaders is not usually a productive approach! You will often be seen as patronising, impractical or irrelevant. Almost invariably, approaches involving poorly constructed or shallow metaphors disengages stakeholders. At best you might be asked 'So what?'

A more effective way to influence those above you (and others) is to use the theory (or a combination of theories) as the foundation of an interactive activity that demonstrates the value of developing relationships. Creating an environment where the stakeholders become embedded in an activity or dialogue they identify with and are (reasonably) comfortable participating in, stimulates interactions that are more likely to influence them. The more uncomfortable, the tighter the participant group needs to be to ensure engagement. A group of participants with strong relationships and deep trust can be pushed well beyond their comfort zone and this can generate strong learnings. However, care must be exercised with groups who do not know or trust each other or who represent widely mixed levels across the organisation. No one wants to look foolish in front of strangers or their boss. It is equally unlikely that participants from different levels of the hierarchy will offer 'out of the box' thinking in front of people higher or lower in the chain of command, as they will play safe. Creating a 'safe-fail' (Snowden and Boone 2007) environment is critical for open exchange. An environment which makes people feel safe and willing to take calculated risks enables the introduction of new concepts, innovation from old ideas and open dialogue to flourish. Trust is earned through working with others, exchange of ideas through *conversations that matter* (Shelley 2009) and finding paths through both successes and failures. Relationships are built over time through collaborating on difficult issues, constructively talking through failures to learn from them and of course celebrating successes.

Many metaphoric models are limited in scope in that they apply to a specific instance. Whilst this is useful for that situation, there is value in having a more flexible and comprehensive model that can be applied across a wide range of contexts. One such model is the *The Organizational Zoo* characters (Shelley 2007) created for the purpose of understanding human behaviours and stimulating constructive conversations about the interactions between them. This model consists of 26 metaphoric characters (25 animals and one plant, one for each letter of the alphabet to make it easy to remember, see Table 9.1). Each character represents a behaviour, not a person. Successful people display a range of behaviours within a context, thereby demonstrating behavioural agility to suit the context. Those who are not able to adapt their behaviour to be appropriate to the situation they are in tend to be less likely to rise through the organisation to senior roles.

Table 9.1   *Organizational Zoo* **characters with primary characteristics**

Character	Behaviour tagline	Is	Is not
Ant	Basic hard worker	Hardworking, loyal, dedicated, territorial, instinctive	Sensitive, thinking, logical, decisive, individualistic
Bee	Knowledge workers	Hardworking, collaborative, communicative, territorial, knowledgeable	Self-aware, individualistic, gullible, political, reflective
Chameleon	Two-faced 'yes person'	Cunning, manipulative, weak, political, intelligent	Loyal, trustworthy, consistent, confident, challenging
Dog	Loyal follower	Loyal, trusting, enthusiastic, boisterous, gullible	Careful, serious, reflective, thinking, streetwise
Eagle	Inspirational leader	Visionary, strong, focused, inspiring, confident	Procrastinating, shy, weak, reclusive, emotional
Feline	Look at me	Individualistic, agile, aloof, vain, selfish	Sociable, friendly, communal, caring, collaborative
Gibbon	Centre of fun	Happy, playful, energetic, highly sociable, cool	Careful, serious, productive, forward-thinking, focused
Hyena	Pack task ambushers	Aggressive, scheming, controlling, manipulative, communal	Trustworthy, caring, considerate, intuitive, shy
Insect (beneficial) yucca moth	Trusted advisor	Helpful, resourceful, positive, forward-thinking, collaborative	Selfish, arrogant, ubiquitous, procrastinating, slow

Table 9.1   *Organizational Zoo* **characters with primary characteristics** *concluded*

Character	Behaviour tagline	Is	Is not
Insect (pestiferous)	Outside intruders	Arrogant, ubiquitous, ravenous, self-interested, costly	Beneficial, trustworthy, caring, productive, shy
Jackal	Elite guards	Territorial, zealous, social, aggressive, controlling	Patient, tolerant, shy, reclusive, caring
Kid	New recruit	Naive, playful, energetic, motivated, expendable	Experienced, reliable, knowledgeable, tough, streetwise
Lion	Aggressive leader	Strong, powerful, aggressive, controlling, territorial	Dedicated, hardworking, caring, shy, emotional
Mouse	Productive back office worker	Agile, productive, economical, reliable, adaptable	Lazy, extroverted, self-centred, aggressive, emotional
Nematode	Lazy parasite	Dependent, invisible, lazy, self-centred, parasitic	Productive, friendly, considerate, communal, beneficial
Owl	Eternal mentor	Wise, dedicated, helpful, intelligent, respected	Lazy, extroverted, self-centred, ambitious, aggressive
Piranha	Aggressive gossipers	Aggressive, ravenous, dangerous, selfish, frustrating	Friendly, trustworthy, approachable, happy, trusting
Quercus robur (oak)	Endangered philanthropist	Knowledgeable, decisive, intelligent, experienced, stimulating	Selfish, disinterested, lazy, emotional, aggressive
Rattlesnake	Noisy politician	Political, sharp, defensive, reactive, insecure	Sincere, trustworthy, loyal, trusting, pleasant
Sloth	Sleepy hermit	Slow, weary, minimalist, submissive, lazy	Sociable, agile, enthusiastic, productive, busy
Triceratops	Resistant dinosaur	Weary, pessimistic, change averse, xenophobic, reclusive	Visionary, adaptable, collaborative, open, opportunistic
Unicorn	Mythical perfect manager (not real)	Believe they are: perfect, visionary, open, honest, collaborative	Project they are not: arrogant, aloof, ambitious, frustrating, insecure
Vulture	Gleeful undertaker	Nasty, opportunistic, scavenging, self-centred, dangerous	Benevolent, trustworthy, happy, collaborative, brave
Whale	Cool techno dude	Intelligent, inspirational, knowledgeable, powerful, social (with whales)	Adaptable, agressive, lazy, arrogant, competitive
X-Breed	Multi-talented hybrid	Arrogant, ambitious, busy, extroverted, educated	Experienced, trustworthy, tolerant, patient, caring
Yak	Bull at a gate	Boisterous, enthusiastic, tactical, friendly, frustrating	Careful, patient, experienced, considerate, modest
Zoo positive	Great organisation	Welcoming, friendly, diverse, open, inspiring, playful, pleasant, productive, respected, balanced, social, stimulating	A place you want to leave (typically workplace, but can be any environment where people interact)
Zoo negative	Disengaging organisation	Political, territorial, negative, backward, divisive, frustrating, change averse, manipulative, nasty, procrastinating, dangerous, draining	A place you want to stay (typically workplace, but can be any environment where people interact)

Collectively the characters represent most of the common behaviours observed in organisational contexts. They were designed to characterise behaviours displayed from the most senior down to the most junior positions, as well as the most passive through to the most aggressive styles. The descriptions are deliberately in an informal style and represent the most extreme versions, as this makes a greater impact and stimulates richer dialogue. The benefit of this approach is more fun (providing that people feel safe) and greater engagement for participants in a fun way. As with any powerful tool, such as a fast car or electricity, it can be used positively to great effect, but if poorly managed it can cause great destruction. As such, the facilitator needs to manage the situation with care to ensure constructive use of the tools.

The beauty of the Zoo metaphors is they are intuitive and applicable across cultures. Most people have some exposure to most of these animals and have a fairly common interpretation of them. The less well-known animals in the list represent the less well-known behavioural types and as such warrant a little thought to recognise in the organisational environment. Table 9.1 lists the characters and the key points associated with them, but reflect the most extreme version of them. Considering what *is* about these behaviours is generally quite easy. However, what is often more insightful is considering what *is not* typical for them. This reflective process encourages us to explore at a greater depth than we normally engage in and often brings out insights that would not have been highlighted without deploying conversations steeped in the metaphor. Any person can display any of these characters, but of course people are more likely to be specific ones in specific contexts. For example, the eagle in the board room may well be the social gibbon at the office party and the lion when sponsoring a tough project and yet a lazy sloth at home. This pattern of behaviours may work for some but not others, depending on their role and desired outcomes. The more we understand our own preferred styles and the styles of others, the more effectively we can improve our own performance and positively influence others. You may not enjoy being a lion, preferring a more subtle collaborative approach, but you need to be able to bring out the lion at times to prevent being taken advantage of when it is important or when it is critical than your position be heard. Aggression is not bad per se, but it can be badly used or overused. Successful and popular leaders understand this and switch smoothly between animals (behaviours) with agility and finesse.

The philosophy of the Organizational Zoo is that the culture of your zoo (organisation, team, club or home) is dependent on which animals inhabit it, where they are in your hierarchy and how they interact. Too much dominance of any type is likely to lead to an unbalanced environment and like the real world environment, unlikely to be sustainable. Organisations, as with individual people, that have a diversity of animals and manage to display them in the right settings in balance with the surroundings are more likely to be successful. That is, the more adaptable the behaviours a person or organisation can employ, the more likely they are to succeed.

Context is critical to success. People behave differently in different contexts and with different people. This is why we need to be able to read the behavioural environment and understand the behavioural dynamics in order to act appropriately. This does not suggest we should not be true to ourselves or our inner values. It is natural for most people to behave differently when in different situations and with different people, the key message here is to decide consciously how to act rather than reacting to the environment. This conscious choice makes a big difference to outcomes and your ability to get what you need (or desire) rather than being influenced (or forced) to accept what others want.

You need to understand who you need to be in what situation. Perhaps you may be primarily owl, gibbon, yak and bee at home with family. However, it seems appropriate to adjust when with senior management to demonstrate more submissive and professional traits such as mouse or dog. It may also be appropriate in a difficult decision-making forum to display more aggression or power through lion style or perhaps be the inspirational eagle to lift the team. The animals used will to a large extent determine the success of the outcome. Displaying your best lion when in the presence of other lions is more likely to cause issues because of the territorial nature that characterises lion behaviour. It may be more productive to show less territorial aggression through being a hyena to command respect without the territorial aspects.

The key point is that behaviour is (or should be) a conscious choice. Successful people decide how to behave to optimise their interactions. Those who don't make conscious behavioural choices (ideally before they engage, with some knowledge of the behaviours of the others involved and the likely outcomes) are driven by the environment rather than managing it to deliver what they need. The discussions using the Zoo metaphors highlight these interdependencies and as such help people to leverage their behaviours more effectively. It is not about right and wrong behaviours, it is about matching behaviours to contexts.

A range of practical interactions has been developed for corporate and government workshops since 2006. These have continued to evolve to suit new situations and have benefited from experience of many implementations with a wide diversity of groups. Some of these interventions are described below to give a sense of what can be achieved using metaphoric techniques. They combine simplified behavioural profile methods with rich animal images and games to make the interactions safe and engaging. Stakeholder relationships, team dynamics and communications were selected as the most widely applied examples of these metaphor-based methods. Research into these techniques is ongoing through the research and practice of the author and through a group of interested practitioners collectively known as the Organizational Zoo Ambassadors Network.[1]

STAKEHOLDER RELATIONSHIPS (ENGAGE, DEVELOP, EVOLVE, LEVERAGE)

Engaging the interests of stakeholders is as much art as it is science. The better you understand your stakeholder(s) the better you are likely to be able to stimulate their interest, influence their mindset and increase the time they invest in thinking about the project, idea or concept you want them to support. The way you behave influences how you interact with them and what level of respect and participation you will receive from them. The outputs of this include:

- their initial level of interest in you or your initiative;

- whether your communications to them get read; and

- how involved you can be in the decision-making processes.

These outputs determine the quality of the (more intangible) outcomes such as:

- relationship;

- credibility;

- trust;

---

1   http://www.organizationalzoo.com/ambassadors.

- engagement;

- acceptance;

- access to their stakeholders, and ultimately; and

- how well you can perform your task with their involvement.

Journalist Matt Lauer (and several others) was attributed with stating '*you never get a second chance to make a first impression*' (ThinkExist.com 2010). This highlights the importance of understanding your stakeholder before you first engage with them: that is, doing your homework. Opening a conversation to get to know an important stakeholder is risky. A far more productive approach is to do some research and find out who they are, some of their successes and 'learning opportunities' (failures), their behavioural style, their key advisors and adversaries and what they choose to do in their discretionary time. Being armed with such knowledge improves the probability of creating a positive first impression. A positive first impression buys more time to build the foundations of a relationship. A negative first impression with a busy senior person probably means opportunities to collaborate or influence them are reduced.

A key to successful stakeholder engagement is to understand the behaviours of the stakeholder before you engage. Knowledge of animal metaphors enables you to have conversations with others about the behavioural profile of the stakeholder in a more objective and non-political way.

STAKEHOLDER MATCHING EXPERIENCE

A team needed to implement a new computer system in a company they had just taken over. They were aware there was a degree of resentment in the acquired company. It appeared likely that any advice they provided for the acquiring company would be treated with disdain. The team realised that they needed to build a sense of trust with the key people in the new business and looked for a way to do this. They instigated a conversation about the behaviours of the key clients with the members of the acquired team using the Zoo character cards as a fun way to engage them in the conversations.

The fact that they focused on the behaviours as an external factor to be managed and on external partners, enabled a constructive conversation that provided them with insights into the behavioural norms of the acquired business. As a result of this initial conversation team members also developed an understanding of the people they were dealing with in the acquired business and began a relationship with them. They were able to target the similarities between members of the two businesses and create alliances. This led to a second stakeholder matching conversation around who in the acquiring business was best placed to support whom from the acquired business.

The fact that they had already engaged on the first dialogue created a positive and fun outlook for the second conversation, leading to constructive outcomes. The awareness of the behavioural strengths and weaknesses of the team as a whole helped them to discuss their approach in some difficult situations. For example, the team was strong on task orientation, but weak on aggression. When the time came to pitch an initiative to some senior decision-makers, they planned who would be best to pitch to achieve the best outcome. This gave the combined team the outcome they required and they realised they were stronger as a collaborating group leveraging their behaviours than as a competing group trying to be territorial about their own expertise areas.

It is possible that the two teams could have developed trusted relationships without the metaphor tools. However, the ability to separate people from behaviours and talk about impacts of behaviours in a non-political and constructive manner seemed to help trigger the right environment and relationships in this case. There have been many examples where the behavioural preferences of stakeholders have been assessed in this way to optimise relationships and sustain their longer-term involvement in projects. It is a simple and enjoyable way to facilitate interactions that lead to deeper understandings and greater influence of those around you.

COMMUNICATION PLANNING FOR TEAM INFLUENCE AND IMPACT

The power of using metaphor in communications is that people very quickly relate to the images from within their own context. This happens because people inherently recognise patterns based on past experiences. Providing an audience or stakeholder with a mental image that seems familiar enables them to:

- grasp the context more quickly;

- visualise the situation in their mind;

- see themselves within that context in a way that they identify with; and

- converse about the types of animals they have in their team (without talking about specific individuals) and how this impacts on the culture, or if the behaviours are appropriate to the tasks required or the desired outcomes.

Typical outcomes of these conversations include statements like: 'We need to be more of a lion when it comes to decision-making time in our meetings' or 'Our stakeholders are a real mix of eagles, lions and owls, so we need to ensure our message is targeted differently for each group to ensure we secure their support.'

The absolute accuracy of the metaphor is not the most important element. Whilst needing to be plausible, the metaphor stimulates the conversations that would not otherwise happen in an open and constructive manner. Metaphoric stories and images serve their purpose by bringing the participants in the conversation to a common point that facilitates 'conversations that matter' (Shelley 2009) in a safe-fail environment. When such images and stories become part of the processes of interactions between team members, stronger bonds, trust and social capital are created leading to enhanced outcomes.

The incorporation of humour reduces political tensions, relaxes the behavioural atmosphere and engages people in the conversation. Figure 9.1 (Shelley 2007) is an example of the use of humour and rich images to assist generation of constructive dialogue between people. This image is shown to team members at kick off meetings to trigger conversations about behavioural diversity of the team and roles within the team. This one simple image introduces many complexities. Each character and the general scene drive a range of topics that are important for the team to discuss early in the project. Each animal represents a specific behavioural style that will be important in the success of the project: the message or desired outcome being that if the right behaviours are displayed at the appropriate time and situation, desired outcomes will be optimised. On the other hand if the same behaviours are applied in the wrong role, time, and context or with the wrong stakeholder, severe damage to the project outputs and outcomes can occur.

The Dragon Boat image represents the team and the boundaries of their responsibility. Discussion about the boat, its direction, who is in and who is out (where is the feline?) can be clarified to ensure there is a common shared vision or mission that is accepted or to be challenged early. What behaviours will be appropriate (tolerated or encouraged) can be discussed with no reference to any individual.

Is the lion (usually the senior stakeholder or sponsor of the initiative, team or project) in the boat with us or somewhere else? Is the boat suitably balanced to ensure the diversity of behaviours can be appropriately leveraged? As a group, does the team have all the behavioural capabilities required to get the job done effectively and efficiently: too much aggression will cause internal tensions, too little will result in poor decision making or delays.

Figure 9.1   The Dragon Boat metaphor for behavioural diversity of teams

TEAM DYNAMICS DIALOGUE EXPERIENCE

There was a team who were being paid lip service from their sponsor. He was saying the right things in meetings, but was not acting on these statements. He was more inclined to distance himself from the project when not in meetings for fear that the project would fail and he would be too closely aligned with it and damage his reputation. The team did an analysis of the stakeholder's behavioural style using the online profiler tool[2] and compared the reports generated. They realised that the common characteristics were around the ego of the lion and the desire to be seen as being perfect like the unicorn.

---

2   http://www.organizationalzoo.com/profiler

After considerable debate the team devised a plan where they could engage the sponsor more heavily with the project (get him into the boat rather than floating along side it like the feline) based on how his direct involvement and association with the project increased the chances of project success. They discussed how others would become more engaged simply because they could see senior support and that if he would do a few simple actions that would confirm his involvement in others perceptions. This support alone would sway the opinions of others in the organisation.

The project was eventually successful because others were more engaged once the leaders support was visible and tangible. The conversations around the animals in the boat and which roles they needed to take on cause the level of support to change and this was the tipping point required for success. This outcome may have been achieved without the use of metaphor, but it was the metaphor that stimulated the interactions that lead to the final successful outcome. In complex situations the relationship between cause and effect is seldom obvious or singular. Each piece of the puzzle is interlinked with every other piece and sometimes subtle changes in the 'feel' of the situation cause a shift that drives a series of actions to move the momentum into a positive direction.

PERFORMANCE, INFLUENCE AND BEHAVIOUR

Although it seems intuitive that behaviour and relationships impact performance, it can be difficult to gather sufficient objective evidence to robustly support this. This highlights the difficulties in objectively measuring behaviour and proving direct cause and effect links between the perceived behaviour to the outcomes. The author has been engaged since late 2009 in a three-year action research programme designed to answer this question more directly. Early results indicate that it is possible to build a body of evidence to support the proposition that behaviours do have a significant impact on performance outcomes.

This research is designed to:

1.   Assess the behavioural environment within projects.

2.   Attempt to influence the behavioural dynamics through specific interventions and then.

3.   Assess their impact on project performance, or at least perceptions of this.

Finding a balance between what is perceived as objective (quantitative) data and subjective (qualitative) interpretation is a challenge. As was stated rather eloquently by Einstein '*Not everything that can be counted counts, and not everything that counts can be counted.*' This research design has led to the development of a new model (Figure 9.2) that combines four separate concepts:

1. reflective practice;

2. conversations that matter;

3. behavioural metaphor; and

4. performance assessment.

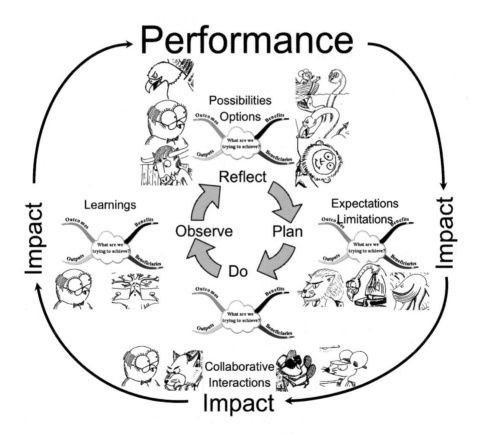

Figure 9.2   Reflective Performance Impact Model

The traditional reflective practice approach of *plan, do, observe then reflect* has the learning at the end of the cycle. The modified approach allows learning through simulation at the beginning to minimise poor interactions with stakeholders through simulations, thereby minimising the potential for relationship damage. Placing reflection at the beginning of the cycle enables creative conversations about possible outcomes with stakeholders before planned interactions or communication. This enables the participants to test a variety of options through conversation and potentially role plays so those trying to influence others can be better prepared.

The interdependence of these four approaches and the synergies they generate with each other make them powerful. Although any of them can be used alone for assessment and influence of stakeholders, together they become much more influential. Using them together through this process also contributes more to personal and team capability development and supports a more productive relationship in the longer term with one's stakeholders. All four concepts help those using them to develop a deeper understanding of themselves and others and the interactions they can then have with them. One significant finding of the research (at the end of 2010) is the incorporation of the terms into the language and practice. Once people become familiar with the animal characters and regularly have reflective conversations with their colleagues, the benefits become apparent. Having a commonly understood structure to converse around which focuses the purpose of the conversation in alignment with the situation they are in provides more clarity, more purposeful participation and better outcomes.

This research is continuing and seeks to understand the extent to which the adoption of this model by a team or organisation will assist to develop emotional intelligence, relationships, trust and ongoing performance improvement. Early results from phase one of the field trials are supportive of this proposition.[3] For example, a research subject used the metaphor characters extensively to manage a difficult relationship difference to minimise the impact of the differences between her and her colleague.

BEHAVIOURAL PERFORMANCE ACTIVITY EXPERIENCE

In the early stages of the research a conversation is held around the performance formula shown in Figure 9.3. The purpose of this conversation is to demonstrate how behaviours impact all aspects of performance, as is

---

3   At the time of writing (end of 2010).

indicated by the callout bubbles on the diagram. The early indications from the research are that this formula, in association with animal metaphor, simplifies the ability to visualise the links between behavioural impacts and performance. Although behavioural interactions are complex and it is dangerous to assume direct cause and effect, the synergies of the metaphor and formula enable a conversation to occur where without these the conversation would not have happened. The lack of conversations in such situations continues to generate a negative spiral which reduces trust, causes political behaviours and creates or reinforces territorial boundaries. All of these implications reduce the transfer of knowledge that should be shared between people and ultimately generate inferior performance. When conversations are stimulated to explore options and generate understandings of the impacts of behaviour, the spiral can be turned around and over time repair some of the negative aspects, providing it is done before permanent damage is caused.

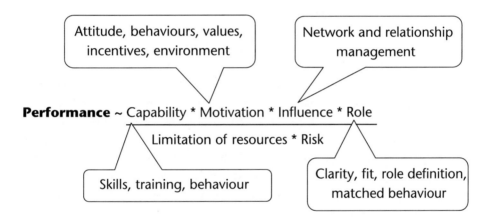

Figure 9.3   Impacts of behaviour on performance
Source: Shelley (2009). Adapted from Clancy and Webber (1999).

One example of such a conversation was conducting of a performance appraisal for a technical expert who was a leader in his field. This expert had the attitude that he was the most capable technical person in the company (and this was correct). However, as a result of his superior attitude he was perceived as being extremely arrogant, which had a negative impact on his work relationships with others in the team and stakeholder group. At performance appraisal time, the formula was used to highlight that his capability and understanding of role were important components of performance and a significant contributor to personal and organisational performance. However, the attitude and behaviours expressed (primarily lion and whale with some elements of vulture when criticising others perceived to be inferior) had a significant negative influence on the rest of the team, demotivating them and decreasing performance across the wider team. Whilst this is a difficult conversation to have in any circumstances, it was much easier to maintain as constructive and objective through the use of the formula in combination with the animal metaphors. These made it possible to separate the various performance components from the person. The capability of the person and his superior understanding of the tasks required (elements of role) could be acknowledged and encouraged. With this acknowledgement forming a constructive foundation and reinforcing their worth, the conversation could focus on the issue of their negative impact on others. In this specific example the attitude of the expert was modified and relationships were able to be improved over time. Other aspects of this formula not covered in this chapter are fully discussed elsewhere (Shelley 2009).

METAPHORIC ROLE PLAYS TO SIMULATE POSSIBLE OUTCOMES

Role plays are becoming more popular as a means of preparing team members for complex unpredictable situations. By playing a number of roles in several scenarios a team member can understand others' perspectives to better understand how to approach a situation. Role plays which identify the target audience are an excellent way to practice an important pitch or test a scenario outcome and solicit feedback before risking this in the real case. They are also a great way to explore other perspectives because they are improvised and somewhat unpredictable.

They are normally done without scripts, with the players being asked to respond in an impromptu manner based on the behaviour of the stakeholder they are playing. Typically they are short with three to five exchanges between the players. The process can be reflective *in* action (stop to discuss observed behaviours and their impacts as you proceed) or reflective *on* action (complete the process and discuss the outcomes afterwards). The advantage of the former is you can immediately respond (for example, 'do you truly believe the stakeholder will react that way?') and the disadvantage is that it disrupts the emergent nature of the role play. The team should discuss if the role play seemed realistic and if the behaviours displayed were true to what could be expected from the stakeholders. Regardless of whether accurate or not, the discussion brings out insights and better prepares all involved for the real event. Playing someone unfamiliar to you and receiving feedback on it is a good way to learn more about them. Inexperienced players often start out playing the role as they would themselves and this is soon highlighted in the discussions. This feedback highlights traits they don't understand in the person or behaviour they are playing, which then helps them to learn how to deal with these more productively. Overall, role plays are fun and insightful and the use of Organizational Zoo metaphor cards can help focus on the likely behavioural interactions outcomes. This increased understanding assists with being more engaging and productive when influencing upwards (and in any other desired direction).

METAPHORIC ROLE PLAY EXPERIENCE

Role plays are fun to do and provide deep insights into the behavioural interactions happening between people. Storytelling is like a form of role play in which an historical event is described through the eyes of the teller. In these cases the outcome is already determined with the known ending being shared with the audience by the teller. In role plays, it can be quite different. The interactions being discussed here are simulations of something that has not already happened and as such the ending is not known by anyone (yet). There may be many versions of the play and the outcome in reality may not be the same ending as any of the rehearsed role-play versions. In this sense role plays seek to discover options and explore possible outcomes that may only emerge through the play itself. As a creative forum involving impromptu interactions by people with different perspectives, it is a medium through which unpredicted opportunities and unforseen issues can be highlighted.

Role plays can be done at any stage of the Reflective Performance Impact Model (Figure 9.2) but are more productive as a 'pre-reflective' simulation at the beginning of a cycle. They can be done generically (predefined characters involved in a set sequence as shown in Figure 9.4) or completely without props. The advantage of using cards is that observers can assess whether the role is being played to character and provide feedback to the actors. This provides them with a different perspective which enhances their depth of knowledge about the stakeholder or behaviour they are playing. The key purpose of the role play is to test assumptions about what might happen in a planned event with others so that any hidden dangers are highlighted along with possible better 'angles' to take. This is likely to increase the probability of achieving your desired outcomes. Whilst some may describe this process as manipulative, that is a negative perspective of what is happening. The aim is to optimise your influence on others. Depending upon your intent, this may be perceived by others as a negative (manipulative) or positive (compelling) interaction.

People's responses to those attempting to influence them are determined by the way it is being done (coercively or openly) according to their values. Metaphor can assist in simplifying your message and making your intent more obvious, creating stronger links to the values of your target audience and thus helping to drive a positive perception of you and your interactions with them. Political parties and advertising agencies are very aware of the science behind such interactions and constantly use these to influence (or is that manipulate?) our voting and buying habits.

The role play example displayed in Figure 9.4 highlights there can be a real difference between what is being said and what are the motivating thoughts behind what is being said. This role play can have a number of plots and outcomes, depending upon the perspectives taken by each of the three players. The two interpretations of the scenario below show the differences between positive and negative outcomes from a similar interaction.

One potential script for the exchange in Figure 9.4:

Frame 1: Eagle speaking to Chameleon 'I have this great idea…' (explains their idea).

Frame 2: Chameleon to Lion 'I have this great idea…' (explains the eagle's idea).

Frame 3: Lion to Eagle 'I had this great idea and implemented it to create value'.

The first interpretation of the script below is usually the chameleon has 'stolen' the idea from the eagle to look good in the eyes of the lion. The eagle at this point is seen as the victim. Consider how they should react upon becoming aware that the chameleon has stolen their idea and the lion is now claiming credit for it. Most participants exposed to this scenario assume they respond with anger.

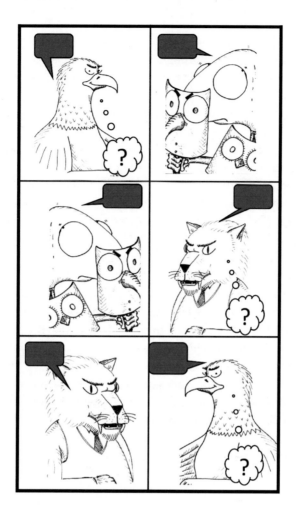

Figure 9.4   Role play sequence example

Certainly if the eagle was to react as a fellow lion there would be heated debates about the ownership and territorial behaviours and the chameleon would be chastised and not trusted in future by the eagle. The chameleon will have effectively chosen sides in this territorial war, but now has a relationship with an important stakeholder. The lion has no qualms about taking credit for the idea as there is a significant power distance between them and the chameleon, so they are unlikely to be challenged by them. They are unchallenged in gaining kudos.

The alternative interpretation is to consider the difference in what was said and the thoughts behind what is being said. It is possible that the initial intent of the eagle is on a far more visionary and strategic level than the chameleon and lion perceived. Assume the eagle knows the idea is good, but they realise they do not have the resources to make it happen. The eagle needs the support of the territorial lion to get it approved and supported for implementation. If they tell the lion to implement it, chances are they would get 'not invented here syndrome' and the idea would be blocked. However, if the eagle leaked the idea through the chameleon who unknowingly becomes the targeted transmitter of the idea to the lion, the idea is more likely to be adopted (as the kudos associated with the idea's value appeals to the ego of the lion). This way the lion adopts the eagle's idea as their own and the eagle effectively gets what he wanted without the political issues and there is strong support and ownership of the idea so it will be sustained. This shows an example of the adage: 'Managers solve problems, leaders avoid them.'

Exploring the differences between stated intent and real intent can be highlighted by role plays as well as a range of other options. This same scenario could be played with a variety of other scripts and with different or more animals. Shorter role plays with emphasis on discussion of implications offer greater value than longer ones because they focus on specific interactions and reduce the variables. The value comes out of both the conversations to create the plays and those discussing the different interpretations of what happened in the play and the likely next steps and implications. The key is to be creative and interactive. We learn more whilst we are having fun and being open minded. It also stimulates innovative ideas.

Conclusion

Metaphor is a powerful tool for advising upwards and for influencing stakeholders generally. It assists in the preparation of team members to optimise outcomes in interaction with stakeholders. Thinking through metaphors enables people wanting to positively influence others to reframe options and see alternatives they would not have otherwise seen. Using metaphoric team interventions, such as the Dragon Boat and stakeholder matching, helps to build relationships within the team and also to better understand those they need to influence outside of the team. When the characters and images are well understood by all involved in the conversations, the exchanges are richer and outcomes are more aligned with desired performance. The Reflective Performance Impact Model provides a strong foundation to develop a common understanding of how and when to incorporate metaphor-based activities into the normal workplace and how to focus these interactions to optimise performance. Using metaphor enables the observed behaviours and their impact on the group to be discussed independently of the people displaying them. This removes perceived blame, politics and personal sensitivities and therefore enables constructive dialogue rather then argument. It also stimulates some conversations to happen that would not have otherwise occurred, thereby relieving tensions and highlighting opportunities for common ground.

Using role plays to practice pitches and simulate likely conversation outcomes helps to prepare for unpredictable twists and to be more adaptable when improvisation is needed to rapidly recover from an unexpected deviation. This helps to build confidence and readiness to take advantage of an unexpected opportunity as well as prepare for the planned events. All of these outcomes help to align your purpose with the desires of the stakeholders and to transfer complex messages in a simple but rich manner. When combined with humour and rich imagery, metaphor generates a fun way to decrease political influences and create a safe trusting environment in which more constructive dialogue can occur. This helps people to strengthen relationships and social capital, ultimately converting into performance improvements and happier, less stressed team members.

References

Chia, J. 2005. Is trust a necessary component of relationship management? *Journal of Communication Management*, 9(3): 277–285.

Denning, S. 2005. *The Leader's Guide to Storytelling: Mastering the Art and Discipline of Business Narrative*. San Francisco, CA: Jossey Bass.

Dictionary.com 2010 http://dictionary.reference.com/browse/metaphor, accessed 3 April 2010.

Disney 2010. *Disney Characters*, http://home.disney.com.au/characters/, accessed 30 March 2010.

Gannon, M. 2004. *Understanding Global Cultures: Metaphorical Journeys through 28 Nations, Clusters of Nations and Continents*, 3rd edn. Thousand Oaks, CA: Sage.

Goleman, D. 2006. *Social Intelligence: The New Science of Human Relationships*. New York: Bantam Dell.

Handy, C. 1978. *Gods of Management. Who they Are, How they Work and Why they Will Fail*. London: Pan Books.

Haley, U.C.V., Low, L. and Toh, M.H. 1996. Singapore Incorporated: reinterpreting Singapore's business environments through a corporate metaphor. *Management Decision*, 34(9): 17–28.

Hofstede, G. 2001. *Culture's Consequences: Comparing Values, Behaviours, Institutions and Organizations across Nations*. Thousand Oaks, CA: Sage.

Inns, D. 2002. Metaphor in the literature of organizational analysis: a preliminary taxonomy and a glimpse at a humanities-based perspective. *Organization*, 9(2): 305–330.

Ivie, S.D. 2003. *On the Wings of Metaphor*. San Francisco, CA: Credo Gap Press.

Lakoff, G. and Johnson, M. 1980. *Metaphors we Live by*. Chicago, IL: Chicago University Press.

Morgan, G. 2006. *Images of Organization*. London: Sage Publications.

Nielsen, C.S. and Mariotto, J.G. 2006. The tango metaphor. *International Studies of Management and Organization*, 35(4): 8–36.

Orwell, G. 1946. *Animal Farm*. New York: Harcourt, Brace and Company.

Schön, D.A. 1993. Generative metaphor: a perspective on problem-solving in social policy. In A. Ortony, ed., *Metaphor and Thought*. Cambridge: Cambridge University Press, pp. 137–163.

Shelley, A.W. 2007. *The Organizational Zoo, A Survival Guide to Workplace Behavior*. Fairfield: Aslan Publishing.

Shelley, A.W. (2009) *Being a Successful Knowledge Leader. What Knowledge Practitioners Need to Know to Make a Difference*. North Sydney: ARK Publications.

Shelley, A.W. 2010. *The Park Ranger and the Leading Lion*. http://organizationalzoo. blogspot.com/2010/01/park-ranger-and-leading-lion.html, accessed 30 March 2010.

Snowden, D.J. 2002. *Archetypes as an Instrument of Narrative Patterning*. www. cognitive_edge.com, accessed 6 May 2008.

Snowden, D.J. and Boone, M.E. 2007. A leader's framework for decision making. *Harvard Business Review*, November: 69–76.

ThinkExist.com. 2010. http://thinkexist.com/quotation/you-never-get-a-second-chance-to-make-a-first/557657.html, accessed 3 April 2010.

Warner Brothers. 2010. *Loony Tunes Characters*, http://looneytunes.kidswb.com/, accessed 30 March 2010.

Vinten, G. 2000. Business theology. *Business Decision*, 38(3): 209–215.

Windsor, R.D. 1996. Military perspectives of organizations. *Journal of Organizational Change Management*, 9(4): 34–42.

10

Intelligent Disobedience: The Art of Saying 'No' to Senior Managers

Bob McGannon

Introduction – Some Definitions

> ***Extraordinary:*** *1) beyond what is usual, ordinary, regular, or established; 2) exceptional in character, amount, extent, degree etc. noteworthy; remarkable.*
>
> *Dictionary.com*

> ***Intelligent disobedience:*** *1) The ability to manage communications, relationships, processes and uphold corporate ideals to accomplish corporate goals; 2) The act of saying no to senior managers, deviating from corporate processes or acting against management direction for the sake of achieving stated objectives or outcomes.*
>
> *Author's definition*

The phrase 'intelligent disobedience' comes from the world of Seeing Eye Dogs.[1] In training these service pets, *intelligent disobedience* is defined as: *a concept where any service animal trained to help a disabled person goes directly against their owner's instructions in an effort to make a better decision.*

This concept is one that would benefit today's leaders. Its core is central to improving the process by which leaders make decisions. The corporate decision-making process is best executed from a set of comprehensive information. However, this process does not always proceed smoothly.

---

1   www.dogtrainertoday.com.

Time pressures, the extent of leadership responsibilities and the fast-paced approach of businesses make communicating sufficient and good information for ideal decision-making challenging. Those same time pressures create stress for leaders who must make decisions and take actions in the best interest of the businesses they serve: hence the need for intelligent disobedience.

Truly *extraordinary* business leaders understand the advantages of complete ownership for the scope of the environments in which they manage. They understand their environments, have a very clear concept of the perceptions of their leadership team, and possess the courage to take action and make decisions that will best further the interests of the business. Sometimes this involves not complying with management directions they have received. Acting in the best interests of the business may also involve a careful examination of the nature of the direction or request against corporate standards and policies. Sometimes the interests of the business are best served by a decision *not* to follow prescribed rules and policies. Corporate processes and procedures are never written with perfect foresight, and cannot cover absolutely every eventuality and every context. Thus, the astute and courageous leader may be faced with a decision to make: do I do 'as I am told'? Do I follow the corporate processes; even through in this instance I believe that it may not be in the best interest of the business?

The essence of being extraordinary is this: having the strength and confidence to ask such questions and not defaulting to 'yes'. This is also the essence of intelligent disobedience. The most successful leaders test situations by asking themselves these questions in specific business and personal circumstances. A decision to act in this way involves some risk taking, but will be managed and made effective within the framework of understanding the business environment and the nature of that specific situation.

Simply put, knowledgeable and action-oriented leaders watch the activities of those around them. These leaders seek information from stakeholders such as their peers, team members, direct reports, customers and competitors. The information is obtained through direct conversations, news reports, interactions with trusted colleagues and attentive observation and should be considered as an essential part of any management task or role.

The leader's manager and other managers in the organisation – 'bosses' – have even larger portfolios to manage. They see a different set of people, bring different information and perspectives and have varying degrees of familiarity with what is going on 'in the trenches' of their own organisations. These differences in awareness and perception may be significant. The astute leader will strive to understand and augment the information and perceptions of their management team, to contribute the best and most comprehensive set of information to the decision-making process. In contrast, weaker or less energetic people in leadership roles do not strive to understand and communicate this information.

Weaker leaders hide behind 'what has always been done', in the form of standard organisational processes, through a fear of being different and rocking the boat. The consequence of such thinking is that they will be reluctant to take action that could advance the position of the businesses that employ them.

This chapter will examine how advising upwards often means being a *courageous follower*. Operating within the principles of intelligent disobedience actively supports the organisation and its goals through commitment to a goal as having greater value over strict compliance with standard approaches and processes. The *intelligent* piece of intelligent disobedience means that where issues of legal compliance, mandatory regulatory constraints and business conduct guidelines are concerned, little to no disobedience reflects intelligence.

To demonstrate appropriate intelligent disobedience in action, a scenario involving a challenging and time-constrained major programme of work is included in the chapter. Case studies will demonstrate common occurrences of intelligent disobedience and how its application can affect the outcome of the programme and the projects within it. It is intended to provide examples that showcase the practice of intelligent disobedience in an organisation, and can be adapted to individual work situations. The nuances of relationships, organisational strategies, personalities and skills inventories need to be considered on an individual basis when contemplating or reflecting actions or potential actions of intelligent disobedience. What may be considered an act of intelligent disobedience in one environment may be a routine action in another. As they say in commercials – *results may vary*. Use of the case study description can provide guidance to forms of advising upwards within the framework of intelligent disobedience through

- actions;

- *inaction;*

- demonstrations of results; or

- demonstrations of a *lack* of results.

A Programme Scenario – PipeCo

This scenario is based on an actual programme and various projects that the author and his colleagues have managed, or been closely affiliated with through consulting engagements. To protect the privacy of the individuals involved all names have been changed, and in some instances the scenario simplified to support efficient analysis.

PipeCo is a small company, but it is well known for its industry expertise and excellent project delivery in the oil and gas pipeline and oil well construction sector. The owner of PipeCo – a large energy conglomerate called Englenergy – was forced to sell the company to an Eastern European oil company called Vortex. Included in the sale agreement between Englenergy and Vortex was the following clause:

> *PipeCo can continue to use Englenergy's information technology infrastructure for a period of 12 months to allow it to develop its own technology infrastructure or to be absorbed into Vortex's corporate IT infrastructure. After 12 months, if PipeCo requires the continued use of Englenergy's IT infrastructure, Vortex will have to pay Englenergy $40,000US per day.*

Vortex has directed the senior leaders of PipeCo to develop their own technology infrastructure. Vortex management decided that this approach would be more efficient than trying to absorb their operations into the Vortex corporate infrastructure. A programme has been launched with the following objectives:

1. Determine the business and technical requirements for PipeCo's information technology development and implementation.

2. Prepare a Request for Proposal (RFP) to solicit proposals to build and manage the technology hardware and network infrastructure.

3. Prepare a RFP for obtaining an Enterprise Resource Planning (ERP) application suite to provide a back office solution for PipeCo.

4. Review and select an organisation to deliver item 1:

    a. review and select the ERP software package;

b. customise the ERP software;

c. integrate, test and install the hardware and software; and

d. implement and run operations for PipeCo using the new infrastructure and application software.

There were delays in starting the programme: information technology expertise in PipeCo was scarce. The first four months was wasted while management was deciding how to *approach* the programme. Pressure on the PipeCo management team started to mount with only eight months remaining before significant IT charges were to be levied against Vortex.

CASE STUDY 10.1

This case study demonstrates one of the principles of intelligent disobedience: when the best interests of the organisation aren't well represented by compliance to its processes, alternative approaches should be considered.

The infrastructure vendor was selected. The next step was to negotiate a contract. A standard Vortex services contract was the basis of the negotiation. The contract detailed a number of specific high-priority performance parameters for the information technology services. Penalties for failure to meet these parameters were included in the standard contract. There were two particular service level objectives for a high visibility customer service system:

- The first defined limits for the number of system outages over each three month period.
- The second defined limitations on the time for completion of the customer support process.
- Other important considerations of the negotiations were that:
  - incremental improvements to the performance of the customer service system were being planned as operational experience was gained; and
  - an outage to the customer service application would be necessary each time new computer code was applied to implement an improvement.

With the planned progressive improvements to processes the programme delivery team anticipated that service improvements should be made in an 'agile' manner with the best approach being small and frequent incremental changes. With this strategy the organisation's infrastructure vendor could easily reach the quarterly limit for the number of outages incurred in any three-month period.

PipeCo management were debating whether to postpone making any improvement to the client's system because of the conditions of the service contract. This approach would have been the easiest course of action, requiring less work from both the infrastructure vendor and the ICT service organisation in the short term; the conditions of the services contract would have validated that action. However, that delay would have extended the improvement process planned for the customer, and delayed the benefits to the customer. There were risks associated with the 'agile' approach, as almost all changes to complicated information technology systems do. In fact, if the installation of the improvements did not go well, penalties could have been levied. Despite this, the delivery management team believed the risks of this approach balanced the potential performance improvement resulting from smaller, frequent improvements.

The programme delivery manager approached PipeCo senior management with a contract proposal incorporating a relaxation of the contractual penalties for outages over a three-month period, placing the potential performance improvement as a higher priority. Management agreed with this proposal, accepting the consequences that could result. Eventually, authorisation to suspend the outage limitation to the customer service system was provided, improvements were installed and worked as intended, delighting the customer and the end users of the system.

ANALYSIS

In this case study, management took a holistic view of the situation, determined that adherence to the strict conditions of the standard service contract in this situation would achieve a suboptimal result. The application of the principle of intelligent disobedience took the form (as it usually does) of advising the organisation's leadership of a situation where processes were not working in both parties' best interest. A positive decision in the best interest of all parties involved could be made after information was made available presenting the risks and benefits.

Case study 10.1 involved eliminating a *hurdle to success*. In some instances applying intelligent disobedience means *becoming* a hurdle, rather than eliminating it. To do this the leader who needs to drive an initiative to successful completion may have to instigate a fight amongst senior leaders. Yes, a *fight*. Case study 10.2 provides an example of the message that: 'many larger initiatives suffer from a lack of a good, rich battle amongst the heavy hitters in the organisation' and shows how a dose of intelligent disobedience can provide the impetus these initiatives need for successful outcomes.

CASE STUDY 10.2

At one point in the customisation of the software for PipeCo, some organisational objectives needed to be clarified to ensure the applications would support the business in an ongoing basis. After a couple of meetings where the objectives were discussed and refined, a high-level set of customisation objectives for the programme were derived by the PipeCo senior management team.

After reading the objectives and proposed approach for the programme, the delivery team was concerned that not all of the managers who directly reported to the programme sponsor were as supportive of the programme. Some were enthusiastic about these customisation objectives, and others appeared to view the customisation approach as detrimental to their personal and divisional objectives. The delivery team was concerned that they would not be able to progress the work very far without encountering considerable resistance. The sponsor and his team appeared to believe the objectives and outcomes of this programme were beneficial, there was a concern that the approach and suggested prioritisation had not been universally accepted by the important stakeholders.

A manager in the programme team approached the sponsor with these concerns. The sponsor's reply was that he and his team were all fully committed to the programme and the proposed application customisations for completing it. Despite this, the delivery team knew that some individual stakeholders were not supportive, and decided an act of intelligent disobedience was required to demonstrate the presence of 'unfought issues'.

The project manager arranged a series of short interviews with the sponsor's direct reports regarding the customisation objectives. Interviews were recorded on a short summary form, capturing a few critical elements. (See Table 10.1 below.) The summary documented:

- Each individual's goals for the programme, in priority order;
- The metric that would be used to determine success; and
- The way that metric would be collected.

Using eight different versions of this stakeholder priority table, one for each of the sponsor's direct reports, the delivery team demonstrated to the sponsor the differing views of his direct reports.

With this new information, the sponsor reconvened his team and addressed the differences (engaged in the battles). The resulting revised programme was delivered without the stress and difficulties that would have occurred if these conflicting expectations had not been resolved.

Table 10.1   Stakeholder priority table

Stakeholder value (priority order)	Customer support process changes	Construction site support productivity	Quality and accuracy increase
Increased staff efficiency	10–20% reduction in processing time per employee	> = 5% increased productivity per site support employee – measured in transactions per person	
Minimise process changes	Less than 4 'core processes' to change with the new system		Decrease transaction errors by 10% to 1 per 50,000
Cost reduction		Decrease site support cost by > = 5%	

ANALYSIS

This case study demonstrates how conflicting stakeholder expectations can be managed successfully when the team understands the joint and individual requirements of its stakeholders. Leaders or team managers don't always have this level of understanding, but they can acquire understanding through the use of information gathering and presentation processes such as the stakeholder priority table. With these processes and practices the leader or manager can gain that understanding, and increase the chance of successful completion of a programme based on a firm foundation of support from key stakeholders.

Situations such as the one outlined in Case study 10.2 surface when an initiative requires major change to how work is done. The benefits of having completed stakeholder priority tables for each key stakeholder include:

- Conflicting stakeholder priorities are identified and understood, leading to their resolution.

- Resource assignment decisions can be aligned with organisational objectives rather than just project objectives.

- The leader or manager has access to vocabulary that has most meaning to each stakeholder: the objectives are recorded in the stakeholder's own words.

- Objectives are clearly understood and are within the defined boundaries of the agreed scope of the work.

The next case study demonstrates how the act of completing the stakeholder priority tables can reveal hidden agendas.

CASE STUDY 10.3

In this case study we examine differences in requirements and expectations of functional managers in the same team.

The stakeholder priority tables also assisted in resolving issues between managers of different PipeCo facilities.[2] After the programme to select, customise and install new IT services had been approved for implementation, stakeholder priority tables were completed for the four main facility managers. Shortly after the programme started, one of the facility managers started to propose changes that appeared to be contrary to what was recorded and approved. The changes

---

2   PipeCo facilities consisted of pipe and pipe support infrastructure manufacturing, inventory and distribution centres and construction sites. PipeCo also performed operational support and consulting so facility managers also include support managers for offshore oil platforms, and oil and gas processing facilities.

were causing obstacles to progress with the initiative. In a private conversation with that facility manager, using the approved stakeholder priority table as the basis for discussion, the delivery programme manager asked that manager to compare his recent change requests to his previously stated and agreed priorities and objectives. That comparison revealed conflict between his new requests and his previous agreements.

During that conversation, the facility manager revealed that one of his primary external customers had requested he deliver another urgent objective unrelated to this current initiative. His focus on this customer request would likely cause him to delay the implementation of the initiative shared and agreed upon by the other facility managers. To balance the needs of the current initiative and the newly discovered needs of the facility manager's customer, a change was proposed to a non-programme-related project that would not impact the overall IT initiative. This action averted the obstacles to the programme, allowing it to progress while saving face for the facility manager and satisfying the request from his customer.

These first three case studies demonstrate actions to ensure the success of a short-term activity. Sometimes there are other drivers for the application of the principle of intelligent disobedience. One of the most significant acts of intelligent disobedience a leader can take is to *allow* something to fail. This is a difficult and emotionally charged action for forcing an action or decision, but often powerfully effective. Similar to letting a stubborn and determined child do something foolish, it can be a very effective way to achieve a long-term gain. The learning that can come from the failure will serve as a catalyst for significant action.

It may appear that allowing something to fail is acting contrary to the objective of ethical behaviour. Consider the following: allowing something to fail should not be the first attempt at moving the organisation forward. The intent of such an action must be a positive step for the organisation, not a vindictive approach to prove somebody wrong. Intervention and supervision to monitor and reduce any unintended impact to the business is crucial and will ensure that the leader still acts with integrity.

Letting something fail to move the business forward is not uncommon. It is accepted as a good thing to 'stretch' an employee by giving them a new, aggressive assignment, and to accept that some mistakes will be made, supporting the employee through any consequences of these mistakes. In the organisational context mistakes come with the learning to help the business in the long run. An *extraordinary* act is when a leader takes a personal risk in allowing something to fail, causing scrutiny on the organisation's actions or decisions. The next case study gives an example of a situation where an aspect of an initiative was *allowed* to fail.

CASE STUDY 10.4

A key stakeholder was very aggressive in his desire to implement a new set of business processes corresponding with the changes to the information technology tools. The stakeholder was advised that a complete set of the current process documentation was required before new processes and the customised IT applications were put in place. The risk presented to the client was straightforward – the current process needed to be analysed to understand how a new process and change to the application systems would affect a current process. It was essential to insure that any departments affected by this change were able to continue to fulfil their responsibilities.

The stakeholder was anxious to move forward and wanted to proceed without performing the appropriate analysis of existing processes. He viewed it as unnecessary, and gave instructions to proceed with a pilot of new process and application changes.

The delivery programme manager approached this situation by suggesting that the pilot be kept small and also suggesting that the support teams prepare to create 'lessons learnt' from the process analysis and documentation steps. Proceeding with the pilot, the technology applications team planned the associated configuration changes for the pilot and was able to manage the large number of *'but what about this'* type of questions that resulted during the testing of the applications changes. Although the process being changed was used by a large team, only a few of those team members were made available to analyse and recommend process changes. This team believed they fully understood the processes and activities, but as the testing progressed it quickly became evident this was not the case. The technology applications team allocated extra process modellers and applications staff (without our client's knowledge) to fix the issues that were expected to surface.

The additional process modelling that the stakeholder rejected was not performed. This led to the failure of the pilot initiative, allowing the predicted knowledge gaps to emerge during reviews. The result of this failed pilot was a new paradigm and clearer understanding of the need for a comprehensive understanding of existing process models. This understanding was instilled in the client's management team as well as the programme sponsor. Modelling was introduced to allow the change team to identify potential gaps ahead of time, and the progression to improved processes and application tools was implemented with minimal unintended and unexpected 'breakages'.

Unlike this last case study, where efforts were hampered by a senior manager's misguided requirement, there are situations where barriers to success are well known, but are not talked about openly. They are often referred to as *sacred cows* or *unmentionables*, and can impose significant burdens on teams. However, due to the influence of culture or the perceived opinions of senior stakeholders, team members and less courageous leaders are reluctant to raise these issues. On the other hand, extraordinary leadership means that the issues will be raised and addressed, even though such discussions will be difficult and politically charged and career threatening. When the issue is raised and addressed satisfactorily, the resulting new approaches and awareness can transform an organisation.

The best approach is to get to the point quickly, positioning the discussion in terms of a business issue or concern, rather than criticising the senior leader. A review of the business responsibilities given to the courageous follower positions the discussion around the conditions for success and opens the discussion for including the unmentionable, and a review of the expectations placed upon the intelligently disobedient follower. When there is agreement, the next step is dealing with the unspoken issue. This dialogue might proceed as follows:

Leader: *'Boss, I believe we need to discuss the X initiative.'*

Boss: *'Proceed.'*

Leader: *'It is my perception that you have entrusted me with bringing Z results from this initiative, am I correct?'*

Boss: *'Yes at a minimum, I believe you can do better than that.'*

Leader: *'Understood. Given that, I believe I have to be aggressive should anything or anyone in the organisation present an obstacle to achieving these results. Would you expect that type of behaviour from me?'*

Boss: ' *Absolutely.'*

Leader: *'Well, given that, <u>it would be irresponsible of me</u> not to mention that the long-standing policy of Y is causing the members of the team to behave in H manner. Can we discuss possibilities for addressing this and potentially reviewing decisions that have been made in the past? Maybe that policy is no longer serving us well.'*

Now, this example is a fairly clean dialogue. A real-life dialogue is unlikely to proceed in such a succinct way. The point of the exchange is to get to the underlined phrase. The point of the conversation is that the leader is addressing this potentially emotionally charged and maybe even embarrassing situation because it is their responsibility to do so. That responsibility has come about because of directions from the very same senior manager who is now participating in this conversation. The intent is to make clear there is no other agenda; the leader is trying to do his job.

A potential impediment to this calm dialogue is the presence of an aggressive senior manager. Despite appropriate and well thought out acts of intelligent disobedience, or just good leadership, some people can be extraordinarily difficult to 'manage'. Although difficult people come in many forms, the aggressive manager seems to be common in the business world.

Chronically aggressive or defensive people are displaying a character trait that others have little chance of penetrating or changing, according to Elaine Krantz, MS, LPC, who works with leaders delivering workshops around the world.[3] She states:

> *Dealing with chronic behaviours needs to be done on your terms, not theirs. Trying to use some form of retort to their aggressiveness,*

---

3   From an interview conducted with Elaine Krantz on 27 August 2007 in Denver Colorado as part of the research for an update of my Intelligent Disobedience Workshop.

or expecting your actions to change them in any manner is a nearly hopeless cause.

The primary piece of advice she provides when dealing with senior leaders with these characteristics is to present only demonstrable data and documented tasks. If the leader does not agree with your evidence:

- continue to present data;

- stick to a focus on the tasks you are managing and the responsibilities of the leader;

- be succinct and precise; and

- don't change your message.

The senior managers who will eventually respond to this do so because they realise their defensive or aggressive approach won't change your view, or the evidence you present. The key is persistence and consistency: don't be deterred by the responses you get. If you are successful the senior manager will react in the manner that you need to make your initiative successful.

There is another possible option in dealing with an aggressive senior manager, which is also a form of intelligent disobedience. If your own personal communication style doesn't work, and the presentation of evidence has no impact, sometimes the best response to aggressiveness is to respond in kind. It may be that the aggressiveness displayed by your key stakeholder is a sign of their passion for a topic, and they want to see that passion in return. Your style, for reasons you may not ever understand, does not represent that expected passion in the eyes of the aggressive key stakeholder. Therefore, a viable strategy may be to imitate the behaviour and style of the manager you are trying to influence. It is uncomfortable; you are stepping out of your own natural communication style, yet it can be a *very* powerful approach. An example of applying 'a style change' occurred in our PipeCo programme and is described in the next case study.

CASE STUDY 10.5

PipeCo's Chief Strategist was one of their few technical staff members. A long-term employee of PipeCo, he was respected by all and feared by many due to his aggressive and coarse manner. He had developed a robust and useful technical strategy for his organisation. The programme team was suggesting a change to this technical strategy as a result of the new information technology suite being installed. The programme manager was assigned the task of negotiating with the Strategist for his approval and endorsement for the necessary changes to the organisation's technical strategy.

The first two attempts of logical and calm reasoning for the case for a change in the infrastructure were unsuccessful. He was very defensive and challenged the data and evidence in support of the change to an architecture that had 'served the company well for a number of years'. Presenting the case a third time, the programme manager mirrored the Strategist's style, attempting to 'reach him' in that way. The conversation went like this:

Strategist: *'You are here to try to convince me to change my strategy again!'*

Programme Manager: *'Yes. I am here to discuss changing the strategy, because the current business direction created a new need. Despite being brilliant 99 per cent of the time, in this instance you are acting like a new graduate holding on to a novel but impractical idea.'*

Strategist: *(Raising his eyebrows) 'OK then, what is the technical basis for your premise.'*

The Programme Manager then explained the rationale for requesting the strategy change, quickly and succinctly. Concluding, the dialogue continued:

Programme Manager: *'Is this an adequate explanation?'*

Strategist: *'Yes it is. I was wondering when or if you were going to come to me with conviction instead of a consultant's "slick approach", and I am glad you did.'*

The Strategist was won over not by different facts but by an emulation of his own communication style. It was uncomfortable for the Programme Manager to approach him in this manner, but ultimately it got his attention and respect and provided the window of opportunity for him to actually listen to the recommendations. After that conversation, the relationship between the Strategist and the Programme Manager improved significantly.

Selecting the Opportunities for Acting in Extraordinary Ways

WHEN TO EMPLOY INTELLIGENT DISOBEDIENCE

The case studies above present examples of the application of the principles of intelligent disobedience. Each situation, organisation and relationship is different so it is important to understand how to assess potential situations that may call for acts of intelligent disobedience. The most successful leaders understand there are very few absolutes, and that every situation needs to be judged on its own merits. Variables to consider will include:

- the extent of the potential gain for the organisation;

- the amount of effort being invested in other initiatives; and

- the availability of critical resources.

Being extraordinary and consciously engaging in acts of intelligent disobedience are not for the meek.

Rare is the leader who is viewed as being special for passionately maintaining the status quo. Intelligently disobedient leaders must constantly assess the risk associated with the actions they take, especially when those actions involve the type of actions that have been described in the case studies:

- breaking or bending organisational norms or rules;

- pointing out issues that senior managers are ignoring; or

- challenging the very culture of a long held business model.

Based on extensive conversations with leaders in workshops delivered around the world,[4] a few common themes start to emerge when these leaders assess their degree of personal risk. These are:

- degree of perceived business gain or loss;

- the presence of other alternatives to accomplish the objective;

- their relationship with senior managers who will be instrumental in the evaluation of themselves and the resulting business change; and

- one's moral stance on the situation – the degree of personal integrity involved in the issue.

DEGREE OF BUSINESS GAIN OR LOSS

The degree of gain or loss is viewed from both a personal and an organisational standpoint. Extraordinary actions and the risks inherent in them should only be taken if the resulting gain – or loss due to a lack of action – is deemed worthwhile. Leaders have shared that taking a long overdue action is the most frequent driver for acts of intelligent disobedience. In many environments, we are told, senior management teams will avoid recognition of a problem because the resulting actions necessary to remedy the problem are difficult. They are difficult because they often counter actions and decisions publicly made by the senior leadership team in the recent past. What is the essential ingredient which instigates action? A compelling sense that: 'Something must be done. Nobody else has the fortitude to do this, so it falls to me.'

THE PRESENCE OF OTHER ALTERNATIVES TO ACCOMPLISH THE OBJECTIVE

The presence or lack of other more traditional alternatives for achieving a valued business goal is the next significant catalyst for acts of intelligent disobedience. These alternatives have either been tried recently or failed, or have been obstructed by reluctant senior leaders or stakeholders with differing objectives as detailed earlier in this chapter. In other instances, someone in the

---

4   Between March 2007 and July 2010, 62 Intelligent Disobedience Workshops have been delivered to over 1100 participants. The workshops have been delivered in the United States, Canada, the United Kingdom, Switzerland, Australia and Singapore.

organisation, lacking other high-level sponsorship, defers to standard policies and approaches which have failed to produce optimal results. The extraordinary leader knows that something different and innovative needs to be attempted, and takes charge. The last two items typically are tied to a passionate and very personal rationale for taking action.

THE RELATIONSHIP WITH SENIOR MANAGEMENT

A strong, trust-based relationship with senior leaders instigates a level of commitment that is not common from the average leader. When a leader fully and completely supports his manager's objectives, and has the desire to protect the senior leader from the consequences of a less than desirable result, the extraordinary leader will consider more extreme actions to achieve these objectives. This is truly personal, and the actions taken are initiated with trust that the senior manager will support the activity, understanding the reason and supporting the intended result.

The most proactive extraordinary leaders will propose or engage in an act of intelligent disobedience as a means of actually *establishing* a relationship with a member of the senior management team. Significant relationships are built as a result of substantial conversations, shared experiences, or both. Discussing a situation of significance with a senior manager, and proposing a bold or non-traditional action to solve it forms a basis for extending and expanding the relationship with that senior stakeholder. The leader that does this – after taking the time to do the appropriate homework – can quickly enrich a relationship. Alternatively, if the conversation goes badly, it provides the leader with a means to engage in other approaches to gain support for extraordinary actions, or to assess whether their intelligently disobedient approach will ever be supported by this manager. The leader can then evaluate their dedication to that organisation, whether they should apply their skills elsewhere in the organisation, or the marketplace at large. That decision is taken based on the last of the personal risk themes; the moral stance or personal integrity invested in the work and approach to personal accomplishment. Many of the attendees of our workshops report they were compelled to take the proposed action anyway, despite concluding that the action wouldn't be condoned by the senior leader.

MORAL STANCE

Of all of the motives for engaging in an act of intelligent disobedience, the simple premise that 'it was simply the right thing to do' is the most compelling and motivating, according to our workshop participants. Leaders whose moral stance is challenged are compelled to ensure the appropriate business outcome is achieved, or to ensure that something they considered to be wrong was quickly corrected.

The most significant acts of intelligent disobedience disclosed by workshop participants have been inspired by a compelling requirement to be true to one's self. This leader simply cannot work with integrity without addressing this compulsion. The extraordinary leader will do this alone, or involve trusted colleagues.

It is important to remember that a detailed understanding of the organisation, its culture, rules and stakeholder expectations is vital. The key to knowing when and how to be intelligently disobedient is embodied in a few critical questions:

1.   Is the rule or process I am going to break or alter tied to a legal compliance requirement?

2.   If I take this action, are the potential process breakdowns that may occur avoidable with quick, proactive communication?

3.   Will I be creating an unreasonable ongoing expectation with my client or my organisation if I change processes in this instance?

4.   Will anyone's integrity, other than my own, be in question if I break the rules in this circumstance?

5.   Is the action I am considering tied to an objective I have in my own mind, rather than a goal that is known and communicated across the organisation?

If the answer to all of the above questions is 'no' then the extraordinary leader should pursue the action they are evaluating. Action is the key, either immediately, or as soon as any other required information is obtained. Either way, with the extraordinary leader, action is taken.

Conclusion

Intelligent disobedience has been defined as a critical approach to satisfying leadership capabilities and as the importance of attainment of goals over strict adherence to policy and standard practices. Through a series of case studies various scenarios describing how an act of intelligent disobedience was appropriate were presented. Lastly, a view to the thought processes a leader might use to assess whether or not to consider an act of intelligent disobedience is defined.

In all cases, it is a matter of understanding the business environment, the personalities, strengths and weaknesses of the stakeholders involved and the individual's personal commitment and risk tolerance. Only after careful consideration should an act of intelligent disobedience be considered.

References

Alberti, R. and Emmons, M. 2008. *Your Perfect Right: Assertiveness and Equality in Your Life and Relationships*, 8th edn. California: Impact Publishers.

Crowe, A. 2006. *Alpha Project Managers: What the Top 2% Know That Everyone Else Does Not*. Georgia: Velociteach

Froling, J. 16 April 2001. Assistance dog tasks. *International Association of Assistance Dog Partners*, http://www.iaadp.org/tasks.html, accessed 22 August 2010.

Prasso, S. (ed.) 2003. Up front. *Business Week*, 24 March, 14

Simons, R., Mintzberg, H. and Basu, K. 2002. Memo to: CEOs. *Fast Company*, June, 117–121.

Index